Palgrave Studies in European Union Politics

Edited by: **Michelle Egan**, American University, USA; **Neill Nugent**, Emeritus Professor, Manchester Metropolitan University, UK; **William Paterson OBE**, University of Aston, UK

Editorial Board: **Christopher Hill**, Cambridge, UK; **Simon Hix**, London School of Economics, UK; **Mark Pollack**, Temple University, USA; **Kalypso Nicolaïdis**, Oxford, UK; **Morten Egeberg**, University of Oslo, Norway; **Amy Verdun**, University of Victoria, Canada; **Claudio M. Radaelli**, University of Exeter, UK; **Frank Schimmelfennig**, Swiss Federal Institute of Technology, Switzerland

Following on the sustained success of the acclaimed *European Union Series*, which essentially publishes research-based textbooks, *Palgrave Studies in European Union Politics* publishes cutting-edge research-driven monographs.

The remit of the series is broadly defined, both in terms of subject and academic discipline. All topics of significance concerning the nature and operation of the European Union (EU) potentially fall within the scope of the series. The series is multidisciplinary to reflect the growing importance of the EU as a political, economic and social phenomenon.

Titles include:

Carolyn Ban
MANAGEMENT AND CULTURE IN AN ENLARGED EUROPEAN COMMISSION
From Diversity to Unity?

Gijs Jan Brandsma
CONTROLLING COMITOLOGY
Accountability in a Multi-Level System

Edoardo Bressanelli
EUROPARTIES AFTER ENLARGEMENT
Organization, Ideology and Competition

Ramona Coman, Thomas Kostera and Luca Tomini (*editors*)
EUROPEANIZATION AND EUROPEAN INTEGRATION
From Incremental to Structural Change

Véronique Dimier
THE INVENTION OF A EUROPEAN DEVELOPMENT AID BUREAUCRACY
Recycling Empire

Helene Dyrhauge
EU RAILWAY POLICY-MAKING
On Track?

Theofanis Exadaktylos and Claudio M. Radaelli (*editors*)
RESEARCH DESIGN IN EUROPEAN STUDIES
Establishing Causality in Europeanization

Eli Gateva
EUROPEAN UNION ENLARGEMENT CONDITIONALITY

Basil Germond
THE MARITIME DIMENSION OF EUROPEAN UNION SECURITY
Seapower and the European Union

Jack Hayward and Rüdiger Wurzel (*editors*)
EUROPEAN DISUNION
Between Sovereignty and Solidarity

Wolfram Kaiser and Jan-Henrik Meyer (*editors*)
SOCIETAL ACTORS IN EUROPEAN INTEGRATION

Christian Kaunert and Sarah Leonard (*editors*)
EUROPEAN SECURITY, TERRORISM AND INTELLIGENCE
Tackling New Security Challenges in Europe

Christian Kaunert and Kamil Zwolski
The EU AS A GLOBAL SECURITY ACTOR
A Comprehensive Analysis beyond CFSP and JHA

Marina Kolb
THE EUROPEAN UNION AND THE COUNCIL OF EUROPE

Finn Laursen (editor)
DESIGNING THE EUROPEAN UNION
From Paris to Lisbon

Kennet Lynggaard, Ian Manners and Karl Löfgren
RESEARCH METHODS IN EUROPEAN UNION STUDIES

Dimitris Papadimitriou and Paul Copeland (editors)
THE EU'S LISBON STRATEGY
Evaluating Success, Understanding Failure

David Phinnemore
THE TREATY OF LISBON
Origins and Negotiation

Ariadna Ripoll Servent
INSTITUTIONAL AND POLICY CHANGE IN THE EUROPEAN PARLIAMENT

Claudia Sternberg
THE STRUGGLE FOR EU LEGITIMACY
Public Contestation, 1950–2005

Yves Tiberghien (editor)
LEADERSHIP IN GLOBAL INSTITUTION BUILDING
Minerva's Rule

Liubomir K. Topaloff
POLITICAL PARTIES AND EUROSCEPTICISM

Amy Verdun and Alfred Tovias (editors)
MAPPING EUROPEAN ECONOMIC INEGRATION

Richard G. Whitman and Stefan Wolff (editors)
THE EUROPEAN NEIGHBOURHOOD POLICY IN PERSPECTIVE
Context, Implementation and Impact

Sarah Wolff
THE MEDITERRANEAN DIMENSION OF THE EUROPEAN UNION'S INTERNAL SECURITY

Jan Wouters, Hans Bruyninckx, Sudeshna Basu and Simon Schunz (editors)
THE EUROPEAN UNION AND MULTILATERAL GOVERNANCE
Assessing EU Participation in United Nations Human Rights and Environmental Fora

Ozge Zihnioglu
EUROPEAN UNION CIVIL SOCIETY POLICY AND TURKEY
A Bridge Too Far?

Palgrave Studies in European Union Politics
Series Standing Order ISBN 978–1–403–99511–7 (hardback) and
ISBN 978–1–403–99512–4 (paperback)
(outside North America only)

You can receive future titles in this series as they are published by placing a standing order. Please contact your bookseller or, in case of difficulty, write to us at the address below with your name and address, the title of the series and one of the ISBNs quoted above.

Customer Services Department, Macmillan Distribution Ltd, Houndmills, Basingstoke, Hampshire RG21 6XS, UK.

European Union Enlargement Conditionality

Eli Gateva

Teaching Fellow, Queen Mary University of London, UK

First published 2015 by
PALGRAVE MACMILLAN

Palgrave Macmillan in the UK is an imprint of Macmillan Publishers Limited, registered in England, company number 785998, of Houndmills, Basingstoke, Hampshire RG21 6XS.

Palgrave Macmillan in the US is a division of St Martin's Press LLC, 175 Fifth Avenue, New York, NY 10010.

Palgrave Macmillan is the global academic imprint of the above companies and has companies and representatives throughout the world.

Palgrave® and Macmillan® are registered trademarks in the United States, the United Kingdom, Europe and other countries.

ISBN 978–1–137–48242–6

This book is printed on paper suitable for recycling and made from fully managed and sustained forest sources. Logging, pulping and manufacturing processes are expected to conform to the environmental regulations of the country of origin.

A catalogue record for this book is available from the British Library.

Library of Congress Cataloging-in-Publication Data
Gateva, Eli.
  European Union enlargement conditionality / by Eli Gateva.
     pages   cm — (Palgrave studies in European Union politics)
  Includes bibliographical references.
  ISBN 978–1–137–48242–6
  1. European Union—Membership. 2. European Union—Europe, Central. 3. European Union—Europe, Eastern. I. Title.
  JN30.G344 2015
  341.242′23—dc23   2015014618

На моите родители Таня и Гриша

Contents

Tables

Acknowledgements

I would like to thank Dimitris Papadimitriou and Peter Humphreys for their unreserved support, invaluable guidance and enthusiastic encouragement throughout the challenging process which led to the creation of this book. I am also obliged to David Phinnemore and Claire Annesley for their valuable comments.

I would like to thank the University Association for Contemporary European Studies for their generous support. I am very grateful to Tom Casier for kindly offering me the facilities of the Brussels School of International Studies. I would like to thank Bojan Savic and Bilyana Petkova for making me feel at home in Brussels. I would also like to express my gratitude to all the interviewees for allowing me to take of their time.

I am indebted to my wonderful family and amazing friends. I would especially like to thank Paul Copeland for his loving friendship and continuous support. George Kyris and Tomas Maltby, thank you for our departmental European community and for sharing your thoughts, comments and coffee. I would like to thank Petar Dochev, Katerina Angusheva, Myriam Mojica Martinez, Sarah Jhumka, Shilpa Patel and Lang'o Odondi for all the great adventures that we have had together. I am also very grateful to Pablo Benito Lopez for teaching me how to make sangria and making me laugh on a regular basis.

Finally, I would like to thank my parents for their unconditional love and support. Words cannot express how much I owe you.

Abbreviations

AAs	Association Agreements
AFET	European Parliament Committee on Foreign Affairs
AL	Albania
AT	Austria
BE	Belgium
BH	Bosnia and Herzegovina
BU	Bulgaria
CDSP	Common Defense and Security Policy
CEE	Central and Eastern Europe
CEECs	Central and Eastern European countries
CFSP	Common Foreign and Security Policy
COWEB	Council Working Group on the Western Balkans
CVM	Cooperation and Verification Mechanism
CY	Cyprus
CZ	The Czech Republic
DE	Germany
DG	Directorate-General
DK	Denmark
EAs	Europe Agreements
EC	European Community
ECSC	European Coal and Steel Community
EE	Estonia
EEA	European Economic Area
EEC	European Economic Community
EFTA	European Free Trade Association
EL	Greece
EMU	Economic and Monetary Union
EP	European Parliament
ES	Spain
EU10	Cyprus, the Czech Republic, Estonia, Hungary, Lithuania, Latvia, Malta, Poland, Slovenia, Slovakia
EU12	Cyprus, the Czech Republic, Estonia, Hungary, Lithuania, Latvia, Malta, Poland, Slovenia, Slovakia, Bulgaria, Romania

EU25	Austria, Belgium, Cyprus, the Czech Republic, Germany, Denmark, Estonia, Greece, Spain, Finland, France, Hungary, Ireland, Italy, Lithuania, Luxembourg, Latvia, Malta, the Netherlands, Poland, Portugal, Sweden, Slovenia, Slovakia, the United Kingdom
EU27	Austria, Belgium, Bulgaria, Cyprus, the Czech Republic, Germany, Denmark, Estonia, Greece, Spain, Finland, France, Hungary, Ireland, Italy, Lithuania, Luxembourg, Latvia, Malta, the Netherlands, Poland, Portugal, Romania, Sweden, Slovenia, Slovakia, the United Kingdom
EURATOM	European Atomic Energy Community
FI	Finland
FR	France
FRY	Federal Republic Yugoslavia
FY	FYROM
FYROM	Former Yugoslav Republic of Macedonia
GFAP	General Framework Agreement for Peace
HR	Croatia
HU	Hungary
ICTY	International Criminal Tribunal for the Former Yugoslavia
IE	Ireland
IPA	Instrument for Pre-Accession Assistance
ISPA	Instrument for Structural Policies for Pre-Accession
IT	Italy
JHA	Justice and Home Affairs
LT	Lithuania
LU	Luxembourg
LV	Latvia
ME	Montenegro
MEP	Member of the European Parliament
MT	Malta
NATO	North Atlantic Treaty Organization
NGO	non-governmental organisation
NL	The Netherlands
NMS	new member states
ODIHR	Office for Democratic Institutions and Human Rights
OSCE	Organization for Security and Co-operation in Europe
PHARE	Poland and Hungary: Assistance for Reconstructing their Economies

PL	Poland
PM	prime minister
PSD	Social Democratic Party (Romania)
PT	Portugal
RO	Romania
RS	Republika Srpska
SAAs	Stabilisation and Association Agreements
SAP	Stabilisation and Association Process
SAPARD	Special Accession Programme for Agriculture and Rural Development
SE	Sweden
SI	Slovenia
SK	Slovakia
SMEs	small and medium-sized enterprises
TCAs	Trade and Cooperation Agreements
TEU	Treaty on European Union
TSEs	transmissible spongiform encephalopathies
TU	Turkey
UK	United Kingdom
UNTAES	United Nations Transitional Administration for Eastern Slavonia
UPFM	United Police Force of Mostar

Introduction

Enlargement has always been an essential part of the European integration project. However, it was the expansion of the European Union (EU) with the ten Central and Eastern European countries (CEECs), together with Cyprus and Malta, unprecedented in scope and scale, which presented the Union with an opportunity to develop a multifaceted set of instruments and transformed enlargement into the EU's most successful foreign policy. However, the direct attribution of EU enlargement policy to the foreign policies of the Union could be contested, as consecutive enlargements have had a significant impact not only on the new member states but also on the makeup of the Union and the development of its internal and external policies. The extensive constellations of networks between Directorate-General (DG) Enlargement and the other DGs, the Council of the EU, the Permanent Representations of the member states and the Permanent Missions of applicant countries further highlight the unique and the highly complex nature of EU enlargement policy. The numerous challenges of the accession process along with the enormity of the historical mission to unify Europe lent speed to the emergence of the study of EU enlargement as a key research area.

The majority of the early studies investigated the puzzle of the EU's decision to enlarge with the CEECs (Baldwin, 1995; Schimmelfennig, 1998; Fierke and Wiener, 1999; Schimmelfennig and Sedelmeier, 2002; Sjursen, 2002; Sedelmeier, 2005) and the costs and benefits of the Eastern expansion (Baldwin, Francois and Portes, 1997; Inotai, 1997). However, the research focus expanded quickly to include other dimensions. The impact of EU enlargement is one of the areas which has blossomed and accumulated a growing body of literature over the last decade, especially with reference to the influence of the EU on applicant

1

and candidate countries, which has not only widened the research focus of Europeanisation studies (beyond the member states of the Union) but also stimulated and shaped the debates on the scope and effectiveness of conditionality. Most of the theoretical discussion of EU conditionality examines the transformative power of the Union by focusing on mechanisms for inducing compliance with EU rules and assessing their impact on the domestic politics of the candidate countries (Smith, 1998; 2003; Grabbe, 2002, 2006; Pridham, 2002; Schimmelfennig, Engert and Knobel, 2003; Hughes, Sasse and Gordon, 2004; Schimmelfennig and Sedelmeier, 2004).

In recent years, research has gradually shifted to studying the sustainability of the impact of EU conditionality after accession by looking into new members' compliance with EU rules (Toshkov, 2007, 2008; Sasse, 2008; Sedelmeier, 2008, 2012; Dimitrova and Toshkov, 2009; Schimmelfennig and Trauner, 2009). The effectiveness of the EU's neighbourhood policy (Lavenex, 2008; Schimmelfennig and Scholtz, 2008; Casier, 2010, 2011) and the diffusion of the EU's impact beyond candidate and potential candidates as well as neighbouring countries (Börzel and Risse, 2012a, 2012b) have also shaped and expanded the debate on the mechanisms and effectiveness of the EU's influence.

The completion of the fifth enlargement and the introduction of the renewed consensus on enlargement as the basis for the EU's strategy towards South-Eastern Europe signalled a new chapter in the development of EU enlargement policy. Furthermore, the recent developments in the relations between the Union and the candidate and potential candidate countries of South-Eastern Europe not only highlight the lack of comprehensive comparative frameworks for the study of EU conditionality but also, as noted by Pridham (2007), the need to examine EU conditionality contextually with reference to the development of enlargement policy. Although Nugent's (2004), Schimmelfennig and Sedelmeier's (2005) and Sjursen's (2006) edited volumes look into the previous enlargement rounds of the Union, the comparative dimension of the studies is limited to highlighting key differences particularly between the Eastern expansion and previous enlargement waves. While recent studies of the impact of EU enlargement conditionality focus exclusively on the Western Balkans (Bieber, 2012; Elbasani, 2013).

The book fills an important gap in the literature on European integration by designing a rigorous conceptual framework for the study of EU enlargement conditionality which allows us to examine its evolving nature at two levels – between different groups of enlargement applicants and across different stages of the accession process. On the basis of the *stage-structured conditionality model*, the study provides the first comprehensive comparative analysis of the development of EU enlargement conditionality across four different enlargement waves – the first (2004) and the second (2007) phase of the Eastern enlargement, the EU enlargement to Croatia (2013) and the ongoing enlargement round with the Western Balkans and Turkey. Furthermore, the relevance of the model is not limited to the macro level of EU enlargement policy, as it establishes a highly comprehensive framework which allows us also to trace the evolution of the EU's enlargement strategy in specific policy areas (such as environment, energy and justice and home affairs). The questions about how and why EU enlargement policy (and respectively EU enlargement conditionality) has changed are crucial not only for understanding the policy dynamics in this area and its legacy on the EU's external policies, but also for assessing its policy outcomes.

A stage-structured conditionality model

The study pursues two key research questions: (1) How has EU enlargement conditionality changed across different stages of the accession process and between different groups of enlargement applicants? (2) Why has EU enlargement conditionality changed over time? Accordingly, the research unfolds in three steps. Firstly, on a basis of the *stage-structured conditionality model*, it discusses the evolution of EU enlargement conditionality. The model relates the examination of EU enlargement conditionality to different steps of the accession process and identifies the following four distinct stages:

- Pre-negotiation stage;
- Negotiation stage;
- Accession stage; and
- Post-accession stage.

Furthermore, building on the literature on EU conditionality (Smith, 1998; Schimmelfennig, Engert and Knobel, 2003; Schimmelfennig and Sedelmeier, 2004; Grabbe, 2006), the model specifies that EU enlargement conditionality has three key elements:

- conditions set out by the EU with which the country aspiring to membership needs to comply;

- an incentive structure, which examines the *reward–threat balance*; and
- monitoring.

In order to complete the second step of the analysis, the book specifies that *EU enlargement policy is a function of differentiated influences from multiple actors and external pressures*. The study investigates continuity and change in EU enlargement policy by analysing the developments of EU enlargement conditionality with reference to the following institutional and exogenous factors: (1) *EU member states*, (2) *EU inter-institutional dynamics*, (3) *public opinion in the EU*, (4) *enlargement countries* and (5) *external pressures caused by economic or security shocks and crises*. Finally, the study summarises the key findings and reflects on their implications for the European integration.

Case studies

The book discusses the evolution of EU enlargement conditionality between three groups of enlargement applicants. The first group includes the countries with which the EU completed the first phase of the fifth enlargement in 2004 – the Czech Republic, Estonia, Hungary, Poland, Latvia, Lithuania, Slovenia, Slovakia together with Cyprus and Malta. The second group consists of Bulgaria and Romania, whose accession to the Union in 2007 led to the completion of the fifth enlargement round. The third group focuses on Croatia's accession and the ongoing enlargement process with Turkey, Montenegro, Serbia, FYROM Albania, Bosnia and Herzegovina and Kosovo.[1]

Although the Union has undergone several expansions, it was the challenge of the Eastern enlargement, unprecedented in scope and scale, which presented the Union with an opportunity to develop a multifaceted set of instruments and transformed enlargement into the EU's most successful foreign policy. The first group of case studies allows us to trace the early development of EU enlargement conditionality. Although Bulgaria and Romania were part of the fifth historic enlargement, they did not accede to the Union in May 2004 together with the other CEECs, Cyprus and Malta. Despite the similarities in the EU's approach to Sofia and Bucharest and the other candidate countries, the Union introduced significant differences, which were not limited to the accession date. They provide important insight into the evolution of the EU enlargement conditionality and motivate pairing Sofia and Bucharest in a separate group. The third group which includes the newest member state of the Union and all of the enlargement countries of South-Eastern Europe allows us not only to highlight the latest developments but also to rigorously test the impact of institutional and external factors on EU conditionality. The case selection strengthens the comparative dimension of the study and allows us to cross-examine the evolution of EU enlargement conditionality at two levels of analysis: different stages of the accession process (pre-negotiation, negotiation, accession and post-accession stage) and across different countries.

The analysis relies on a wide range of primary sources: key EU documents (such as Conclusions of the European Council, Association Agreements (AAs), Stabilisation and Association Agreements (SAAs), Accession Partnerships, Enlargement Strategies, Regular and Progress Reports), Eurobarometer surveys and news articles. The analysis is supplemented by the examination of the statements and speeches by the European Commission Presidents, Commissioners for Enlargement and leading European politicians. The study also draws on more than 115 extensive semi-structured interviews with high-ranking officials from DG Enlargement and the Cabinets of Commissioners: van den Broek, Verheugen; Rehn and Füle (See Appendix II); European Parliament Committee on Foreign Affairs (AFET); the General Secretariat of the Council of the EU; and national officials from the permanent representations of existing member states and missions of candidate countries to the EU.

Structure

The book is structured in five chapters. The first chapter briefly discusses the development of EU enlargement policy, provides a review of the academic literature on EU enlargement conditionality and outlines a conceptual framework for comparative examination of EU enlargement conditionality. The study proceeds with three empirical chapters: Chapter 2, Chapter 3 and Chapter 4. Each of them examines the evolution of EU enlargement conditionality by focusing respectively on:

- the first phase of the fifth enlargement, which expanded the Union with the Czech Republic, Estonia, Hungary, Poland, Latvia, Lithuania, Slovenia, Slovakia together with Cyprus, and Malta;
- the second phase of the fifth enlargement, which led to the accession of Bulgaria and Romania;
- Croatia's accession and the ongoing enlargement process with Turkey, FYROM, Montenegro, Serbia, Albania, Bosnia and Herzegovina and Kosovo.

Chapter 5 analyses the research findings and draws conclusions on the evolutionary nature of EU enlargement conditionality and the varying mechanisms for shaping the Union's most successful policy, and it reflects on their wider implications for the ongoing enlargement process and the advancement of the research agenda on EU enlargement.

1
Conditionality and EU Enlargement: A Conceptual Overview

The aim of this chapter is threefold. Firstly, it briefly sketches the development of the EU enlargement policy by focusing on the history of enlargement rounds (Table 1.1), the nature of the accession process and the development of membership conditions. Secondly, the chapter discusses the emergence of EU enlargement as a prominent research area and reflects on the key questions and debates in the literature on EU conditionality. Finally, it outlines a *stage-structured conditionality model*, which provides a conceptual framework for comparative study of EU enlargement conditionality.

EU enlargement waves

Enlargement has always been an important part of the European integration project. The Schuman Declaration of 9 May 1950, which promoted the idea of 'a united Europe' and inspired the creation of the first European Community (EC), acknowledged that:

> Europe will not be made all at once, or according to a single plan. It will be built through concrete achievements which first create a de facto solidarity. The coming together of the nations of Europe requires the elimination of the age-old opposition of France and Germany. Any action taken must in the first place concern these two countries.
>
> (Schuman Declaration, 1950)

On 18 April 1951, France, West Germany, Italy, Belgium, the Netherlands and Luxembourg took the first steps towards unifying the continent by signing the Treaty establishing the European Coal and

Table 1.1 Enlargement rounds

Date	Enlargement rounds	Countries
01.01.1973	First enlargement	United Kingdom, Ireland and Denmark
01.01.1981	Second enlargement	Greece
01.01.1986	Third enlargement	Spain and Portugal
01.01.1995	Fourth enlargement	Austria, Finland and Sweden
01.05.2004	Fifth enlargement (first phase)	Cyprus, Czech Republic, Estonia, Hungary, Poland, Latvia, Lithuania, Malta, Slovenia and Slovakia
01.01.2007	Fifth enlargement (second phase)	Bulgaria and Romania
01.07.2013	Sixth enlargement	Croatia

Steel Community (ECSC) or the Treaty of Paris. Article 98 confirmed the inclusive nature of the process by specifying that:

[a]ny European State may request to accede to the present Treaty. It shall address its request to the Council, which shall act by unanimous vote after having obtained the opinion of the High Authority. Also by a unanimous vote, the Council shall fix the terms of accession. It shall become effective on the day the instrument of accession is received by the government acting as depository of the Treaty.

(Treaty of Paris, 1951)

In a similar manner, Article 237 of the Treaty establishing the European Economic Community (EEC) and Article 205 of the Treaty establishing European Atomic Energy Community (EURATOM) stated that '[a]ny European State may apply to become a member of the Community' (EURATOM Treaty, 1957; Treaty of Rome, 1957).

First enlargement

Churchill was one of the first to advocate the idea of a united Europe. In his Zurich speech in 1946, he noted that 'to recreate the European fabric, or as much of it as we can, and to provide it with a structure under which it can dwell in peace, safety and freedom. We must build a kind of United States of Europe' (Churchill, 1946). Although he argued that '[i]f Europe were once united in the sharing of its common inheritance there would be no limit to the happiness, prosperity and glory which its 300 million or 400 million people would enjoy', he did not envisage the participation of the United Kingdom in the European unification (Churchill, 1946). Great Britain was reluctant to take part in the European Communities. However, in the 1960s United Kingdom's policy towards Europe changed and the country applied for EEC membership on 9 August 1961.

The British government flagged 'the special Commonwealth relationship as well as [of] the essential interests of British agriculture and of the other Members of the European Free Trade Association [EFTA]' as difficult matters and expressed the belief that:

> Member Governments will consider these problems sympathetically and therefore have every confidence in a successful outcome to the negotiations. This would constitute an historic step towards that closer union among the European peoples which is the common aim of the United Kingdom and of the Members of the Community.
>
> (*Bulletin of the European Economic Community*, 1961)

The United Kingdom's commitment to European integration also influenced Ireland's decision to seek membership. Denmark and Norway followed suit and also applied to join the EEC (see Table 1.2). In January 1963, the French President De Gaulle reflected on the differences between the British and the continental European economic interests and their implications for the future of the Community and declared his opposition to the United Kingdom's application. Although the French veto brought the 1961–1963 enlargement negotiations to an abrupt end, the United Kingdom, Ireland, Denmark and Norway applied for a second time in 1967. Following the devaluation of the British pound in November 1967, De Gaulle vetoed again the British application. It was only after his resignation that the French position changed and accession negotiations were launched in 1970.

The membership talks included a number of challenging issues such as the United Kingdom's financial contribution to the Community and its participation in the Common Agricultural Policy. In the case of Denmark, solutions needed to be found with regard to the Faroe Islands and Greenland. Norway raised concerns about the implications of membership for its agriculture and fishing industry. The Accession Treaty was signed on 22 January 1972 in Brussels. The referenda in Ireland and Denmark showed strong support for European membership, respectively, with 80% and 63% in favour of accession to the European Communities. The result of the referendum in Norway was unexpected

Table 1.2 Application for membership of the EEC/EU

Applicant	Date of application	Application outcome/date of accession
Ireland .	31.07.1961	Withdrawn due to veto on United Kingdom
	11.05.1967	01.01.1973
United Kingdom	10.08.1961	Vetoed by France
	10.05.1967	01.01.1973
Denmark	10.08.1961	Withdrawn due to veto on United Kingdom
	11.05.1967	01.01.1973
Norway	30.04.1962	Withdrawn due to veto on United Kingdom
	21.07.1967	Rejected by Norway in referendum
	25.11.1992	Rejected by Norway in referendum
Greece	12.06.1975	01.01.1981
Spain	28.06.1977	01.01.1986
Portugal	28.03.1977	01.01.1986
Turkey	14.04.1987	Negotiating accession
Morocco	20.07.1987	Rejected
Austria	17.07.1989	01.01.1995
Cyprus	03.07.1990	01.05.2004
Malta	03.07.1990	01.05.2004
Sweden	01.07.1991	01.01.1995
Finland	18.03.1992	01.01.1995
Switzerland	25.05.1992	Frozen
Hungary	31.03.1994	01.05.2004
Poland	05.04.1994	01.05.2004
Romania	22.06.1995	01.01.2007
Slovakia	27.06.1995	01.05.2004
Latvia	13.09.1995	01.05.2004
Estonia	24.11.1995	01.05.2004
Lithuania	08.12.1995	01.05.2004
Bulgaria	14.12.1995	01.01.2007
Czech Republic	17.01.1996	01.05.2004
Slovenia	10.06.1996	01.05.2004
Croatia	21.02.2003	01.07.2013
FYROM	22.03.2004	Candidate country
Montenegro	15.12.2008	Negotiating accession
Albania	28.04.2009	Candidate country
Iceland	17.07.2009	Suspended accession negotiations
Serbia	22.12.2009	Negotiating accession

Sources: Commission of the European Communities (1976, 1989); European Commission (1993a, 1993b, 1994, 1997, 2004a, 2005b, 2010c, 2010d, 2010e, 2011a); Council of the European Union (2009, 2014).

with 53.5% against EEC membership. Although the outcome of the referendum was not legally binding, it led to the rejection of the Treaty by the Norwegian Parliament. The first enlargement took place on 1 January 1973 with the accession of the United Kingdom, Ireland and Denmark. Although the British public was not initially consulted, the results of the 1975 referendum – 67.2% in favour and 32.8% against – confirmed the approval of the electorate for the EEC membership of the country.

Second enlargement

In the 1980s, the Communities expanded to the South. Greece was the first country to seek and establish an association 'involving reciprocal rights and obligations, common action and special procedures' with the Community (Treaty of Rome, 1957). The AA which was signed on 9 July 1961 envisaged the development of a customs union between Athens and the EEC over a period of 22 years. Furthermore, Article 72 of the Agreement stated that 'as soon as the operation of this agreement has advanced far enough [...] the contracting parties shall examine the possibility of the accession of Greece to the EEC' (Official Journal, 1961). However, following the military coup of 21 April 1967 and the establishment of military dictatorship, the Community froze the AA. After the restoration of democracy, Athens formally applied to join the European Communities in 1975. The Commission recognised that the AA 'was explicitly aimed at paving the way for eventual full membership' and stressed 'that the Community must now give a clear positive answer to the Greek request' (Commission of the European Communities, 1976). Nevertheless, the Commission opposed swift accession and called for a preparatory phase by noting that '[i]n the case of Greece, where structural changes of a considerable magnitude are needed, it would seem desirable to envisage a period of time before the obligations of membership, even subject to transitional arrangements, are undertaken' (Commission of the European Communities, 1976). In addition to reflecting on the economic implication of the Greek accession, the Commission also acknowledged the consequences of the Greek membership for the relations between the Community and Turkey and for the development of the Community. Despite the negative recommendation, the Council 'agreed that the preparatory talks essential to the establishment of a common basis for negotiation should take place as soon as possible in a positive spirit' (Council of the European Communities, 1976). Although the member states imposed a seven-year transitional period on the free movement of Greek workers and some agricultural products, they agreed to grant Athens a five-year transitional period in order to allow the Greek economy to comply with the Community rules. The accession negotiations were completed in May 1979, and Greece became the tenth member state of the Communities on 1 January 1981.

Third enlargement

The 1970s signalled the beginning of important political transformations in Spain and Portugal. Following the collapse of the dictatorships, Lisbon and Madrid submitted their applications for EEC membership in 1977. The Commission not only issued favourable opinions on the applications of both countries, but also identified a number of challenges in the areas of agriculture, fisheries, industry, social aspects, regional aspects and external relations. The membership negotiations with Portugal were launched in October 1978. Four months later, the Community started negotiating with Spain. Although the size of the Spanish agricultural sector and fishing fleet turned out to be particularly problematic issues, the French opposition to further enlargement and the debates surrounding the British Budgetary Question also protracted the accession process with Madrid and Lisbon (Council of the European Union, 2009).

In December 1982, the Commission analysed the enlargement process and drew up a list of proposals with the aim of overcoming the existing obstacles. The Commission identified the general principles of the accession negotiations:

- clarity of the terms of accession (particularly with reference to the transitional measures);
- adoption of the *acquis communautaire* (short: *acquis*) in full; and
- simultaneous accession of Portugal and Spain.

The Commission's communication recognised that some 'traditional problems' 'arise from the fears engendered in the Member States by the prospect of change in an established situation, the increased openness of their markets to external competitors and the concomitant adjustments in terms of specialization' (*Bulletin of the European Community*, 1982). The major issues referred to Mediterranean agricultural products, fisheries, textiles and iron and steel. The free movement of workers from the applicant countries also caused concern. Moreover, the accession process was conditioned by internal considerations. The Commission stressed the growing burden of existing common policies on the Community budget and urged the member states to address the own resources problem. It also called for a more flexible approach to decision-making, including the extension of majority voting (*Bulletin of the European Community*, 1982).

In October 1983, an informal summit of the prime ministers of France, Italy, Greece, Portugal and Spain proved crucial for the advancement of the membership talks (Council of the European Union, 2009). In March 1985, the Community, Spain and Portugal reached a political agreement on a range of difficult issues including agriculture, fisheries and the government of the Canary Islands. The Fontainebleau European Council settled the British question and increased the Community's own resources thus clearing the way for the third enlargement. The Accession Treaty was signed on 12 June 1985, and Spain and Portugal acceded to the European Communities on 1 January 1986.

Fourth enlargement

Turkey and Morocco submitted their applications for membership in 1987. Although the Commission concluded that 'it would not be useful to open accession negotiations with Turkey straight away', it recommended 'a series of substantial measures' which would allow for increased interdependence and integration (Commission of the European Communities, 1989). The outcome of Rabat's application was not successful. The Council rejected Morocco's request on the grounds that it was not a European state. The fall of the Berlin Wall on 9 November 1989 marked a turning point in the European and world history. It is interesting to note that some have described the reunification of Germany as 'enlargement without accession' despite the fact the historic event did not take place within the framework of the enlargement policy of the Communities (*EurActiv*, 2010a). Following the end of the Cold War, the queue of membership applicants grew, and Cyprus, Malta as well as countries of the EFTA expressed their desire to join the European Communities.

Austria applied to become a member of the Community in July 1989. Twelve months later, Sweden also submitted its application for EEC membership as it was no longer considered to be incompatible with its policy of neutrality. Finland and Switzerland followed suit in 1992. In the meantime, the ministers of the Community and the EFTA states had embarked on negotiations with the aim of establishing European Economic Space. Although reaching consensus on fisheries, transit traffic, judicial and institutional issues proved to be very difficult, the agreement creating the European Economic Area (EEA) was signed in

May 1992. The Lisbon European Council noted that 'the EEA Agreement has paved the way for opening enlargement negotiations with a view to an early conclusion with EFTA countries seeking membership of the European Union' (Council of the European Communities, 1992). After the Swiss electorate refused to join the EEA, the country withdrew its application for membership. The Union launched accession negotiations with Austria, Finland, Sweden and Norway in early 1993.

The Copenhagen European Council urged 'the Commission, the Council, and the candidate countries to ensure that the negotiations proceed constructively and expeditiously' and confirmed 1 January 1995 as target date for the accession of the four EFTA countries. Although candidates had already accepted a significant part of the *acquis* under the EEA Agreement, the accession negotiations were particularly difficult with regard to agriculture, fisheries, regional aid and budgetary contributions. A Commission official stressed that some 'imaginative solutions' were necessary for the completion of membership talks, including a 'third option' on environmental issues (which allowed the candidate countries to maintain their higher environmental standards) and the creation of a new regional policy Objective 6 – for Arctic areas with a low-density population (Granell, 1995). The challenging issues between the candidate countries and the member states were resolved by March 1994. However, the British and Spanish insistence on changing the proportion of votes required for the blocking minority in the Council threatened to delay the accession process. Although the Ioannina compromise provided a complex solution to the heated institutional issue, it reinforced the need to reform the EU's institutional architecture.

Austrian, Finish and Swedish citizens supported the accession of their countries to the Union respectively, with 66.6% and 56.9% and 52.2% in favour of EU membership. The Norwegian electorate rejected EU membership for the second time in 1994 with 52.2% against and 47.8% in favour. The fourth enlargement of the Union to Austria, Finland and Sweden took place on 1 January 1995.

Fifth enlargement

In the meantime, the number of the countries aspiring to become member states increased dramatically. Hungary, Poland, Romania, Slovakia, Latvia, Estonia, Lithuania, Bulgaria, the Czech Republic and Slovenia submitted their applications for EU membership. The Union embarked on an unprecedented enlargement, described as 'both a political necessity and a historic opportunity for Europe' (Council of the European Union, 1995b).

The Luxembourg European Council, in December 1997, officially launched the overall enlargement process and decided to start accession negotiations with Cyprus, Hungary, Poland, Estonia, the Czech Republic and Slovenia. Two years later, the Helsinki European Council reaffirmed 'the inclusive nature of the accession process, which now comprises 13 candidate States within a single framework' and decided to open membership talks with Romania, Slovakia, Latvia, Lithuania, Bulgaria and Malta. Furthermore, the European Council confirmed that:

> Candidate States which have now been brought into the negotiating process will have the possibility to catch up within a reasonable period of time with those already in negotiations if they have made sufficient progress in their preparations.
>
> (Council of the European Union, 1999b)

Following a lengthy and complex pre-accession process, eight CEECs – the Czech Republic, Estonia, Hungary, Poland, Latvia, Lithuania, Slovenia, and Slovakia together with Cyprus and Malta (also known as the 'Laeken Ten' after the Laeken European Council which confirmed 2002 as a target date for the completion of their accession negotiations) – joined the EU in May 2004. The accession of Bulgaria and Romania in January 2007 marked the end of the fifth enlargement.

Sixth enlargement and ongoing enlargement

Enlargement remained a vital part of the EU's external policies, and the Union extended the membership perspective to South-Eastern Europe. In 2005, the Union started negotiating accession with Croatia and Turkey. The European Council has repeatedly reaffirmed its commitment to the membership of all Western Balkan countries[1] and Turkey (Council of the European Union, 2000a, 2003a, 2005a, 2006a, 2008, 2011a, 2011b, 2013, 2014). In July 2009, in the midst of an economic and banking crisis, Iceland applied for EU membership. The Union started the accession negotiations with Reykjavik in July 2010. Although the accession process advanced at a good pace, the Icelandic government decided to put the membership talks on hold in May 2013 (*EurActiv*, 2013a). In the meantime, Croatia finalised the accession negotiations and became the 28th member state of the Union on 1 July 2013.

After a three-year hiatus, the accession negotiations with Ankara 'regained momentum' with the opening of Chapter 22 (Regional Policy and Coordination of Structural Instruments) in November 2013

(Council of the European Union, 2013). However, since the start of the membership talks in 2005, Turkey has opened 14 chapters and provisionally closed only one – Chapter 25 (Science and Research) (European Commission, 2014a). Furthermore, there are only three chapters which are not blocked either by the Council of the European Union or by member states. Despite the slow pace of the accession negotiations, there has been progress between the EU and Ankara on the visa-liberalisation dialogue. The EU–Turkey readmission agreement entered into force in October 2014 (Council of the European Union, 2014). The membership talks with Montenegro – first country to negotiate under the 'new approach' which the Commission launched in 2012 – have advanced well. Podgorica has opened 16 chapters, including Chapter 23 (Judiciary and Fundamental Rights) and Chapter 24 (Justice, Freedom and Security) and provisionally closed two chapters (European Commission, 2014a). The EU urged Montenegro to intensify its efforts to further develop a solid track record of implementation in the area of the rule of law and fight against corruption (Council of the European Union, 2014).

The historic agreement between Belgrade and Pristina cleared the way for advancing their relations with the Union. The EU started the negotiations for a Stabilisation and Association agreement with Kosovo in October 2013, and two months later the EU ministers agreed to begin the membership talks with Serbia on 21 January 2014 (Council of the European Union, 2014). In line with the new approach, the EU set opening benchmarks for Chapters 23 and 24 which ask Belgrade to prepare comprehensive action plans. The relations between FYROM and the EU have been strained by the name dispute between Athens and Skopje. There has been limited progress in the advancement of the EU relations with FYROM. This was the first country to sign an SAA and has been a candidate country since 2005. In 2014, the Commission recommended for the sixth time in row the opening of accession negotiations with Skopje, but it was blocked by Greece (European Commission, 2014a). Albania applied for membership in 2009. The Netherland's veto prevented the Council from granting Albania a candidate status, despite the Commission's unconditional recommendation (*EurActiv*, 2013b). The EU ministers agreed to reward Tirana with a candidate status in June 2014, however, the Union was cautious to stress that '[c]andidate status does not mean that the EU will automatically start accession negotiations with Albania' (Europa Press Releases, 2014). The progress in Bosnia and Herzegovina – another aspiring member – has been rather slow, and the Council has openly criticised the lack of political will on the part of the political leadership in the country (European Commission, 2014a).

In December 2014, the EU launched a renewed approach towards Sarajevo with 'the objective to establish functionality and efficiency at all levels of government and allow Bosnia and Herzegovina' (Council of the European Union, 2014). The recent developments in the relations between the EU and the candidate and potential candidate countries show that the enlargement process remains at the heart of the EU agenda.

EU accession process

This section briefly outlines the main stages of the EU accession process. Firstly, any country which aspires to join the Union submits its membership application to the Council of the EU. The Council forwards the application to the Commission. In order to evaluate the application, the Commission compiles a questionnaire and delivers it to the applicant country. The questionnaires for the Western Balkan applicants illustrate the scope of the Commission's enquiry: Serbia was asked to answer 2483 questions and sub-questions; Montenegro – 2178; Albania – 2280; Croatia – 4560; and FYROM – almost 4000 questions (Government of the Republic of Serbia, 2015). On the basis of the answers, the Commission draws up an Opinion (Avis) evaluating the country's compliance with EU membership conditions. Although previously a positive opinion from the Commission would lead to a Council decision on the opening of the accession negotiations, the ongoing enlargement process illustrates the emergence of two separate steps: (1) the Council recognises the applicant as a candidate country and (2) the Council decides to launch accession negotiations. The EU can also establish certain conditions which the applicant country should meet in order to start negotiating accession.

The membership talks are a key element of the accession process as they are aimed at the adoption and the implementation of the *acquis* by the candidate country. The *acquis* is the body of EU laws and obligations, which consists of more than 160,000 pages. It covers virtually all areas of the EU policies and is divided into 35 chapters (see Appendix I). The negotiations, which are governed by a negotiating framework unanimously agreed by the member states, take place at bilateral intergovernmental conferences between the member states and the candidate country. The preparatory phase of the accession negotiations, known as screening, involves the analytical investigation of the legislation of the applicant country and its conformity with the *acquis*. On the basis of the screening, the Commission prepares a screening report which includes recommendations for the opening of individual chapters and, if necessary, outlines conditions (opening benchmarks) which should be met prior to the opening of the chapter. After the member states have unanimously agreed that the opening benchmarks have been fulfilled, the Council invites the candidate country to present its position (which could include a request for transition period and derogation) on the specific chapter. The next step involves the preparation of the EU common position, which for most chapters includes closing benchmarks.

In 2012, the New Approach to accession negotiations placed Chapter 23 (Judiciary and Fundamental Rights) and Chapter 24 (Justice, Freedom and Security) at the heart of the accession process. The Commission:

- confirmed that Chapters 23 and 24 are to be opened early and closed late;
- introduced the application of interim benchmarks for these two chapters; and
- linked the advancement of the accession negotiations to the progress in the areas of covered by the chapters.

The negotiations on individual chapters vary depending on the issues discussed and the preparedness of the candidate country. The membership talks operated on the principle that 'nothing is agreed until everything is agreed', which means that individual chapters are provisionally closed and the agreements reached are finalised at the end of the entire negotiating process (European Commission, 2007c).

In 1961, when announcing the government's decision to apply for EC membership, the British Prime Minister Harold Macmillan (1961) noted: 'These [enlargement] negotiations must inevitably be of a detailed and technical character, covering a very large number of the most delicate and difficult matters. They may, therefore, be protracted and there can, of course, be no guarantee of success.' More than 50 years later, his description remains very accurate.

The accession negotiations are highly asymmetrical as applicants are bound by the logic of enlargement 'to accept the pre-existing set of rules before getting a chance to take part in shaping them' (Raik, 2006: 85). As Olli Rehn, the former Commissioner for Enlargement, stated: 'Negotiations are not about whether a candidate country will adopt the EU legislation. The rules of the club have indeed to be accepted. Negotiations are about determining when and how it will happen' (Rehn, 2006e).

When negotiation of all chapters is completed, the Council, after receiving the opinion of the Commission and the assent of the European Parliament (EP), decides unanimously whether to conclude the process or not. The conclusion of the accession negotiations is followed by the signing of an Accession Treaty. After signature, the Accession Treaty is submitted to the member states and to the acceding country for ratification by them in accordance with their own constitutional procedures. When the ratification process has been concluded and the Treaty takes effect, the candidate becomes a member state.

Membership conditions

In order to conclude the accession negotiations and to become a member of the EU, the applicant state has to fulfil certain conditions. As the European Communities have evolved, so have the conditions for membership. Before the first enlargement took place, the only condition for membership was 'European identity'. According to Article 237 of the Rome Treaty, '[a]ny European state may apply to become a member of the Community' (Treaty of Rome, 1957). However, with respect to the applicant countries from Southern Europe (Greece, Portugal and Spain), the European Council in April 1978 set out additional conditions by stating that 'respect for and maintenance of representative democracy and human rights in each Member State are essential elements of membership in the European Communities' (Council of the European Communities, 1978). Furthermore, as Smith notes, 'in the case of Greece, an early version of the "good-neighbourliness" condition appeared ... as the Commission and the Council declared that Greece accession should not adversely affect the Community's relations with Turkey' (Smith, 2003: 110).

In the light of the EU enlargement with the countries of the EFTA, the Lisbon European Council in 1992 confirmed that 'any European State whose system of government is founded on the principle of democracy may apply to become a member of the Union' (Council of the European Communities, 1992). The decisions taken at the Copenhagen European Council in June 1993 had important consequences for the development of EU enlargement policy and particularly for the development of its membership conditions. The European Council took a decisive step towards the fifth enlargement by concluding that 'the associated countries in central and eastern Europe that so desire shall become members of the European Union' (Council of the European Union, 1993). Furthermore, the European Council laid down membership conditions, known as the Copenhagen criteria, which a candidate country must satisfy before it could join the Union. The membership criteria require that the candidate country must have achieved:

• stability of institutions guaranteeing democracy, the rule of law, human rights and respect for and protection of minorities;
• the existence of a functioning market economy as well as the capacity to cope with competitive pressure and market forces within the Union; and
• the ability to take on the obligations of membership, including adherence to the aims of political, economic and monetary union.

The Copenhagen European Council set out another membership condition. It was not designed for the applicant countries, but for the EU itself. According to the conclusions of the Council, 'the Union's capacity to absorb new members, while maintaining the momentum of European integration, is also an important consideration in the general interest of both the Union and the candidate countries' (Council of the European Union, 1993).

The membership conditions were revised at the Madrid European Council in 1995. The Presidency conclusions confirmed that membership requires the creation of the conditions for integration through the adjustment of administrative and institutional structures guaranteeing effective implementation of the *acquis*. However, neither the Copenhagen European Council nor the Madrid European Council established a hierarchy among the membership requirements. In December 1997, the Union stated that:

[c]ompliance with the Copenhagen political criteria is a prerequisite for the opening of any accession negotiations. Economic criteria and the ability to fulfil the obligations arising from membership have been and must be assessed in a forward-looking, dynamic way.
(Council of the European Union, 1997a)

Furthermore, the Commission introduced the first detailed explanation of scope and range of the membership conditions in 'Agenda 2000 – For a Stronger and Wider Union', which presented a comprehensive far-reaching project aimed at preparing the Union for the eastern expansion (see Chapter 2 for a detailed discussion).

In addition to the Copenhagen and the Madrid criteria, the EU gradually elaborated on the fundamentals of another condition: 'good-neighbourliness'. The Essen European Council noted that:

[b]eing aware of the role of regional cooperation within the Union, the Heads of State and Government emphasize the importance of similar cooperation between the associated countries for the promotion of economic development and good neighbourly relations.

(Council of the European Union, 1994b)

The EU also stressed the principle of peaceful settlement of disputes in accordance with the United Nations Charter and urged 'candidate States to make every effort to resolve any outstanding border disputes and other related issues' (Council of the European Union, 1999b). After the European Council extended the membership perspective to the countries of the Western Balkans, the Union specified that the policy of good neighbourliness was:

based on the negotiated settlement of disputes, respect for the rights of minorities, respect for international obligations, including with regard to the ICTY, a lasting resolution of the problem of refugees and displaced persons and respect for States' international borders.

(Zagreb Declaration, 2000)

In addition to outlining the key aspects of the principle of good neighbourly relations, the EU confirmed that:

[t]he prospect of accession is offered on the basis of the provision of the Treaty on European Union, respect for the criteria defined at the Copenhagen European Council in June 1993 and the progress made in implementing the stabilisation and association agreements, in particular on regional cooperation.

(Zagreb Declaration, 2000)

In 2003, the Union expanded the scope of conditions by confirming the importance of the Stablisation and Association Process (SAP) for the accession of the Western Balkans. The SAP conditionality included (among other requirements) co-operation with the International Criminal Tribunal for the Former Yugoslavia (ICTY) and regional co-operation, return of refugees and displaced persons, democratic reforms, and free and fair elections. Furthermore, the Commission has also provided Turkey and the Western Balkan applicants with country-specific lists of conditions at different stages of the accession process (see Chapter 4 for a detailed discussion). In 2012, the EU altered the dynamics of the accession process by confirming that 'the chapters Judiciary and fundamental rights and Justice, freedom and security will be tackled early in the negotiations to allow maximum time to establish the necessary legislation, institutions, and solid track records of implementation before the negotiations are closed' (European Commission, 2012a).

The analysis illustrates that the EU has gradually elaborated on the scope of EU membership conditions. The new policy developments provide more evidence for the evolutionary nature of EU enlargement conditionality and point to a very important progression in the EU's requirements for membership: from the adoption of the *acquis* and policy alignment to the development of a sustainable track record of implementation. Furthermore, the questions about tracing and measuring the irreversibility of reforms in challenging areas (such as judiciary reform and fight against corruption) are bound to prompt more policy innovations.

Literature on EU enlargement conditionality

The numerous challenges and the great political significance of the unique historical enlargement of the Union to the East lent speed to the emergence and development of the study of EU enlargement as a key research area. Although the majority of the early studies investigated the puzzle of the EU's decision to enlarge to the CEECs (Baldwin, 1995; Schimmelfennig, 1998; Fierke and Wiener, 1999; Sjursen, 2002; Sedelmeier, 2005), the research focus expanded quickly to include other dimensions. The impact of EU enlargement is one of the areas which has blossomed and accumulated a growing body of literature over the last decade, which has not only widened the research focus of Europeanisation studies (beyond the member states of the Union), but also stimulated and shaped the debates on the scope and effectiveness of conditionality (see the following section).

Types of conditionality

Conditionality is one of the main concepts which has been applied in examining the enlargement policy of the EU towards the applicant countries of Eastern Europe. Conditionality is a broad concept and it varies according to the context applied. Enlargement conditionality (Hughes, Sasse and Gordon, 2004), membership conditionality (Smith, 2003, 2004), accession conditionality (Grabbe, 2002, 2006), *acquis* conditionality (Grabbe, 2002; Schimmelfennig and Sedelmeier, 2004), democratic conditionality (Pridham, 2002) and political conditionality (Smith, 1998) are some of the categories of conditionality defined in the literature on European integration. It is important to note that the application of conditionality is not limited to the accession process, as the EC was among the first international organisations which started to apply political conditions in their relations with third countries in the late 1980s (Dimier, 2006; Börzel and Risse, 2009). The use of economic and political criteria in the dispersal of development aid was established with the fourth Lomé Convention in 1989, which confirmed that development was specifically linked to the promotion of human rights (Dimier, 2006: 263). Furthermore, the decisions of the Rome Summit in December 1990 made democracy promotion and human rights protection a normative principle of EC's external relations (Council of the European Communities, 1990).

The increasing application of political conditions indicates that conditionality has evolved from 'first generation' of economic conditionality to a 'second generation' of combined economic and political conditionality (Hughes et al., 2004: 15). Although the Communities applied conditionality to third countries, it was the desire of the CEECs to join the EU which triggered the development of complex conditions which the applicants must satisfy before they are allowed to become members. As Grabbe notes, 'the conditions for accession set for the CEE countries were the most detailed and comprehensive ever formulated' (2002: 251). Hughes et al. (2004: 18) stress that it is the 'totality of economic and political elements and the attempt to operationalize them simultaneously across a whole region that makes the EU conditionality exceptional in its scope and intent'. However, the ongoing enlargement round with the Western Balkan countries and Turkey shows that 'the conditions or the thresholds for becoming a member have become ever-increasingly tougher' (Interview 23, 2014).

Application of EU conditionality

Smith examines EU conditionality and particularly membership conditionality applied towards the CEECs. She notes that 'membership conditionality is used by the EU as a foreign-policy instrument to influence applicant (and future applicant) countries' domestic and foreign policies' (Smith, 2003: 108). Although membership conditionality is limited in geographical and temporal terms as EU membership is open only to 'European states' which will eventually become members, 'the EU has wielded the instrument, at times quite assertively and to great effect' (Smith, 2003: 109).

Smith notes that setting membership conditions is a way to protect the achievements of the Union in various policy areas from radical change brought on by membership expansion (2003). Furthermore, she argues that the strict application of membership conditionality is a partial solution to the 'widening versus deepening' dilemma, as membership conditions protect the future integration process (Smith, 2003). Grabbe argues that the conditions set out at the Copenhagen European Council have a dual purpose. She notes that the conditions were designed not only to minimise the risk of new entrants becoming politically unstable and economically burdensome and thus to reassure reluctant member states, but also to guide the applicant countries (Grabbe, 2002: 254). However, Grabbe points out that the accession conditionality established by the Copenhagen criteria is not a straightforward case of conditionality because the linkage between fulfilling particular tasks and receiving particular benefits is not clear as most of the tasks are complex and not amenable to quantitative targets (Grabbe, 2006: 32).

In the analysis of the EU's transformative power, Grabbe investigates the mechanisms used by the EU to effect change through conditionality and the accession process. Grabbe (2006: 76) identifies five groups of mechanisms:

- gate-keeping: access to negotiations and further stages in the accession process;
- benchmarking and monitoring;
- models: provisions of legislative and institutional templates;
- money: aid and technical assistance; and
- advice and twinning.

Grabbe argues that the EU's most powerful conditionality tool is the access to different stages of the accession process. She specifies that achieving candidate status and starting the accession negotiations are the two most important stages (Grabbe, 2001: 1020).

Geoffrey Pridham notes that 'conditionality is one of the most resonant and deliberate efforts to determine the process's outcome through external pressure' (Pridham, 2002: 956). He specifies that the outcomes are achieved by setting conditions or preconditions for support, which include either a promise of material aid or political opportunities. Pridham notes that democratic conditionality is a special version of conditionality which emphasises respect for and the furtherance of democratic rules, procedures and values (Pridham, 2002: 956). Other researchers argue that democratic conditionality is 'the core strategy of the EU to induce non-member states to comply with its principles of legitimate statehood' (Schimmelfennig, Engert and Knobel, 2003: 495;

Schimmelfennig and Sedelmeier, 2004). Smith claims that '[p]olitical conditionality entails linking by a state or international organisation, of perceived benefits to another state (such as aid) to the fulfillment of conditions relating to the protection of human rights and the advancement of democratic principles' (Smith, 1998: 256).

Hughes, Sasse and Gordon examine the application of conditionality in the context of the EU regional policy. They argue that EU conditionality is not 'a uniformly hard rule-based instrument, but rather a highly differentiated' one (Hughes et al., 2004: 256). Furthermore, they state that the nature of conditionality has been shifting and transforming depending on the content of the *acquis*, the policy area, the country concerned and the political context in which it is applied. They distinguish two main categories of conditionality: formal and informal. Hughes et al. (2004: 256) specify that formal conditionality includes 'the publicly stated preconditions as set out in the broad principles of the Copenhagen criteria and the legal framework of the acquis', whereas, informal conditionality refers to 'the operational pressures and recommendations applied by actors within the Commission during interactions with their CEEC counterparts in the course of the enlargement'.

According to Schimmelfennig and Sedelmeier (2004), EU enlargement conditionality includes two main types: democratic and *acquis*. Democratic conditionality is aimed at the compliance of the applicant country with the political criteria for membership and takes place at the initial stage of the accession process. *Acquis* conditionality requires that the non-member state adopts the Community *acquis* prior to its accession to the Union. Although *acquis* conditionality may take place at the very early stages of the accession, it is characteristic of the accession negotiations.

Gaps in the literature

The analysis of the academic literature shows some important characteristics of the research on EU conditionality. Firstly, there is no commonly agreed definition of EU (enlargement) conditionality. However, the literature tends to agree that the concept of conditionality entails the linkage between fulfilling particular tasks (conditions) and receiving particular benefits (rewards), and that conditionality operates in an environment of power asymmetry.

Secondly, most of the theoretical discussion of conditionality focuses on the conditionality established by the Copenhagen criteria and the *acquis*. It is important to note that EU conditionality is not limited to the membership conditions established at the Copenhagen European

Council, as the Community started to apply conditionality towards the CEECs in the late 1980s. The Trade and Cooperation Agreements (TCAs), which officially established the relations between the Community and the CEECs, as well as the AAs were made conditional on satisfying certain criteria, including democracy, the rule of law, human rights and respect for and protection of minorities. Similarly, the relations between the EU and the countries from the South-Eastern Europe were developed in the framework of rigorous conditionality. The adoption of the Zagreb Declaration, which reaffirmed the European perspective of the countries from the Western Balkans, launched the SAP. In addition, to the existing Copenhagen criteria, the Declaration established a set of conditions (known as the SAP conditionality) which should be fulfilled by the countries prior to their accession.[2] In the framework of the SAP, the EU initiated and signed SAAs with the countries from the Western Balkans.[3] The agreements were similar to the AAs signed with the previous candidates.

Thirdly, most of the research is aimed either at explaining how the EU conditionality influences the domestic structures in the applicant countries or at evaluating the effectiveness of EU conditionality in particular policy areas. The fundamental problems of the nature and the scope of EU conditionality remain very weakly analysed. Although the key modalities of the accession process have remained the same, EU enlargement policy has undergone a dramatic transformation since the establishment of the Copenhagen criteria in 1993. The questions about how and why EU enlargement policy (and respectively EU enlargement conditionality) has changed are crucial for understanding not only the policy dynamics in this area and its legacy on EU Neighbourhood policy, but also for assessing its policy outcomes. The strong comparative dimension of this book allows us to trace policy evolution beyond key historical milestones and identify key trajectories of policy development. Furthermore, the introduction of the new approach to accession negotiations and the renewed EU approach to Bosnia and Herzegovina show that the transformation of EU conditionality is still far from being completed.

Towards a stage-structured model for comparative examination of EU enlargement conditionality

With a view to investigating two areas which have been largely neglected by the academic literature – the evolution of EU enlargement conditionality and the impact of institutional and external factors on the development of EU enlargement policy – the book outlines a conceptual framework for comparative study of EU enlargement conditionality. The *stage-structured conditionality model*, which relates the examination of EU enlargement conditionality to different stages of the accession process, follows an inclusive approach and does not distinguish between different categories of conditionality based on the context of their application (such as membership conditionality, accession conditionality and democratic conditionality).

Although the EU has not formally identified these stages, some of the achievements on the way to accession can be regarded as key turning points. The first step which has strong political significance is the formal agreement of the European Council on the membership perspective of the potential candidate country. Another milestone which intensifies the relations between the EU and the aspiring member state is the opening of the accession negotiations. The conclusion of the accession negotiations is another turning point which is central to the dynamics of the process. Finally, the accession of the new member state to the EU marks the completion of the process. On the basis of these achievements, the conceptual model outlines the following four distinct stages of the accession process:

- Pre-negotiation stage;
- Negotiation stage;
- Accession stage; and
- Post-accession stage.

The pre-negotiation stage starts with the formal agreement of the European Council on the membership perspective of the potential candidate country and ends with the start of the accession negotiations. Although making a formal application for EU membership is considered to be the first step of the accession process, the EU's experience of the fifth and the ongoing enlargement indicates that this is not always the case. Relations between the Union and the CEECs as well as the Western Balkan countries, for example, were structured on the basis of conditionality prerogatives prior to these countries formally applying for EU membership.[4] As the membership talks mark an important phase in the development of the relations between the EU and the candidate country, the *stage-structured conditionality model* specifies that the accession negotiations make up the second stage of the enlargement process. The third stage includes the period after the conclusion of the membership talks and before the formal accession of a country to the Union.

The accession stage includes the signing of the Accession Treaty and its ratification, and it is characterised by thorough examination of the would-be-member's compliance with EU conditions. The fourth stage refers to the period after the accession of a candidate country to the EU. The safeguard clauses, included in the Act of Accession for the countries which became members in 2004, attached significant relevance to the post-accession stage by specifying that the safeguard measures may be applied 'until the end of a period of up to three years after accession' (Official Journal, 2003a).

Although the Act of Accession for Bulgaria and Romania included the same safeguard clauses (with the exception of the postponement clause), the establishment of the Cooperation and Verification Mechanism (CVM) and the conclusions of the July 2009 reports that the mechanism 'needs to be maintained until these reforms are achieved' (European Commission, 2009f, 2009g) extended the post-accession stage beyond the period of three years after accession. Therefore, the model specifies that the post-accession stage starts with accession of a state to the EU and ends with the suspension of any post-accession monitoring mechanism or, in the absence of any post-accession monitoring mechanism, with the expiry of the applicability of the safeguard measures included in the Treaty of Accession.

In addition to identifying the key stages of the accession process, the model outlines the key elements of EU enlargement conditionality. The literature highlights the significance of the conditions laid down by the EU as well as the particular benefits (rewards) which the applicant states receive as a result of their compliance (Smith, 1998; Schimmelfennig et al., 2003; Schimmelfennig and Sedelmeier, 2004; Grabbe, 2006). However, the completion of the fifth round of enlargement with the CEECs, Cyprus and Malta has proved that there are other elements which are also essential for the application of EU conditionality.

The *stage-structured conditionality model* specifies that EU enlargement conditionality has three key elements:

- conditions set out by the EU with which the country aspiring to membership needs to comply;
- an incentive structure that examines the *reward–threat balance*; and
- monitoring (see Table 1.3).

The first element includes the conditions set out by the EU with which the country aspiring to membership needs to comply. During

Table 1.3 Stage-structured (EU enlargement) conditionality model

Stages	Conditions	Incentive structure		Monitoring
		Rewards	**Threats**	
Pre-negotiation	– Conditions for applying for membership (conditions of accession) – Conditions for opening accession negotiations – Additional (country-specific) conditions	**Accession advancement rewards:** – Providing membership perspective – Signing AA – Implementing AA – Granting candidate country status – Opening accession negotiations **Financial rewards**	**Explicit threats:** Financial sanctions Preventive and remedial sanctions **Implicit threats:** Delays of the accession advancement rewards	Regular progress reports
Negotiation	– Copenhagen criteria – Opening benchmarks (conditions for opening chapters) – Interim benchmarks – Closing benchmarks (conditions for closing chapters) – 31/35 chapters – Areas of serious concern (highlighted in the monitoring reports)	**Accession advancement rewards:** – Opening chapters – Closing chapters – Credible membership perspective – Completion of accession negotiations – Signing accession treaty **Financial rewards**	**Explicit threats:** Financial sanctions Preventive and remedial sanctions **Implicit threats:** Delays of the accession advancement rewards	Regular progress reports

Table 1.3 (Continued)

Stages	Conditions	Incentive structure		Monitoring
		Rewards	Threats	
Accession	– Copenhagen criteria – Areas of serious concern (highlighted in the monitoring reports)	**Accession advancement rewards:** – Accession **Financial rewards**	**Explicit threats:** **Preventive and remedial sanctions:** – Internal market safeguard clause – Justice and home affairs (JHA) safeguard clause – Super safeguard clause – Additional clause(s)	Comprehensive monitoring reports
Post-accession	– Benchmarks (individual country-specific conditions)	**Financial rewards**	**Explicit threats:** **Preventive and remedial sanctions:** – Economic safeguard clause – Internal market Safeguard clause – JHA safeguard clause	Progress reports Interim reports

the pre-negotiation stage, the potential candidate country must satisfy two sets of conditions: *conditions for applying for membership* and *conditions for opening of accession negotiations*. Article 49 of the Treaty on European Union (TEU) sets out the conditions for enlargement by stating that any European state which respects principles of liberty, democracy, respect for human rights and fundamental freedoms and the rule of law may apply to become a member of the Union. The conclusions of the Helsinki European Council in December 1999, which confirm that 'compliance with the political criteria laid down at the Copenhagen European Council is a prerequisite for the opening of accession negotiations', do not limit the scope of the *conditions for opening of accession negotiations*, as the EU can establish country-specific conditions (Council of the European Union, 1999b).

In order to complete the accession negotiations, the candidate country needs to fulfil all the Copenhagen criteria. Furthermore, the EU can establish specific conditions for the opening and/or provisional closure of individual chapters, known respectively as opening and closing benchmarks.[5] During the accession stage the EU urges the acceding countries to fully meet all the commitments and requirements arising from the membership talks and can use the monitoring reports to highlight areas of serious concern. Furthermore, the establishment of an unprecedented monitoring mechanism for Bulgaria and Romania confirms that the Union can specify individual sets of benchmarks even after accession.

The EU has developed a wide range of incentives in order to induce compliance with its conditions. Although the Union has favoured the use of carrots over sticks, it has also established mechanisms for punishing non-compliance by introducing a range of threats. The *stage-structured conditionality model* specifies that the second element of EU conditionality is the incentive structure, which examines the *reward–threat balance*. The model outlines two categories of rewards: *accession advancement rewards*, which reflect the progress of the candidate country in the accession process, and *financial rewards* (or financial assistance). The main *accession advancement rewards* include:

- granting membership perspective;
- signing an AA;
- implementing an AA;
- granting candidate country status;
- opening accession negotiations;
- opening a specific negotiating chapter;

- provisionally closing a chapter;
- committing to a credible membership perspective;
- completing of accession negotiations;
- signing an accession treaty;
- ratifying an accession treaty; and
- accession to the EU.

The stage-structured conditionality model limits the definition (and the examination) of the credibility of the membership perspective to a commitment to target dates/timetables for the advancement of the accession process. It is important to note that this reward can be attributed to both pre-negotiation and negotiation stage.

The financial rewards refer to the financial assistance provided by the EU to the candidate country through the pre-accession financial instruments such as PHARE, SAPARD and ISPA programmes.[6] Although the book will acknowledge the financial assistance granted by the EU to the applicant countries at different stages of the enlargement process, it will not provide a detailed discussion of the sums allocated to each of the case studies. A previous research has noted that closer contractual relations provide stronger incentives for compliance with EU conditions rather than financial assistance (Grabbe, 2002). Furthermore, the vast majority of the interviewees commented that the allocation of pre-accession funds was not a controversial issue among the candidate countries of Central and Eastern Europe (CEE). One senior Commission official observed that the pre-accession financial assistance was 'peanuts' compared to the funding available to countries through structural and cohesion funds after they have become full-fledged members of the Union (Interview 20, 2009).

The *stage-structured conditionality model* divides the threats into two groups: *implicit* and *explicit*. The *implicit threats* sanction non-compliance by delaying the receiving of the *accession advancement rewards*. Unlike *implicit*, *explicit threats* introduce specific penalising measures. There are two types of *explicit threats* based on the nature of the measures which they introduce. The first type refers to *financial sanctions* which penalise non-compliance with EU rules by suspending or withdrawing funds. The second type of *explicit threats* refers to *preventive or remedial sanctions* which include specific precautionary measures (safeguard measures). The EU has developed numerous precautionary measures ranging from economic and internal market safeguard clauses to specific measures in the areas of food safety and air safety.

With a view to analysing the shifting nature of the incentive structure, the *stage-structured conditionality model* highlights the relevance of *accession advancement rewards* and *explicit threats* and establishes two main points of reference:

- the incentive structure is positive if the *reward–threat balance* is dominated by *accession advancement rewards*; and
- the incentive structure is negative if the *reward–threat balance* is dominated by *preventive and remedial sanctions*.

As the significance of monitoring the applicants' compliance with EU conditions has increased substantially since the publication of the first Regular Reports in 1998, the *stage-structured conditionality model* specifies that monitoring is the third key element of EU enlargement conditionality. The rigorous approach of the Commission to reporting on the progress made towards accession by each of the candidate countries (which were part of the fifth round of enlargement) as well as potential candidate countries (since 2005) has transformed the scope and nature of the Regular Reports from brief general assessments into detailed evaluation analyses. More importantly, it has helped the Commission to establish significant expertise in providing a comprehensive assessment of the EU hopefuls' compliance with EU conditions and, thus, legitimising the impartiality of the Commission's recommendations. The Commission significantly increased the relevance of monitoring reports as it started to use them not only as a basis for its recommendations (whether to grant a reward or impose a sanction), but as an instrument for prioritising conditions and as well as for establishing new conditions and introducing new threats. On the basis of the functions which the monitoring reports fulfil, the *stage-structured conditionality model* distinguishes between two groups of reports: *evaluation reports* and *advanced reports*. The *evaluation reports* include the monitoring reports which assess progress and/or prioritise conditions. The *advanced reports* refer to the reports which, in addition to evaluating progress, establish new conditions and/or threats.

The *stage-structured conditionality model* allows us to analyse in a systematic and comprehensive manner the empirical data, to identify key developments of EU enlargement conditionality and to complete the first step of the analysis. Despite the growing body of literature on EU conditionality, policy-making in the area of enlargement remains under-researched.

The role of member states' preferences has featured extensively in the academic literature on EU enlargement. Although some analyses look into the impact of individual member states such as Germany, France and Spain, the focus of most studies is limited to one dimension of EU enlargement policy – decision-making regarding the Eastern expansion of the Union (Tewes, 1998; Hyde-Price, 2000; Piedrafita, 2007). Similarly, research on the activism of the Commission is predominantly confined to the development and implementation of EU enlargement strategy towards the CEECs (Sedelmeier, 2005; O'Brennan, 2006). However, the literature has witnessed the emergence of studies advocating multi-dimensional approaches to investigating the development of EU enlargement policy, which highlight the continuity and change in the EU's enlargement strategy across the CEECs, Turkey and the Western Balkans (Pridham, 2007; İçener, Phinnemore and Papadimitriou, 2010).

With a view to explaining the evolution of EU enlargement policy (and respectively enlargement conditionality), the book draws on public policy literature. Richardson's (2012) edited volume, which features an impressive selection of sectoral studies, demonstrates that there is a wide range of actors shaping the development of EU policies. Furthermore, no single theoretical framework can satisfactorily explain EU policy-making in all policy areas. However, Richardson (2012) notes the significance of institutions and stresses the relevance of the idea of policy entrepreneurship and importance of crises as windows of opportunity.

In order to examine the evolution of EU enlargement policy and complete the second step of the analysis, this book develops a comprehensive approach to policy dynamics and specifies that *EU enlargement policy is a function of differentiated influences from multiple actors and external pressures*. The definition highlights the complex constellations of actors involved in the accession process and emphasises their relevance by focusing on the influence which they can exert rather than on their competences. As it is virtually impossible to account for all the groups of actors and external shocks which affect the development of EU enlargement policy, the book follows a selective approach. The scope of the study is limited to analysing the impact of two sets of factors: institutional and exogenous. The former set analyses the institutional dimension and traces the impact of (1) *EU member states* and (2) *EU inter-institutional dynamics* on the development of EU enlargement conditionality. Furthermore, the study is strengthened by the analysis of external pressures and focuses on the following factors: (3) *public opinion in the EU*, (4) *enlargement countries* and (5) *external pressures caused by economic or security shocks and crises*.

The discussion of the impact of EU institutions is structured in two sections. The study dissects the role of the Council of the European Union, undoubtedly the most powerful non-unitary actor in the accession process, by analysing the influence of individual member states. The examination of member states' preferences is not limited to the impact of their attitudes towards enlargement (in general) or the accession of a/group of candidate country/ies (in particular). It also investigates the relevance of bilateral relations between member states and candidate countries by focusing on the implications of bilateral issues for the advancement of the accession process.

With a view to analysing the policy outcomes of inter-institutional dynamics, the book outlines the competences of the main EU institutions – the Council of the EU, the European Commission and the EP – and highlights the complexity of the inter-institutional interactions. Furthermore, as the study is concerned with the influence which the institutions can exercise, the discussion reflects particularly on the fruitfulness of the Commission's entrepreneurship and the activism of the EP. It also reflects on the relevance of the Presidencies of the Council of the EU for the advancement of the accession process.

Although the crucial relevance of institutional factors for the development of enlargement policy is unquestionable, the EU as a political system is not immune to external pressures. The relevance of public opinion has grown dramatically over the last ten years. European integration is often viewed as an elite-centred project that has failed to engage with its public. In a similar vein, the Eastern expansion of the Union is described as an elite-led process decided above the heads of the European citizens. Therefore, it is not surprising that the impact of the public opinion in the EU member states on the Eastern enlargement did not attract much scholarly attention (but see Eichenberg and Dalton, 1993). However, the failed constitutional referenda in France and the Netherlands not only questioned the future development of the European project but also pushed the EU to reflect on its relationship with the European citizens. The Commissioner for Enlargement Olli Rehn noted that '[t]he EU's enlargement fatigue started and became a scapegoat in June 2005, after the two failed referenda on the Constitutional Treaty' (Rehn, 2006d). The renewed consensus on enlargement, which provided the basis for the new enlargement strategy of the Commission, insisted that '[i]t is essential to ensure public support for enlargement' (European Commission, 2006g). In recent years, research on the public attitudes towards Turkey – probably the most controversial candidate country – has become very prominent (Dalhman, 2004; Ruiz-Jiménez and Torreblanca, 2007; Schoen, 2008). However, the academic literature on EU enlargement lacks in-depth systematic examinations of the impact of public opinion on the development of

EU enlargement policy. With a view to investigating if and how public opinion can influence enlargement conditionality, the book examines the variation in EU public support for enlargement and the shifts in the attitudes towards the accession of individual applicant countries in a comparative perspective. The analysis draws on the data from the Standard Eurobarometer surveys, published in the period between 1990 and 2014.

The literature concerned with the effectiveness of the EU influence on applicant states has stressed the importance of domestic politics particularly with reference to veto players and administrative capacities (Hughes et al., 2004; Schimmelfennig and Sedelmeier, 2004; Toshkov, 2008). However, the analytical frameworks aimed at investigating the dynamics of policy-making have neglected the impact of the EU hopefuls. Although enlargement takes place in an environment of power asymmetry and applicant states have very limited bargaining power in the accession process, the EU enlargement strategies show that candidate countries not only inform but also shape the parameters of EU enlargement policy (see European Commission, 1997, 2006g).

In order to investigate how the profile of the candidate countries can influence EU conditionality, this study looks into the following two aspects:

- the impact of problematic issues and reform challenges, which the applicant states need to address, on the scope and range of the EU conditions; and
- the implications of the existence or lack of group dynamics (analysed with reference to number of candidate countries at similar stages of the accession process) for the development of the incentive structure, particularly with reference to the *accession advancement rewards*.

The analysis of the impact of exogenous factors on EU enlargement policy also discusses the relevance of economic or security shocks and crises as windows of opportunity. The study follows a selective approach and focuses on pivotal events – whose significance for the transformation of Europe is undeniable – the end of the Cold War, the Yugoslav wars, Kosovo crisis and the Eurozone crisis.

Conclusion

The book proceeds with a comparative examination of EU enlargement conditionality. The following three chapters focus respectively on:

- the first phase of the fifth enlargement (Chapter 2);
- the second phase of the fifth enlargement (Chapter 3); and
- Croatia's accession and the ongoing enlargement process with the Western Balkans and Turkey (Chapter 4).

The study capitalises on the case study selection and traces the evolution of EU enlargement conditionality not only across different stages of the accession process (pre-negotiation, negotiation, accession and post-accession stage), but also across different countries. Furthermore, the two-step analysis strategy allows us to rigorously investigate continuity and change by examining the impact of a mixed set of internal and external factors.

2
EU Conditionality in the Context of the 2004 Enlargement

This chapter examines the evolution of EU enlargement conditionality by focusing on the first phase of the fifth enlargement, which expanded the Union by ten countries on 1 May 2004. The analysis of EU enlargement conditionality towards the Czech Republic, Estonia, Hungary, Poland, Latvia, Lithuania, Slovenia and Slovakia together with Cyprus and Malta is highly relevant for the examination of the evolution of EU conditionality. The 2004 enlargement was not only unprecedented in scale and scope but also represented the EU's initial response to the high number of requests for membership from the former communist states. Thus, the case study selection allows us to trace the early developments and test the impact of institutional and external factors on the EU conditionality of a uniquely exceptional enlargement round.

The chapter is structured into two parts. On the basis of the *stage-structured conditionality model*, the first part, which traces the transformation of EU conditionality between the stages of the accession process, is divided into four sections:

- Pre-negotiation stage;
- Negotiation stage;
- Accession stage; and
- Post-accession stage.

With a view to looking at the elements of EU enlargement conditionality, each section[1] is divided into the following three subsections:

- conditions set out by the EU with which the country aspiring to membership needs to comply;
- an incentive structure, which examines the *reward–threat balance*;
- monitoring.

The second part of the chapter examines the relationship between the developments of EU conditionality and the following factors: (1) *EU member states* (2) *EU inter-institutional dynamics*, (3) *public opinion in the EU*, (4) *enlargement countries* and (5) *external pressures caused by economic or security shocks and crises*.

Tracing the evolution of EU conditionality towards the 'Laeken Ten'

The EC was linked with Malta and Cyprus in the early 1970s by AAs, which provided for the establishment of a customs union (European Commission, 1993a, 1993b). However, relations between the EC and the CEECs followed a different trajectory. In order to contextualise the analysis of EU enlargement conditionality, this section briefly accounts for the development of relations between the EU and the 2004 candidates, prior to the establishment of their membership perspective.

Unlike the Mediterranean islands, the first contractual relation between the EC and the former communist countries[2] were established in the late 1980s and early 1990s by the signing of TCAs. The main objectives of these agreements were:

- to reinforce and diversify economic links;
- to contribute to the developments of economies and standards of living; and
- to open up new sources of supply and new markets.[3]

It is important to note that only the TCAs with Estonia, Latvia and Lithuania included a 'human rights clause', which confirmed that:

> [r]espect for the democratic principles and human rights established by the Helsinki Final Act and the Charter of Paris for a new Europe inspires the domestic and external policies of the Community and Estonia and constitutes an essential element of the present agreement.
>
> (*Official Journal*, 1994a, 1994b, 1994c)

Relations between the EC and Poland, Hungary and Czechoslovakia entered a new phase in December 1991 with the signing of the AAs, also known as Europe Agreements (EAs). The EAs not only strengthened the links between the Community and Warsaw, Budapest and Prague, but also recognised that 'the final objective' of the associated countries was 'to become a member of the Community' (*Official Journal*, 1993a, 1993b). The EAs signified 'the beginning of an entirely new era in bilateral relations' between the Community and the CEECs and were the first EC agreements to contain both a political dialogue dimension and a cultural co-operation dimension (Pinheiro, 1993).

The Copenhagen European Council on 21–22 June 1993 marked a crucial turning point by establishing that 'the associated countries in Central and Eastern Europe that so desire shall become members of the European Union' (Council of the European Union, 1993). Several days later, the Commission presented its opinions on Cyprus' and Malta's application, which confirmed their eligibility for membership (European Commission, 1993a, 1993b).

Pre-negotiation stage

Conditions

This section discusses the evolution of EU enlargement conditionality with reference to the development of two sets of conditions: *conditions for applying for membership* and *conditions for opening of accession negotiations* in the period from the establishment of the membership perspective to the start of the accession negotiations.

Article 98 of the Treaty of Paris, Article 237 of the Treaty of Rome and Article 205 of the EURATOM Treaty specified that '[a]ny European State may apply to become a member of the Community'. Following the enforcement of the TEU on 1 November 1993, Article O confirmed that 'Europeanness' was the only *condition for applying for membership* by stating that '[a]ny European State may apply to become a Member of the Union'. However, the Union did not provide a definition for 'Europeanness'.

The Copenhagen European Council not only gave the green light to enlargement with the CEECs, but also laid down the requirements which the associate countries should satisfy in order to become members. According to the Presidency conclusions,

> [m]embership requires that the candidate country has achieved stability of institutions guaranteeing democracy, the rule of law, human rights and respect for and protection of minorities, the existence of a functioning market economy as well as the capacity to cope with competitive pressure and market forces within the Union. Membership presupposes the candidate's ability to take on the obligations of membership including adherence to the aims of political, economic and monetary union.
>
> (Council of the European Union, 1993)

In addition to the political, economic and the *acquis* criteria, the European Council noted that 'The Union's capacity to absorb new members' was 'also an important consideration in the general interest of both the Union and the candidate countries' (Council of the European Union, 1993). Although, the EU refrained from officially establishing absorption capacity as an explicit institutional condition for enlargement, it was often referred to as a prerequisite for enlargement. The significance of the institutional arrangements for the advancement of the accession process was emphasised by the Corfu European Council in June 1994 which concluded that '[t]he institutional conditions for ensuring the proper functioning of the Union must be created at the 1996 Intergovernmental Conference' (Council of the European Union, 1994a).

The Essen European Council adopted a comprehensive pre-accession strategy, which provided 'a route plan for the associated countries as they prepare for accession' and emphasised the primary significance of 'their progressive preparation for integration into the internal market through the phased adoption of the Union's internal market acquis' (Council of the European Union, 1994b). Although the strategy was tailored to the needs of the countries with which Europe Agreements were concluded, the EU confirmed that it would 'be applied to other countries with which such Agreements are concluded in the future' thus highlighting the inclusive nature of the accession process (Council of the European Union, 1994b). The pre-accession strategy reaffirmed the importance of the EU's absorption capacity and stated that respecting the internal cohesion of the Union and its fundamental principles was also an important consideration (Council of the European Union, 1994b).

The adoption of the 'White Paper: Preparation of Associated Countries of Central and Eastern Europe for Integration into the Internal Market of the Union Internal Market' was the next step in the development of the membership conditions, which reaffirmed the importance of the economic criteria and set out a programme for meeting the obligations of the internal market. Furthermore, the paper identified key measures[4] in each sector and suggested the sequence in which the approximation should to be tackled without establishing any hierarchy between the sectors or imposing any timetables (European Commission, 1995).

The Madrid European Council introduced a new dimension to the third Copenhagen criteria, also known as the *acquis* criteria, which referred to the ability to take on the obligations of membership, including adherence to the aims of political, economic and monetary union.

The EU reaffirmed the importance of the incorporation of the *acquis* into national legislation and emphasised the importance of 'the development of the market economy, the adjustment of their administrative structures and the creation of a stable economic and monetary environment' that the harmonious integration of the CEECs required (Council of the European Union, 1995b).

The adoption of the Commission communication 'Agenda 2000 for a stronger and wider Union'[5] presented three new significant developments in the evolution of the conditions set out by the EU with which the applicant countries must comply. First, the Communication acknowledged the amendment of the *conditions for applying for membership*, specified in Article 49 (ex Article O) of the TEU. Agenda 2000 announced that following the preparation for the Amsterdam Treaty, the Intergovernmental Conference decided to modify Article 49, so that it included the constitutional principle, enshrined in Article 6 (ex Article F), that 'the Union is founded on the principles of liberty, democracy, respect for human rights and fundamental freedoms and the rule of law',[6] thus making respect for the founding principles of the Union an explicit *condition for applying for membership*. Second, with regard to the *conditions for opening accession negotiations*, the Commission confirmed that the respect of the political criteria 'is a necessary, but not a sufficient condition for opening accession negotiations' and specified that the recommendations for the opening of the accession negotiations were to be based on applicants' sufficient progress in satisfying the conditions of membership defined by the European Council in Copenhagen and their preparedness to satisfy the conditions for membership in the medium term (European Commission, 1997: 38). Last but not least, Agenda 2000 acknowledged that 'the Copenhagen criteria are broad in political and economic terms and go beyond the acquis communautaire' and provided the first detailed explanation of the membership conditions (European Commission, 1997: 37).

The Communication confirmed that democracy and the rule of law; human rights and minority rights were the main elements of the political criteria and specified further the conditions which each sub-criterion included (see Table 2.1).

The Commission followed the same approach to clarifying the other membership criteria. It confirmed that the first economic criterion refers to the existence of a functioning market economy and that the second economic criterion was evaluated with reference to the capacity of the applicant countries to withstand competitive pressure and market forces

Table 2.1 Key elements of Copenhagen political criteria

Sub-criteria	List of conditions
Democracy and the rule of law	• Constitutions guaranteeing democratic freedoms, including the freedom of expression and the freedom of religion; • Democratic institutions; • Independent constitutional and judicial authorities; • Free and fair elections, permitting the alternation of different political parties in power; • Recognition of the role of the opposition.
Human rights	• Guaranteeing respect for fundamental rights; • Adoption for the Council of Europe's Convention for the Protection of Human Rights and Fundamental Freedoms and the Protocol; • Freedom of expression and of association; • Independence of radio and television.[7]
Respect for minorities	• Satisfactory integration of minority populations into society – a condition for democratic stability; • Signature and ratification of a number of text governing the protection, in particular the Framework Convention for the Protection of National Minorities and recommendation 1201 adopted by the Parliamentary Assembly of the Council of Europe in 1993.

Source: European Commission (1997).

within the Union. The Commission also provided a detailed list of the conditions for each of the economic criteria.

The EU acknowledged the complexity of the third membership criterion by stating that the adoption and the implementation of the *acquis* was 'a far greater challenge than in earlier enlargements' as a result of the new obligations which had arisen regarding the Single Market, Common Foreign and Security Policy (CFSP), the EMU and justice and home affairs (European Commission, 1997).

In order to comply with the aims of the economic and monetary union, the applicants were expected to meet a number of conditions (see Table 2.2). Additionally, the Commission stressed that '[t]he applicant countries' administrative and judicial capacity is of crucial importance for the adoption, implementation and enforcement of the acquis and for the efficient use of financial support in particular from the structural funds' and established another list of steps to be taken (see Table 2.3).

The Helsinki European Council in December 1999 amended the *conditions for the opening of the accession negotiations* by confirming that

Table 2.2 Key elements of first economic criteria

Sub-criteria	List of conditions
Existence of a functioning market economy	• Equilibrium between demand and supply is established by the free interplay of market forces, prices and trade are liberalised; • Significant barriers to market entry (establishment of new firms) and exit (bankruptcies) are absent; • The legal system, including the regulation of property rights, is in place; laws and contracts can be enforced; • Macroeconomic stability has been achieved including adequate price stability and sustainable public finances and external accounts; • Broad consensus about the essentials of economic policy; • The financial sector is sufficiently well developed to channel savings towards productive investment.
Capacity to withstand competitive pressure and market forces within the Union	• The existence of a functioning market economy, with a sufficient degree of macroeconomic stability for economic agents to make decisions in a climate of stability and predictability; • A sufficient amount, at an appropriate cost, of human and physical capital, including infrastructure (energy supply, telecommunication, transport, etc.), education and research, and future developments in this field – the extent to which government policy and legislation influence competitiveness through trade policy, competition policy, state aids, support for small and medium-sized enterprises and so on; • The degree and the pace of trade integration a country achieves with the Union before enlargement, and this applies both to the volume and the nature of goods already traded with member states; • The proportion of small firms, partly because small firms tend to benefit more from improved market access, and partly because a dominance of large firms could indicate a greater reluctance to adjust.

Source: European Commission (1997).

Table 2.3   Key elements of second economic criteria

Sub-criteria	List of conditions
Aims of the Economic and Monetary Union	– Achieve further progress in the structural reform (particularly in relation to maintaining macroeconomic stability in the long run); – Adopt the *acquis* of Stage 2 of EMU, which implies independence of central bank, co-ordination of economic policies (national convergence programmes, multilateral surveillance, excessive deficit procedure) and adherence to the relevant positions of the Stability and Growth Pact; – Forego any direct central bank financing of public sector deficits as well as privileged access of public authorities to financial institutions; – Complete liberalisation of capital movements; – Participate in an exchange rate mechanism and avoid excessive exchange rate changes.
Administrative and judicial capacity	– The applicants' administrations to be modernised so that they can implement and enforce the *acquis* (this will often require new administrative structures as well as properly trained and remunerated administrators); – The applicants' judicial system must be capable of ensuring that the law is enforced (this requires the retraining, and in some cases, replacing of judges to ensure that courts are able to operate effectively in cases involving the Community law); – These countries' courts should be able, from accession, to apply the principles of Community, law such as primacy over national law or the direct effect of some legislation; – It is also essential for these courts to have a sufficient number of judges trained in Community law in order to make use of the preliminary ruling procedure in Article 177 and to ensure effective co-operation with the Court of Justice of the European Communities.

Source: European Commission (1997).

compliance with the political criteria laid down at the Copenhagen European Council was a prerequisite for the opening of accession negotiations (Council of the European Union, 1999b).

The review of the conditions set out by the EU during the pre-negotiation stage shows that the first couple of years following the

Union's decision to embark on a historical enlargement with the CEECs were characterised by remarkable activism and intensity, especially on the part of the Commission. The analysis highlights three key features of the first element of EU enlargement conditionality. Firstly, the Union briefly reflected on the widening versus deepening debate by noting the relevance of the institutional arrangements for the success of the accession process but did not establish the EU's absorption capacity as an explicit condition for membership. Secondly, as evidenced by the *conditions for applying for membership* and the *conditions for opening accession negotiations*, the EU followed a very uniform approach in establishing the range of the conditions with which the applicant countries had to comply. However, following complaints about the broad and vague nature of the Copenhagen criteria, Agenda 2000 presented a significant step in explaining and defining the scope of the membership criteria, which illustrates another important feature of the pre-negotiation conditionality – the gradual expansion and detail specification of EU requirements.

Incentives structure

This subsection explores the evolution of the second element of EU conditionality – the incentives structure, which examines the *reward–threat balance*. On the basis of the *stage-structured conditionality model*, the study traces the developments in two categories of rewards: *accession advancement rewards* and *financial rewards* (or financial assistance) and two categories of threats: *implicit threats* which sanction non-compliance by delaying the receiving of the accession advancement rewards and *explicit threats* which introduce specific penalising measures.

When examining the scope of the incentive structures provided by the EU for the 'Laeken Ten' during the pre-negotiation stage, it is difficult to establish the exact ascending order of granting *accession advancement rewards*. Both Cyprus and Malta had their membership perspective confirmed in the early 1990s, which was more than 20 years since the establishment of the contractual relations between the Mediterranean islands and the EC in the framework of the AAs. However, Hungary, Poland and Czechoslovakia were the only three countries to have signed EAs in 1991, prior to the confirmation of the membership perspective of the CEECs at the Copenhagen European Council in June 1993. Following the dissolution of Czechoslovakia, the EU signed separate AAs with the Czech Republic and Slovakia in October 1993. The three Baltic States signed Europe Agreements on 12 June 1995 and Slovenia was the last CEEC to sign AA in June 1996. The ratification of the AAs took on average two years.

The first steps towards establishing a credible membership perspective by setting a timetable for the enlargement process were taken at the Essen European Council in December 1994 by stating that the accession negotiations would take place after the creation of the institutional conditions for ensuring the proper functioning of the Union at the 1996 Intergovernmental Conference (Council of the European Union, 1994b). Six months later, the Cannes European Council established the date for the start of the enlargement process by confirming that 'the accession of Malta and Cyprus to the Union will begin on the basis of Commission proposals, six months after the conclusion of the 1996 Intergovernmental Conference and taking the outcome of that Conference into account' (Council of the European Union, 1995a). However, it was the Madrid European Council, which set the timetable for accession by linking the preliminary stage of negotiations with the CEECS to the start of negotiations with Cyprus and Malta. The timetable was confirmed at the Dublin European Council in December 1996 (Council of the European Union, 1996).

The Luxembourg European Council in July 1997 provided the next *accession advancement reward* by confirming the candidate status of the countries.[8] Furthermore, it announced the EU's decision 'to convene bilateral intergovernmental conferences in the spring of 1998 to begin negotiations with Cyprus, Hungary, Poland, Estonia, the Czech Republic and Slovenia' (Council of the European Union, 1997a). Thus, the EU provided the Luxembourg group of countries with another *accession advancement reward*.

Although, the General Affairs Council on 7 December 1998 did not make any recommendations to the European Council to extend the accession negotiations, it noted the Commission's intention to propose the opening of negotiations with Latvia before the end of 1999 (Council of the European Union, 1998). Furthermore, the Council commented on the prospect of opening accession negotiations with Lithuania and Slovakia following the positive developments in the countries. The Helsinki European Council decided to open accession negotiations with Bulgaria, Latvia, Lithuania, Slovakia, Romania and Malta in February 2000. The summit not only provided the next *accession advancement reward* for the countries which were not included in first group, but it reinforced the credibility of the membership perspective by introducing the EU's commitment 'to welcome new Member States from the end of 2002 as soon as they have demonstrated their ability to assume the obligations of membership and once the negotiating process has been successfully completed' (Council of the European Union, 1999b).

The examination of the second element of the incentives structure – the threats during the pre-accession stage indicates that the EU used mainly *implicit threats* to induce compliance with its conditions. The advancement of the accession process, in particular the decisions for the start of the accession negotiations, were conditional on sufficient progress in meeting the membership conditions. The application of *explicit threats* was limited to financial sanctions. According to Article 4 of Council Regulation (EC) No 622/98 of 16 March 1998,

> [w]here an element that is essential for continuing to grant pre-accession assistance is lacking, in particular when the commitments contained in the Europe Agreement are not respected and/or progress towards fulfilment of the Copenhagen criteria is insufficient, the Council, acting by a qualified majority on a proposal from the Commission, may take appropriate steps with regard to any pre-accession assistance granted to an applicant State.
>
> *(Official Journal, 1998)*

The Accession Partnerships[9] between the EU and the candidate countries, which were the key feature of the enhanced pre-accession strategy, further specified that 'failure to respect these general conditions could lead to a decision by the Council on the suspension of financial assistance'.[10]

The investigation of the pre-negotiation incentive structure shows that the EU used a wide range of *accession advancement rewards* in order to induce compliance with its conditions. It is worth mentioning that from a very early stage the Union made commitments to a credible membership perspective by agreeing on a date for the start of the accession negotiations. However, the Luxembourg decision to open membership talks with only six of the candidate countries and delay the advancement of other candidates reflects the difference between the incentive structures offered to the 'ins' and the 'pre-ins'. Nevertheless, the Union did not introduce any *explicit threats*. Furthermore, the *reward–threat balance* was dominated by *accession advancement rewards* and *financial rewards*.

Monitoring

This subsection reviews the third key element of EU enlargement conditionality – monitoring. On the basis of the functions which the monitoring reports fulfil, the *stage-structured conditionality model* distinguishes between two groups of reports: *evaluation reports* and *advanced reports*. The *evaluation reports* include the monitoring reports which assess progress and/or prioritise conditions. The *advanced reports* refer to the reports which, in addition to evaluating progress, establish new conditions and/or threats.

The Commission presented its Opinions on the CEECs' applications for membership of the European Union on 15 July 1997 (European Commission, 1997). The Individual Opinions provided the first comprehensive evaluation of the applicants' progress towards complying with the membership conditions established by the Copenhagen European Council. The analysis of the political criteria, which reflected the current situation in the candidate countries, went beyond a formal account of the political institutions in order to examine how democracy and the rule of law operated in practice. It is important to note that the examination of the economic and the *acquis* criteria (the capacity to assume the *acquis*) included a prospective assessment. The analysis, which was based on a medium-term time horizon of approximately five years, aimed at evaluating at the progress which was expected from the applicants in the years before accession. The Commission cautiously noted that the medium-term time horizon did not prejudge the actual date of accession and that it took account of the fact that 'the acquis itself will continue to grow' (European Commission, 1997). Agenda 2000 confirmed that 'The Commission will report periodically to the Council on the progress achieved by the applicant countries in the programme for adopting the acquis, particularly through the Accession Partnerships, with a view to fulfilling the Copenhagen criteria' (European Commission, 1997).

The conclusions of the Luxembourg European Council confirmed that:

> [f]rom the end of 1998, the Commission will make regular reports to the Council, together with any necessary recommendations for opening bilateral intergovernmental conferences, reviewing the progress of each Central and East European applicant State towards accession in the light of the Copenhagen criteria, in particular the rate at which it is adopting the Union acquis.
>
> (Council of the European Union, 1997a)

Furthermore, they specified that the Commission's reports, which were to follow the method adopted by Agenda 2000 would serve as a basis for taking, in the Council context, the necessary decisions on the conduct of the accession negotiations or their extension to other applicants (Council of the European Union, 1997a).

The Opinions prepared by the Commission provided the first detailed evaluation, which was of crucial importance not only for the advancement of the accession process but also for the development of the monitoring instruments. However, they did not set out key priorities or list of conditions.

Negotiation stage

Conditions

This subsection discusses the development of the scope and range of the EU conditions during the negotiation negotiations with the 'Laeken Ten'. In November 1998 the Commission presented a 'Composite Paper: Reports on Progress towards Accession by each of the Candidate Countries', which elaborated on the scope of the membership conditions. With regard to the first element of the *acquis* criteria – the aims of the economic and monetary union – the Commission reaffirmed that the EMU was an integral part of the community *acquis* and new members were not expected 'to adopt the single currency upon accession' (European Commission, 1998b).

The 1999 Strategy paper introduced another development by establishing the conditions for the provisional closure of the accession chapters. They included:

- full acceptance of the EU *acquis*;
- absence of requests for transitional periods;
- satisfactory answers to EU questions;
- the global character of the negotiations (nothing is agreed until everything is agreed); and
- the need for satisfactory progress in the preparations for accession in each of the candidate countries.

(European Commission, 1999)

The strategy established a strong link between the negotiations and the preparatory process by revising the procedures for provisional closure of chapters. The Commission confirmed: 'No chapter would be provisionally closed (or closed again after re-opening) unless the EU is satisfied that the candidates' preparations are in line with their commitments in terms of preparation for accession' (European Commission, 1999). Furthermore, the Commission reaffirmed that transition periods but not derogations could be agreed on.

The Nice European Council adopted a new approach to accession conditionality by introducing a new instrument of the enlargement strategy – the 'road map'. The road map, which referred essentially to chapters in which the candidates requested transitional measures, identified priorities for the negotiations for three semesters (the beginning of 2001 – the end of the first half of 2002). Additionally, the Commission reaffirmed that the provisional closure of negotiations on chapters would depend on all parties making the necessary contributions and that the progress in the negotiations depended more on the quality of preparation made by each member state than on the number of chapters opened (European Commission, 2000a). The Regular Reports published by the Commission in 2001 identified the following areas which required further progress: internal market, competition, transport and energy, environment, social policy and employment, justice and home affairs, customs and taxation, agriculture, structural policy and financial control and included a detailed list of measures.

Furthermore, the Commission stressed the importance of institution building and adopted a plan for administrative and judicial capacity. The plan identified a number of chapters related to the *acquis* and specified the four priorities: functioning of the market economy, sustainable living conditions, protection of EU citizens and proper management of community funds (European Commission, 2001).

The analysis of EU conditions during the negotiation stage highlights the growing entrepreneurship of the Commission and illustrates the gradual shift from broad and vague conditionality to more detailed and targeted conditionality. As evidenced by key policy documents the EU elaborated considerably on the scope of the Copenhagen criteria. Furthermore, the EU followed a uniform approach to establishing the parameters of the membership requirements.

Incentives structure

The evaluation of the *accession advancement rewards* provided by the EU for the eight CEECs, Cyprus and Malta during the negotiations stage focuses on the progress of the accession negotiations, particularly on the chapters opened and provisionally closed; and the credibility of the membership perspective. The EU formally opened the accession negotiations with the Luxembourg six (Hungary, Poland, Czech Republic, Estonia, Slovenia and Cyprus) on 31 March 1998. The screening of 16 out of the 31 negotiating chapters was completed between 27 April and the end of October 1998 (European Commission, 1998b). On 10 November 1998, the negotiations started on seven of the chapters: Science and Research; Education and Training; Small and Medium-Sized Enterprises; Culture and Audio-visual Policy; Telecommunications; Industrial Policy;

and Common Foreign and Security Policy. During the first semester of 1999, eight additional negotiating chapters were opened: Company Law; Statistics; Consumer and Health Protection; Fisheries; Competition Policy; Free Movement of Goods; Customs Union; and External Relations. By the end of September 1999, seven[11] of the 15 chapters (which were opened) were provisionally closed with all the six countries. The chapter on fisheries was provisionally closed with Hungary, the Czech Republic and Slovenia. Cyprus managed to provisionally close three other chapters – culture and audio-visual, external relations and customs union.

The EU opened the accession negotiations with the Helsinki group (Slovakia, Latvia, Lithuania Malta, Bulgaria and Romania) on 15 February 2000. It is important to note that the EU started the detailed examination (screening) of the *acquis* with all CEECs and Cyprus in April 1998. Following the reactivation of Malta's membership application, Malta started the screening process in February 1999. The first round of negotiations with the Helsinki group was held on 14 June 2000 (European Commission, 2000a). The EU managed to open up to 17 and provisionally to close 11 to 16 chapters with each of the Helsinki group of countries by the end of 2000. At the same time, 29 chapters (all chapters with the exception of Institutional questions and Other questions) were opened and 11 to 16 chapters were provisionally closed with each of the Luxembourg group of countries (European Commission, 2000a). During the Swedish Presidency, the EU opened 13 chapters with Latvia, 12 chapters with Lithuania and Slovakia and 11 chapters with Malta. By October 2001, Institutional Questions and Other Question were only two chapters left to be opened with the eight CEECs and Cyprus. The EU granted the 'Laeken Ten' the penultimate *accession advancement reward* by concluding the accession negotiations with them at the Copenhagen European Council in December 2002. The last advancement on the way to the completion of the enlargement process was the signing of the Accession Treaty on 16 April 2003 (Council of the European Union, 2003a).

The EU provided the candidate countries with *accession advancement rewards* not only by opening and closing negotiating chapters, the credibility of the membership perspective was reinforced by making commitments to a timetable for the completion of the accession process and setting target dates. The Nice European Council presented a Road Map based on the Helsinki timetable that the EU would be 'in a position to welcome those new Member States which are ready as from the end of 2002' (Council of the European Union, 2000b). The Laeken European

Council not only confirmed the end of 2002 as the target date for the successful conclusion of the accession negotiations but also stated for the first time that 'Cyprus, Estonia, Hungary, Latvia, Lithuania, Malta, Poland, the Slovak Republic, the Czech Republic and Slovenia could be ready' to join the EU (Council of the European Union, 2001b). Furthermore, the Laeken Council decided that 'Proceedings on the drafting of the accession treaties will begin in the first half of 2002' (Council of the European Union, 2001b).

The examination of the second element of the incentive structure reveals that the EU did not change the scope of both *implicit* and *explicit threats*. The latter were confined to *financial sanctions* which allowed for the suspension of financial assistance on the basis of Article 4 of Council Regulation (EC) No. 622/98 of 16 March 1998. The suspension clause, which was included in the first[12] Accession Partnerships between the EU and the applicant countries, was also incorporated in the Accession Partnerships signed in 2001. The EU did not introduce any new *explicit threats*. Furthermore, as the advancement of the accession process was made conditional on sufficient progress in complying with the Copenhagen criteria, we can confirm that the Union used mainly *implicit threats* to induce compliance with its conditions during the negotiation stage.

The analysis shows that the *reward–threat balance* during the negotiation stage was dominated by accession advancement rewards and financial rewards, which in turn created a positive incentive structure. In addition to opening and closing negotiation chapters, the EU provided the eight CEECs, Cyprus and Malta with another important *accession advancement reward* – credible membership perspective. The provisional timetable, prepared by the Commission and strongly supported by the EP, was endorsed by the Nice European Council. As the timetable for the completion of the accession process further solidified the EU's commitment to the European future of the countries.

Monitoring

During the accession stage the Commission prepared five series of monitoring reports. The first were published in the end of 1998. The reports followed the same structure as the Opinions published by the Commission. The 1999 Regular Reports built on the existing assessment format and started to highlight priorities and include recommendation for action in particular areas. The 2000 Regular Reports introduced two separate subsections, which evaluated the candidates' progress towards meeting the short-term and medium-term priorities of the Accession

Partnerships. One Commission official commented on the importance of prospective evaluation by pointing out that:

> it is a judgement one has to make also about the credibility of the country – whether they are on sustainable process that will take them there, even if they are not there in two, three or four years and for that you need to have different elements. You need to have political consensus on this [EU membership], you need to have capable people who can draft laws, who can come and talk to us here, understand what we talk about, you need to have functioning institutions that allow you to get to that stage [...]. It is not only a question of where this country is at the moment but what the prospects of which this country is progressing are.
>
> (Interview 5, 2009)

In addition to assessing the preparedness of the candidate countries, the monitoring reports allowed the Commission to apply political pressure. One EU official noted that:

> countries are also very keen to have a positive report and sometimes they are willing to try to fix a couple of things just before [the report is published], so we have the whole process, they tell us where they are, we ask them questions, and at an early stage, we indicate, we have seen a problem at a, b and c and very often the country will try to fix these problems before we produce the report.
>
> (Interview 5, 2009)

The developments during the negotiation stage show that the rigorous approach of the Commission to reporting on the progress made towards accession by each of the candidate countries transformed the scope and nature of the Regular Reports from general assessments into detailed evaluation analyses. Furthermore, the study confirms the growing relevance of monitoring for the advancement of the accession process and highlights the multi-functionality of the monitoring instruments.

Accession stage

Conditions

Following the completion of the accession negotiations, the acceding countries were expected to finalise their preparations for assuming the responsibilities of membership, which included compliance with the Copenhagen criteria and the specific arrangement for each of the 29 *acquis* chapters. However, the Commission elaborated on the scope of the membership criteria by establishing individual country specific conditions.

The 2003 Comprehensive Monitoring Reports assessed the overall state of preparedness of the countries, flagged the remaining gaps and arranged them in three categories: minor (largely technical) issues, issues requiring enhanced efforts and issues of serious concern. The third category included 39 issues, which the ten countries needed to address urgently. They were grouped broadly into two types of cases: issues affecting the proper functioning of the internal market and issues affecting the delivery of EU funds to beneficiaries in the acceding countries. Some of the benchmarks included: the introduction of the minimum training requirements and mutual recognition rules for a number of professions; the implementation of the necessary measures for inspection and control of their fisheries fleet and for ensuring application of EU resource and fleet management rules; the adoption and implementation of the necessary veterinary legislation; implementation of the *acquis* in respect of TSEs and animal waste; the upgrade the agri-food establishment; setting up a Paying Agency; and the implementation the Integrated Administration and Control Systems (central elements for payments of common agricultural policy funds to farmers).

The study highlights the importance of benchmarking for the development of EU enlargement policy during the accession stage. The examination of the scope of the conditions during the accession stage reveals two important changes in the EU's approach towards establishing conditions. By preparing individual lists of benchmarks, the Commission introduced the use of differentiated conditionality. Furthermore, the fact that the reports presented specific policy items illustrated a move away from the EU's traditional approach to establishing uniform sets of conditions and highlighted the growing relevance of targeted conditionality.

Incentive structure

The examination of the accession incentive structure reveals significant changes in the *reward–threat balance* after the signing of the Accession Treaty. The rewards provided by the Union were mainly *financial rewards*, as the only *accession advancement reward* was the actual accession of the countries to the Union. Although the EU did not introduce any *implicit threats*, it established a wide range of *explicit threats* by specifying, for the first time in the accession process with the eight

CEECs, Cyprus and Malta, *preventive or remedial sanctions* in the form
of safeguard clauses.

The Treaty of Accession included one general economic safeguard
clause and two specific safeguard clauses: internal market and justice and home affairs (JHA) safeguard clause. The economic safeguard
clause[13] allowed member states to apply for authorisation to take protective measures with regard to 'Laeken Ten' in the event of serious
economic difficulties.[14] Article 37 of the Act of Accession specified that
the Commission may establish appropriate measures if the acceding
countries caused, or risked causing, a serious breach of the functioning of the internal market. This safeguard clause referred not only to the
internal market but also all sectoral policies which concern economic
activities with cross-border effect (e.g. competition, agriculture, transport, telecommunications, energy, environment). According to Article
38 of the Act of Accession, the Commission may establish appropriate measures if there were serious shortcomings or any imminent risk
of such shortcoming in the transposition and implementation of the
acquis in the area of justice and home affairs. Although all three safeguard clauses could be activated 'until the end of a period of up to three
years after accession', the treaty specified that the internal market and
the JHA safeguard clause 'may be invoked even before accession' (*Official
Journal*, 2003a).

The developments during the accession stage illustrate the remarkable
transformation of the incentive structure. The completion of the membership talks is a crucial turning point, which signals the final stage of
the European journeys of the applicant states. However, as the advancement of the accession process is inherently bound to 'strip' the Union
of its *accession advancement rewards*, the finalisation of the negotiations
limits significantly the range of the available rewards. Furthermore, the
study shows that the EU provided for the application of *explicit threats* in
the form of safeguard measures for the first time in the accession process
with the CEECs, Cyprus and Malta. The combined effect of both trends
(less *accession advancement rewards* compensated by more *explicit threats*)
significantly altered the *reward–threat balance* during the accession stage
and produced a negative incentive structure. Unlike the pre-negotiation
and negotiation stage, the Union relied on negative conditionality to
induce compliance with its conditions.

Monitoring

During the accession stage the Commission published a 'Comprehensive Monitoring Report on the state of preparedness for EU membership

of the Czech Republic, Estonia, Cyprus, Latvia, Lithuania, Hungary, Malta, Poland, Slovenia and Slovakia'. Its preparation was envisaged in the Strategy Paper 'Towards the enlarged Union', which specified that the Commission should 'produce six months before the envisaged date of accession a comprehensive monitoring report for the Council and the European Parliament' (European Commission, 2002a). The report was also a response to request made at the Copenhagen European Council in December 2002 that monitoring should continue up to accession, and that it should give further guidance to the acceding states in their efforts to assume the responsibilities of membership and give the necessary assurance to current member states (Council of the European Union, 2002).

The report, which reflected the situation at the end of September 2003, included individual country reports which not only assessed the state of the overall preparedness of the acceding countries, but also identified the remaining gaps and presented policy options for dealing with them. The individual Comprehensive Monitoring Reports assessed the state of preparedness for each of the 29 chapters 'both in terms of transposition of legislation and from the perspective of implementing structures, administrative capacity and enforcement' (European Commission, 2003). It is important to note that in the conclusions for each chapter, the Commission highlighted the issues which required further progress by devising a system with three categories. The first category outlined the 'issues where a country is ready or where minor issues remain to be addressed'; the second category included 'issues requiring enhanced efforts and an increased pace of progress to ensure that they are resolved by the time of accession', and the third category emphasised 'issues of serious concern where immediate and decisive action needs to be taken for the country to be ready by the date of accession' (European Commission, 2003).

The examination of the Comprehensive Monitoring Report reveals that following the completion of the accession negotiations monitoring remained an essential element of the enlargement process. It is important to note that the Commission firmly established its expertise in providing objective comprehensive assessment of the EU-hopefuls' compliance with EU conditions thus legitimising the impartiality its recommendations. Furthermore, the Commission increased significantly the relevance of monitoring reports as it used them not only as a basis for its recommendations and an instrument for prioritising conditions but also as an instrument for establishing new conditions.

Post-accession stage

This section discusses the scope of the post-accession conditionality applied to the eight CEECs, Cyprus and Malta. Unlike, the previous sections, the analysis is limited only to the second element of EU conditionality – the incentive structure – as the EU neither established any specific conditions for the new member states, nor introduced any special monitoring mechanisms.

The first significant difference in the *reward–threat balance* (in comparison to the earlier stages of the accession process) is that after the accession of the new member state, the rewards provided by the Union for compliance with its conditions were limited to *financial rewards*. It is important to note that most of the post-accession financial assistance is part of the financial assistance previously agreed and allocated in the framework of the pre-accession programmes (PHARE, ISPA and SAPARD). During the post-accession stage, the EU is 'stripped' of its strongest incentive for inducing compliance – the membership perspective. Furthermore, all the *accession advancement rewards* are no longer available as a result of the accession of the new member state to the Union.

The assessment of the second element of the incentives structure – the threats during the post-accession stage indicates that the EU does not rely on the use of *implicit threats* to induce compliance with its conditions. However, the lack of *implicit threats* is compensated by the establishment of a wide range of *explicit threats*. It is essential that we distinguish between the *preventive and remedial sanctions* established in the framework of EU enlargement conditionality and the sanctions which are applicable to all member states. The latter include safeguard measures based on the *acquis* in areas such as transport, food safety, aviation; safeguard measures in relation to the EU funds, including financial corrections; competition policy measures and infringement procedures. In order to differentiate these measures from the *financial sanctions* developed in the framework of post-accession conditionality, we classify them as *general financial sanctions*.

The EU specified the scope of the *explicit threats*, applicable to the 'Laeken Ten' by confirming that the *preventive and remedial sanctions*, introduced by the three safeguard clauses,[15] included in the Accession Treaty, could be evoked 'until the end of a period of up to three years after accession' (*Official Journal*, 2003a).

Although this enquiry of the post-accession conditionality focuses exclusively on the incentive structure, it is highly relevant for the analysis of the EU enlargement conditionality, as it shows that its application is not confined to the accession process and continues after candidate countries have become fully fledged member states. Furthermore, as the analysis shows that the *reward–threat balance* was dominated by *preventive and remedial sanctions* (unlike the early stage of the accession process), the incentive structure during the post-accession stage was negative.

Conclusions

The comparative study of the key elements of EU enlargement conditionality identifies important evolutionary developments in the application of EU enlargement conditionality towards the 'Laeken Ten'. The broad set of the Copenhagen membership criteria shows that the Union initially followed a very uniform approach to setting out the conditions with which the applicant countries needed to comply. The EU gradually elaborated and clarified the scope and the range of the membership requirements during the pre-negotiation and negotiation stage. Furthermore, the introduction of closing benchmarks and the identification of the areas of serious concerns during the accession stage marked the gradual transition from one-size-fits-all to a more tailor-made approach. The establishment of country specific conditions indicates the increasing application of differentiated and targeted conditionality, which reflects the Commission's growing expertise with regards to the candidate countries. Furthermore, benchmarking enhances the quality of the accession process by providing detailed guidance on the steps which candidate countries needed to implement in order to meet the Copenhagen criteria.

The incentive structure also underwent a significant transformation. During the pre-negotiation and negotiation stage, the EU used only *implicit threats* and a wide range of *accession advancement* and *financial rewards*. Although the Union favoured the use of carrots over sticks to induce compliance with its conditions, the advancement of the accession process inevitably limited the range of the available rewards. After the completion of the accession negotiations, the EU introduced *explicit threats* by providing for safeguard clauses in the Accession Treaty. Consequently, the *reward–threat balance* was dominated by *remedial and preventive sanctions*, in stark contrast with the pre-negotiation and negotiation stage. The alteration in the balance between rewards and threats illustrates the transformation from a *positive* incentive structure to a *negative* incentive structure, which in turn reflects the gradual shift from positive conditionality, which the Union applied in the early stages of the process, to negative conditionality in the accession and post-accession stage.

The Commission gradually expanded the scope of the Progress and Regular Reports. Their increasing sophistication and frequent publication confirm the growing relevance of monitoring for the advancement of the accession process. Furthermore, the 2002 Regular Reports and the Comprehensive Monitoring Reports show that the EU extended the functions of the monitoring reports beyond measuring the compliance of the candidate countries with the EU conditions. In addition to evaluating progress and providing the basis for further recommendations, the reports specified further the scope of the membership conditions and acted as instruments for political pressure.

The two-level analysis on the basis of the *stage-structured conditionality model* confirms that the evolution of the EU enlargement conditionality towards the eight CEECs, Cyprus and Malta is characterised by three distinct trends. Firstly, examination of the developments of the EU conditions illustrates a shift from broad uniform conditionality to targeted and differentiated conditionality. Secondly, the alternation in the *reward–threat balance* indicates another important change: from positive to negative conditionality. Last but not least, the analysis highlights the growing relevance and multipurpose instrumentalisation of the monitoring reports.

Explaining EU conditionality towards the 'Laeken Ten'

With a view to analysing the evolution of EU enlargement conditionality, the book specifies that *EU enlargement policy is a function of differentiated influences from multiple actors and external pressures*. The definition highlights the complex constellations of actors involved in the accession process and emphasises their relevance by focusing on the influence which they can exert rather than their competences. Although the book stresses the leading role of the main EU institutions, it delves deeper into policy dynamics by analysing key policy developments with reference to the following factors: (1) *EU member states*, (2) *EU inter-institutional dynamics*, (3) *public opinion in the EU*, (4) *enlargement countries* and (5) *external pressures caused by economic or security shocks and crises*.

EU member states

This section discusses the impact of the Council of the EU on the development of EU enlargement conditionality by looking into the influence of individual member states. Although it acknowledges the scope of the competences of the Council, the research is concerned with examining more subtle channels for applying political pressure and focuses on two key aspects:

• the impact of member states' preferences for the advancement of the accession process and
• the implications of bilateral issues between member states and candidate countries.

The debates prior to the Luxembourg Summit conclusions provide a very interesting snapshot of the complex nature of the decision-making in the Council. The Commission's recommendation to launch accession negotiations with only six of the applicant states – the Czech Republic, Estonia, Hungary, Poland, Slovenia and Cyprus – provoked very strong reactions among the member states and the applicant countries. In July 1997, Italy's foreign minister, Lamberto Dini, stated that the opening of membership negotiations with applicant countries must 'take place like the Tour de France: everyone starts at the same time, even if some go faster afterwards' (*Agence Europe*, 1997b). However, certain member states disagreed. In a joint statement the German and Austrian foreign ministers Klaus Kinkel and Wolfgang Schüssel (in their capacity as the then future successive Presidents of the Council) insisted that the membership negotiations must be a dynamic process and noted that 'the countries that have already made major progress in their reform efforts must not be obliged to wait for the applicant countries that have made less progress' (*Agence Europe*, 1997a). While the Swedish foreign minister Lena Hjelm-Wallen pointed out that Lithuania, Latvia and Estonia had to begin accession negotiations with the EU together (*Agence Europe*, 1997c).

The new round of discussions in October 1997 showed that there was 'wide support given by a large majority of Member states' (more precisely Germany, Belgium, France, Italy, the Netherlands and the United Kingdom) for the Commission's recommendation; 'only Denmark and Portugal openly took position in favour of starting negotiations with all the applicant countries (nonetheless Denmark excluded Slovakia), while Greece kept a low profile on the matter and Italy defended the principle of "differentiation"' (*Agence Europe*, 1997d). The discussions in November 'confirmed the existence within the 15 of very different ideas about how to give concrete substance to the principles of inclusivity, progressiveness and globality which, from the EU's point of view, must characterise the enlargement process' (*Agence Europe*, 1997e). Jacques Poos, the President of the Council of Ministers, noted that

'[a] "large majority" of delegations "continues to support a differentiated approach", but a few States still favour a "simultaneous approach"'
and pointed out that ' "political inventiveness is needed to find a mid-
dle way between the two" and several possibilities have already been
discussed' (*Agence Europe*, 1997f). In the meantime, the Danish government launched the idea of beginning the screening of the *acquis*
(the initial phase of the accession negotiations) with all CEECs (*Agence
Europe*, 1997f). The idea quickly became an initiative jointly submitted
by Denmark and Sweden to the Council, the proposal specified that 'the
EU should begin talks in 1998 with all the applicant countries so as
to check the extent to which they are capable of adopting the Community acquis, while negotiations proper would begin in January 1999
with the best prepared countries' (*Agence Europe*, 1997g). Although accession negotiations with the Luxembourg group were officially launched
in March 1998, all candidate countries were included in the screening
process.

The continuous debates illustrate the polarising effect of the question
with which countries to start accession negotiations and reveals that it
was difficult for the 15 member states to reach a unanimous decision. EU
officials and national official agreed that good and particularly strong
relations between a member state or a group of member states and a candidate country or a group of candidate countries had a positive impact
on the advancement of the accession process. One senior Commission
official reflected on the Luxembourg conclusions by commenting that:

the Visegrád three (Poland, the Czech Republic, Hungary) were bor-
dering on Germany, were very central, and [they] had been playing
key roles for the downfall of the wall, so there was a particular famil-
iarity and historical interest [...]. The Nordics felt that this was a
moment for a kind of North-European solidarity, that we should not
leave the Baltics outside of this. It was in fact divisive between the
Nordic countries, Finland was the one country pushing very much for
Estonia, based on the assessment, that first of all Estonia was maybe
in a slightly better shape but not that much in 1997 [...] If you try to
include all three countries, it is easier to block them and it may have
the undesired result that they would all stay out. So, rather make sure
that you bring in one in the original pack and then it will be easier
to extend and draw the other two. Whereas Sweden and Denmark
were scandalised by this and they thought that they can't separate
between the different Baltics, just bring them all in together.

(Interview 10, 2009)

The comments were echoed by another high-ranking official who noted that:

it was relatively political, there were some elements which were clearly given elements, so the most advanced such as Slovenia, Hungary were clearly seen as the ones which should start. Poland was to a certain extend a given element because it was the biggest in that context, Czech Republic was also in there, but there were questions as much as the Baltics were concerned and then we ended up with this decisions of taking Estonia but not Latvia and Lithuania.

(Interview 18, 2009)

Another Commission official outlined the member states preferences by saying that '[t]he Baltic States had the Scandinavians. The Czechs and the Slovaks had their friends in the centre' (Interview 3, 2009). Although 'Poland was to a certain extend a given element because it was the biggest', it is universally agreed that she was strongly supported by Germany (Interview 18, 2009). One senior official noted that '[t]he major actor was Germany, obviously, and then the Commissioner in charge of enlargement was also German national and the major partner for [the] 2004 [enlargement] was of course Poland, so the German-Polish relationships were the key to the whole exercise' (Interview 6, 2009).

The complex nature of the enlargement process provides further evidence for the significance of the member states' preferences as one senior EU official pointed out:

[i]t is not just a process run by bureaucrats [who say:] 'these are the conditions tick them off, if it takes one year or if takes twenty years'. This is how we are set up at the working level, but the big decisions are taken at the heads of state level for enlargement always, and there of course the reasoning is somehow different, you can see that certain countries support other countries.

(Interview 5, 2009)

One senior official further highlighted the role of the member states for the development of the accession process by saying that:

Germany was driving the process of the fifth enlargement as a geo-strategic necessity. That does not mean to say that it was done blindly. There is no comparable positive driving force for the current enlargement. Germany, the UK and France to an extent, you had all of the major member states, they were driving the fifth enlargement.

(Interview 20, 2009)

Another Commission official reflected on the attitudes of member states towards enlargement by noting that 'UK was always a very strong supporter, Germany definitely for Poland and some others, and you always had the traditional divide between the UK and the Nordics in favour then, and the centre and the southern countries'(Interview 5, 2009). Similar observations were made by another EU official who recollected that 'the only countries really wanting enlargement were Sweden, Denmark, for specific reasons, and then the UK, for their specific reasons. The others they all agreed to it in principle, as a good idea' (Interview 11, 2009).

However, the preference of the member states can also have a negative impact on the development of the accession process, especially if the relations between them and the candidate countries are hindered by unresolved disputes. One senior Commission official summarised the implication of bilateral issues on the first phase of the fifth enlargement by commenting that:

> [f]irst of all the Beneš decrees and then the Temelín nuclear plant made the negotiations really difficult and there were crises between the Czech Republic and Austria. But others issues [such as] the German-Polish border issue – the Oder-Neisse border issue was settled, there were border problems with Russia, between the Baltics and Russia, but Russia is not a member state. There was the Kaliningrad issue, Russia was not candidate [and] it did not really matter, but Russia put a lot of pressure [on the EU] to allow the free movement of its nationals from Kaliningrad to Russia, but apart from this we did not have big problems.

(Interview 8, 2009)

Another senior member of the Commission also confirmed that 'there were bilateral issues but they never dominated the agenda, never blocked the progress' (Interview 12, 2009).

The examination of the role of the Council for the development of the first phase of the EU enlargement shows that the influence of the member states on the accession process is not confined to their veto powers in the accession process. As evidenced by the decisions of the Luxembourg Summit, member states' preferences are highly relevant for

EU enlargement conditionality and strong support for a candidate or a group of candidate countries can significantly improve the incentive structure, whereas unresolved disputes bilateral issues can put a strain on the development of the enlargement process. Furthermore, analysis shows that most of the member states have proactively shaped the development of the enlargement policy.

Inter-institutional dynamics

The aim of this section is to contribute to the discussion about the impact of institutional factors on the evolution of EU enlargement conditionality. It complements the analysis of the influence on member states by discussing the complexity of the inter-institutional dynamics of the Union. The book acknowledges the leading position of the Council in decision-making, but focuses on the crucial role of the Commission for the formal launch of the Eastern enlargement and the impact on of the Presidencies of the EU and the EP on the advancement of the accession process. The discussion is supported by the reflections and the comments of senior EU officials on the significance of their respective institutions for the completion of the 2004 enlargement.

The debates prior to the EU's decision to launch accession negotiations with Czech Republic, Estonia, Hungary, Poland, Slovenia and Cyprus (also referred as the Luxembourg six) were very intense not only among the member states but also in the Commission, whose task was to prepare the recommendations for the Council. One senior EU official acknowledged the complexities of the political situation and noted that:

> [w]e were confronted with such a big group of countries, completely different economic background, completely different political history and at the political level [...] it was a bit like, let's be cautious to see how things go, and I think it was a mixture of caution on the side of the Commission foreseeing the enormous challenges from human resources point of view, from, you know you have to invest in getting the reforms on track, from the financial point of view and then the purely political considerations, which were certainly stated by countries like Germany and Austria.
>
> (Interview 21, 2009)

Another Commission official summarised the essence of the decision by stressing that '[i]t has always been one of the big dilemmas, should we actually take a country when it has met the criteria, purely on its own merit, or is there a political adjustment to go along fine?' (Interview 3,

2009). Another high-ranking EU official discussed the complex nature of the inter-institutional dynamics by noting that:

[t]here was a political compromise. It is always a political decision. Now I have to say that already in the very early stage, there was some indication that some of the countries are more ahead than the others, I mean clearly Hungary, the Czech Republic. Poland because of the backing of Germany was always pushed in the first group. Slovenia [was] clearly [advanced]. So there was a distinction that was made on the basis of the factual information that we had with regard to their: economic performance, financial performance, privatisation process which in fact was far more advanced than in other countries, probably also [the differences in the development of] the political environment, the extent to which it was stable. I think it's all elements which in the end inspired the Commission to take decisions one way or another.

(Interview 21, 2009)

However, it is also important to reflect on the some difficulties which the Commission faces as a result of its unique role in the enlargement process. One senior EU official highlighted the special position of the Commission vis-à-vis the Council, particularly with reference to the recommendations for the start of the accession negotiations with the six 'pre-ins':

We are a little bit the book-keeper at the Commission. We are the honest broker. We should not have our strategic political thoughts. If we say yes to these [countries], what happens to the others? It is not our task, the presidency can do it, the Council can do it. We are asked to have an opinion, we should look at the facts: is the country prepared or not prepared? We are not the first institution who should think about that [which countries to start accession negotiations]. Having said that, we are not politically blind either.

(Interview 4, 2009)

Another senior EU official commented on a similar aspect of the Commission's role which also calls for fine balancing acts and has important implications for the development of the EU enlargement conditionality:

Our job is to make sure that you have another benchmark, another milestone, after the accession negotiations start and at some point, the countries started to get frustrated because they thought that the countries were not going fast enough and the chapters were not being opened and closed at the rhythm they want.

(Interview 5, 2009)

Another high-ranking official also noted some of the wider implications surrounding the preparations of the recommendations by reflecting on the complexity of the inter-institutional and intra-institutional dynamics:

> the Commission is not autonomous in all these things and all the member states who are looking over our shoulders and there would have been a European Council meeting in June and there would have been a European Council meeting in December, there would have been signals from the member states whether they feel they are ready to conclude or they are not ready, you know this is all there in the background.
>
> (Interview 5, 2009)

When dissecting the relationship between the Commission and the Council and its implications for EU enlargement policy, it is essential that we look into the role of the presidency. One senior official was keen to stress that:

> [i]t can be very important in a given circumstance, Presidency has only the power to set the agenda and lead the meetings but this setting-the-agenda power is very, very powerful. It is very, very strong because it means you can achieve a lot of what you want to happen by setting the agenda. So by preparing and of course working with the Commission, making sure that that the common positions for the countries that were catching up came in a very strong stream from the Commission, with all the evidence necessary to open and close chapters, [we] gave the latecomers a re-boost during the Swedish presidency. [We had] to set the agenda of having these chapters on the agenda, but if only one member state would have said: 'I don't agree', it would not have happened, so you can push and press things to a certain degree'.
>
> (Interview 11, 2009)

The enthusiasm and the crucial relevance of the presidencies for the advancement of the accession negotiations were highlighted by another senior EU official who recollected that:

[t]here was a continuous discussion between the Presidency and the Commission. Every Presidency who came along would say with country X we want to open three new chapters and close another three, and the Commission would say, you cannot do that, it is only realistic to open this two, this is why you cannot open the third that you want to open, as for closing these three, well maybe this one, do you really think you can do that one or that one? And each Presidency wanted to be able to say we are supporting the accession of this country, you know, we are achieving, we are moving forward down the path.

(Interview 20, 2009)

It is interesting to note that, in contrast to the significance of the Commission, the Council and the Presidencies for the 2004 enlargement, the role of the Parliament is a much more contested issue. One Commission official noted that:

[t]he Parliament in the enlargement is not really a serious player [...]. There are few individuals who take personal interest in it [enlargement] and you have the Foreign Affairs Committee where the Commission goes every once in a while to tell them how things are going and you have some bogus debates but the Parliament does not really have the same institutional standing in the enlargement process, as it has in legislative processes within the Community.

(Interview 10, 2009)

Whereas, another EU official stressed the influence of the EP rather than its competences by noting that:

[t]he most important idea the Parliament introduced was the date for the entry into force of the accession treaties: first of all – [the year] 2004, [whereas] 1 May was the idea of the Commission. There was in one [EP] report that new member states should be ready to participate to this election as fully-fledged member states and this was absolutely genius, because never, neither the Commission nor the Council dared to say we want to have these countries in this year in the EU [...]. So the Parliament said [our] target date [is] the next elections and it was a very good idea [...]. It was intelligent because it was the way to take one contribution of the Parliament and then everything was organised – the tempo of the accession negotiations – to meet this deadline of next European elections of June 2004. This

is a very concrete example of how the Parliament can do something in the enlargement process.

(Interview 6, 2009)

The study of the influence of the Council of the EU, the Commission and the EP on the 2004 enlargement provides interesting insights into the inter-institutional dynamics of the Union. The analysis acknowledges the leading role of the Council in decision-making. However, it also illustrates the strong influence of the Commission and illuminates the difficulties which the Commission faces while trying to balance the technocratic nature of its responsibilities with the political agendas of the member states. Furthermore, the research confirms that the Parliament, which is the least powerful of the three main institutions with regard to enlargement, can successfully channel political pressure and shape significantly the advancement of the accession process.

Public opinion

This section focuses on the variation in EU public support for enlargement and analyses the attitudes towards the accession of the Czech Republic, Estonia, Hungary, Poland, Latvia, Lithuania, Slovenia, Slovakia, together with Cyprus and Malta, in comparative perspective. It draws on the data from the Standard Eurobarometer surveys. As questions regarding enlargement were not included in all of the Eurobarometer reports since 1990, the analysis of public attitudes briefly comments on the earlier developments and focuses primarily on the period between the spring of 1996 and the spring of 2004. The wide range of the data allows us to identify the key trends in EU public opinion and reflect on their relevance and implications for the development of EU enlargement policy.

Eurobarometer first surveyed the attitudes of the citizens of the EC towards the changes in Central and Eastern Europe in March/April 1990. The report revealed that 63% of the interviewees supported the accession of each of the CEECs that 'requests to join the EC as soon as democracy and open economy have been established' whereas 16% of the interviewees were against it (Eurobarometer, 1990). In 1992, the findings of a co-operative venture of 24 leading European newspapers[16] showed that absolute majorities of EC citizens wanted only three of the soon-to-be applicants – Poland, Hungary and Malta – to be members by 2000. The survey indicated that relative majorities supported the accession of the Czech Republic (47:34), Cyprus (44:36), Estonia (42:36) and Lithuania (41:38), Latvia[17] (40:38), but this was not the case with Slovakia (36:42) and Slovenia (33:44) (Eurobarometer, 1992).

Following the establishment of the membership perspective of the CEECs, the 1994 Autumn Eurobarometer also confirmed that many respondents differentiated between the countries, particularly between Hungary, Poland and the Czech Republic on one hand and Bulgaria, Slovakia, Slovenia and Romania on the other (Eurobarometer, 1994). Favourable opinions about membership of all of these CEECs outweighed the unfavourable in seven member states: Greece, Spain, Ireland, the Netherlands, Portugal, the United Kingdom and Italy (Eurobarometer, 1994).

The comparative examination of the public attitudes towards enlargement in the period between the spring of 1996 and the spring of 2004 (see Appendix III) reveals three distinct trends. Firstly, the support for enlargement varied and varied greatly depending on which country the respondents come from. In some of the member states, particularly in Sweden, Denmark and Greece, the attitudes towards enlargement were quite favourable and support was generally above the EU average. In other countries like France, Austria and Belgium the levels of support were consistently below the EU average for all applicant countries.

Secondly, attitudes towards enlargement varied also depending on the candidate country in question (see Appendix IV). Support was consistently higher for Malta (49%–52%), Hungary (46%–52%) and Poland (43%–49%). However, most of the other candidate countries did not manage to secure the approval of the EU public. More people were opposed to than in favour of the membership of Estonia, Latvia, Lithuania, Slovenia and Slovakia in autumn of 1997, the spring of 1999, the spring and the autumn of 2000 and in the spring of 2002 (with only exception of Slovakia then its membership equally was supported and opposed by 38%). Support for Slovenia was the least widespread ranging from 33% to 39%. Furthermore, it was only in the spring of 1999 that the people opposed to Slovenia's membership were less than those in favour of it.

Thirdly, the average support for the EU enlargement, as illustrated by Appendix III, was not particularly high, it fluctuated between 38% (in the spring of 2000) and 47% (in the autumn of 2003) and peaked only once above 50% in the autumn of 2001 when support reached 51%.

The assessment of the developments of EU conditionality confirms that public opinion did not have any substantial positive or negative effect on the first phase of the fifth enlargement. The levels of support did not reflect the conclusions of the Luxembourg European Council, which established two groups of candidate countries ('ins' and 'pre-ins'). Even though support for enlargement was declining, the EU not only continued but also accelerated the completion of the accession process. Despite the fact that some of the applicants did not receive much support from the EU citizens and in some cases more people were against than in favour of their accession, all ten candidate countries completed the accession negotiations and joined the EU in 2004. The comparative analysis of the implications of the public opinion on the development of EU enlargement policy confirms that it was not a decisive factor in the case of the fifth enlargement, as it did not influence any of the decisions of the Union regarding the advancement of the process.

Enlargement countries

This section reflects on the relationship between the profile of the 'Laeken Ten' and the evolution of the EU enlargement conditionality, by focusing on the following two aspects:

- the impact of the problematic issues and reform challenges (the applicants need to address) on the scope and range of the EU conditions; and
- the implications of the existence or lack of group dynamics (which is examined with reference to the number of applicant states at the same stage of the accession process) for the development of the incentive structure, particularly with reference to the *accession advancement rewards*.

It is undeniable that the first key development with reference to the conditions set out by the EU for the candidate countries of CEE was the establishment of the Copenhagen criteria. Although some have argued that the conditions were set out in order to protect the achievements of the Union (Smith, 2003), we can also advance the argument that the membership conditions reflect the key challenges which the former communist countries were facing in early 1990s. It is interesting to note that in addition to carrying out major political and economic reforms, the candidate countries shared another common feature, as one senior EU official pointed out, 'There was this sense that these countries had to come back and they were unknown, if you think how many of us have actually been to these countries and how many actually understood how they function' (Interview 3, 2009).

However, things quickly changed, as an another senior EU official noted, 'It was recognised quite early on that you were dealing with a fundamental change, dealing with the ten East European countries, you were dealing with a fundamental change in the entire structure of the government' and pointed out that

> [t]he genesis of the Copenhagen criteria was, on one hand a recognition that for geostrategic reasons, political reasons, but also for loads of other reasons, we wanted to consolidate democracy in the whole of Central and Eastern Europe.
>
> (Interview 20, 2009)

He also emphasised that '[t]he logic of the Copenhagen criteria was that the accession process needed to be much more focused on governance and administrative capacity rather than merely looking at what was down on paper' (Interview 20, 2009). The distinct approach of the Commission towards the CEECs and Cyprus and Malta and the preparation of separate enlargement strategies provide further evidence for the significance of the profile of the candidate countries.

It is important to mention that it was not only the nature of the issues which the applicants needed to address but also their number which had a strong impact on the enlargement process. As one senior Commission official noted, 'this is the first time, that you have first of all, so many countries, secondly, countries with such a different levels of development, with such a different background' (Interview 5, 2009). He stressed that 'we doubled the size, with totally different countries' and also remarked that there 'was a realisation that it was a different type of event, we needed a different approach with this emphasis on preparation before joining' (Interview 5, 2009).

The number of candidate countries also had important implications for the EU's decisions to grant key *accession advancement rewards*, particularly for the start of the accession negotiations. There were heated debates prior to the publication of the Commission's Opinions on the applicant countries. As one senior EU official noted, 'there were clearly discussions between the Commission and the member states on how to form the different groups whether [there] should be one negotiation or whether [there] should be a number of different negotiations' (Interview 18, 2009). Another senior Commission official confirmed that '[i]t has always been one of the big dilemmas. Should we actually take a country when it has met a criteria purely on its own merit or is there a political adjustment to go along fine?' (Interview 3, 2009). Another Commission official summarised the main considerations by saying that:

it was more a question of the choice between, until the very end, between those who felt that it should be individual, regatta style approach, where the faster you run, the quicker you enter the EU and the others who felt it was not fair to have this kind of race and you would not get a balanced outcome, if you get some countries and other are left out and might get disappointed or unmotivated.

(Interview 5, 2009)

Although some member states like Denmark wanted to open negotiations with all countries, the Luxembourg European Council gave the green light to the start of the accession negotiations with only six countries – Poland, Hungary, the Czech Republic, Estonia, Slovenia and Cyprus (Council of the European Union, 1997b). However, the decisions of the Helsinki European Council to open negotiations with all candidate countries (with the exception of Turkey) established a new group dynamics and introduced the catch-up principle. One senior Commission official reflected on the significance of the Helsinki conclusions by saying:

I think that you have seen a gradual shift from an approach which was truly based on the country meeting the first of the Copenhagen economic criteria – market economy – that was differentiating criteria and was the one that most of the discussions were focused on, pre-Helsinki.

(Interview 3, 2009)

Further, she stressed that 'it was a significant policy shift to say that we take everybody in and we adjust that criteria in the process' (Interview 3, 2009).

It is evident that the size of the newly unified group of negotiating countries also had important implications for another *accession advancement reward* – the credibility of the membership perspective and the establishment of a provisional timetable for the completion of the process. One EU official recollected, 'In the 2004 enlargement we had this kind of an "armada" approach ... there was group of countries, so there was a need to have at least an indicative schedule for things to happen, so that everybody was drawn on board' (Interview 12, 2009). He further highlighted the relevance of the group dynamics by specifying that 'there was peer pressure amongst the candidates themselves and then there was a schedule from our side and that gave a rhythm and pace for our work and then there was a target that worked' (Interview 12, 2009).

There is also evidence for the significance of the group dynamics for the completion of the accession process. As one senior EU Commission official pointed out, with regard to Latvia, Lithuania and Slovakia (which started accession negotiations in 2000 and managed to complete them in 2002):

[w]e were a bit generous with them as well. They did not go through a similar vigorous process, as did the Estonians and the Czechs and others. To be honest, we gave certain discounts to them, because it became a political will not to separate, not to draw away these countries.

(Interview 10, 2009)

He noted that 'if we had applied exactly the same methodology, as the one we applied with the six, with whom we started in March 1999, the Helsinki countries, as you call them, the second group of countries would have become members a little later' (Interview 10, 2009).

The comparative analysis of the impact of the candidate countries on EU enlargement conditionality confirms that although applicant states have a narrow scope for manoeuvring in the accession process, they do indirectly shape the development of EU enlargement policy. The findings reveal that the profile of the candidate countries (particularly the problematic issues or the deficiencies that they need to address or improve) influences the range and scope of EU conditions. Furthermore, the study underlines the crucial role of the group dynamics among applicant states. As evidenced by the European journeys of the eight CEECs, Cyprus and Malta, the existence of strong group dynamics affects the EU's decisions regarding the granting of accession advancement rewards. The analysis reveals that the profile of the enlargement countries is an important conditioning factor for the development of EU enlargement policy.

External pressures

It is inevitable that the external context has always had a significant impact on the development of the EU. However, it is also true that some events might have been more important than others. In order to examine the relationship between external factors and the evolution of EU enlargement policy, this section follows a selective approach. It focuses on two pivotal events – the end of the Cold War and the Yugoslav wars – whose significance for the transformation of Europe is undeniable.

After the fall of the Berlin Wall and the collapse of communism in the late 1980s and early 1990s, there was an urgent need to reinvent Europe. In 1994, the Commissioner for External Relations Hans van den Broek pointed out that 'Europe today is not a geographic expression but rather a political aspiration, the desire of the diverse peoples of our continent to live and work together in conditions of political and economic freedom' (Van den Broek, 1994). It is not surprising that the Community focused on tackling the problems of post-Cold War Europe, particularly by developing new instruments and new policies. Some have argued that the Union was slow to officially establish enlargement with the CEECs as one of its goals (at the Copenhagen European Council in June 1993). However, one senior Commission official noted that:

> [w]e forget what a change it was. Four years... it was not massively long. Look back at the political situation: worry about Russia, what to do... and it was a very hectic period politically.
>
> (Interview 3, 2009)

The official pointed out that:

> once there was a recognition that Europe was the direction, they [CEECs] were looking, they were in and we had a definite responsibility to bring them back in.
>
> (Interview 3, 2009)

The relevance of the end of the Cold War for the significant development of EU enlargement policy was confirmed repeatedly by the members of the Delors Commission, who were consistent in establishing strong links between the new political context and the need for the EU enlargement to the East.

The Commissioner for External Relations noted that '[t]he end of the Cold War appeared, at first, to confirm the achievement of a new age of well-being, which could now progressively be extended to the Community's less fortunate neighbours to the east' (Van den Broek, 1993). With reference to the disappearance of the old block system, Van den Broek commented that the CEECs which 'look forward to eventual membership' were left 'feeling rather exposed, particularly given instability in the former Soviet Union and the tragic war in the former Yugoslavia' (Van den Broek, 1993). He insisted that '[a] clear vision of Europe's future is all the more needed as others are already knocking at the Community's door' (Van den Broek, 1993). His comments were echoed by another Commissioner – Christiane Scrivener – who acknowledged that '[n]ew challenges are arising and important political and economic changes are taking place' and that in Europe, 'we are at a turning point' (Scrivener, 1994). She also highlighted the need for European integration by saying that '[a] small and federal Europe is no longer our future. We may regret it, but it is too late for that. Times have changed in Europe and the European Union must keep in pace with all internal and external changes that have rapidly occurred for the last years' (Scrivener, 1994).

The Vice-President of the Commission Henning Christophersen also acknowledged the new role of the EU by noting that 'the Union has become a pole of attraction for other European states' and insisted that:

> the Union cannot be regarded as a closed club. It must continue its enlargement process towards the East. This will be essential to give our Central and East European Neighbours the right signal and would indeed help to stabilise the region.
>
> (Christophersen, 1994)

Christophersen raised some of the issues related to the dissolution of the 'monolithic block under the control of the Soviet Union' by pointing out that '[w]e have witnessed the emergence of 27 independent nations. Seven of those countries are now at war with each other or dominated by Civil war' (Christophersen, 1994). The Vice-President highlighted the significance and the scope of the Eastward enlargement by noting that 'the stabilization and integration of this region is perhaps the biggest challenge of this century' (Christophersen, 1994).

Although 'the end of the Cold War has led to profound political and economic changes', the Yugoslav wars in the early 1990s posed new challenges to the stability of the continent (Pinheiro, 1993). On 3 July 1993 in Corfu, Commissioner Pinheiro noted that 'a few hundred kilometres away from us a war is raging which has already cost hundreds of thousands of lives, has turned into one of the most cruel conflicts since 1945 and is threatening the stability of the entire Balkan peninsula, if not Europe as a whole' (Pinheiro, 1993).

The painful realisation that 'war has returned to Europe, and returned with a vengeance' caught the EU and the international community 'in general unprepared' (Van den Broek, 1993). The Yugoslav conflicts had significant implications for the new European democracies, as Van den Broek pointed out; the instability in former Yugoslavia made 'our Eastern neighbours feel particularly vulnerable' (Van den Broek, 1993).

Although the Yugoslav tragedy had an impact on a number of EU policies, its relevance to EU enlargement policy is very significant. The Commissioner for External Relations insisted, 'We do not intend to wait for more Yugoslavias before offering real support to our neighbours in central and eastern Europe' (Van den Broek, 1993). Furthermore, he pointed out that 'the Yugoslav tragedy has shown that the European Union must identify its geopolitical interests and build a consensus on how best to protect them' (Van den Broek, 1993).

The analysis of the implications of the end of the Cold War and the Yugoslav wars for the Union highlights the importance of external factors for the internal dynamic of the EU. Although the collapse of communism and the Yugoslav conflicts had a significant impact on the political climate (not only in Europe), their relevance to the development of EU enlargement policy is undeniable. It is important to note their role particularly for the EU's crucial decision to establish accession of the CEECs as a shared objective, which marks the beginning of a new approach to the EU's enlargement policy.

Conclusions

The chapter confirms that the evolution of the EU enlargement conditionality towards the eight CEECs, Cyprus and Malta is characterised by three distinct trends. Firstly, examination of the development of the EU conditions illustrates a shift from broad uniform conditionality to targeted and differentiated conditionality. Secondly, the alternation in the *reward–threat balance* indicates another important change: from positive to negative conditionality. Last but not least, the findings highlight the growing relevance and multi-functionality of the monitoring reports. In order to explain these developments, the two level analysis dissects the influence of a mix of institutional and external factors.

The study confirms the essential relevance of EU institutions for the development of the scope and range of EU requirements. Furthermore, it illustrates the impressive entrepreneurship of the Commission which has led to the growing application of detailed, targeted conditionality. The analysis also points to the attempts of some of the member states to shape the scope of EU conditions in order to advance their position in bilateral disputes with candidate countries. However, the findings reveal that the development of EU requirements is not fully monopolised by EU-internal factors, as the candidate countries themselves influence the scope of the requirements. Although the scope of the

Copenhagen criteria was not actively engineered by the EU hope-fuls, it reflects the Union's acknowledgement of the specific challenges which the applicants need to address and points to the growing rel-evance of external actors. Furthermore, it proves that despite their limited bargaining power in the accession process, candidate coun-tries are a decisive factor, shaping the evolution of EU enlargement conditionality.

The evaluation of the factors affecting the developments of the incen-tive structure reveals a very complex picture. Similarly to the discussion of the evolution of EU conditions, the analysis confirms the crucial role of the institutional factors – namely, member states' preferences and inter-institutional dynamics. The research findings also highlight the strong influence of the Parliament in setting 2004 as a target date for accession. However, we also need to acknowledge that the commitment to provisional timetables and target dates as well as the confirmation of the inclusive and irreversible nature of the enlargement process would not have been possible without the seal of approval from the member states. The study also points to the growing influence of the Commis-sion over shaping the development of the accession process. It firmly cemented its position as a policy driver, which is reflected not only by its responsibilities for the preparation of the Union's enlargement strategies but also by its impact on the Council, as the latter followed all of the Commission's recommendations regarding the first phase of the fifth enlargement.

In addition to reflecting on the impact of the institutional factors, the book highlights the relevance of external pressures and actors. The findings confirm that the EU's most successful foreign policy is exposed to the pressures cause by external crises and shocks. Although it is difficult to precisely measure the intensity of their impact, the empirical evidence identified herein shows that security shocks and crises had a catalysing effect on the development of EU enlargement conditionality towards the eights CEECs, Cyprus and Malta. However, external pressures cannot on their own account for the developments of the incentive structure. The same observation applies to the impact of the enlargement countries. The analysis confirms the relevance of group dynamics for the incentive structure. It illustrates that the strong group dynamics contributed to the establishment of strong commitments to provisional timetables and accelerated the advancement process. Although public opinion was carefully surveyed and integrated in the enlargement strategy of the Union, the research findings confirm that public attitudes did not have any unequivocally positive or negative impact on the development of enlargement policy. Furthermore, the examination of the evolution of monitoring reveals that it was exclusively modified by the Commission with the aim of assessing the applicant states' progress towards meeting the Copenhagen criteria.

3
EU Conditionality in the Context of the 2007 Enlargement

This chapter examines the evolution of EU enlargement conditionality by focusing on the second phase of the fifth enlargement, which was completed with the accession of Bulgaria and Romania on 1 January 2007. Although both countries were 'part of the same inclusive and irreversible enlargement process', they did not accede to the Union in May 2004 together with the other CEECs, Cyprus and Malta (Council of the European Union, 2003a). The chapter notes the similarities in the EU's approach to Sofia and Bucharest and the other candidate countries, but concentrates on the scope and implications of three far-reaching changes: the introduction of additional country-specific conditions; the incorporation of a 'super' safeguard clause in the Accession Treaty; and the establishment of an unprecedented post-accession monitoring mechanism. As the EU's Bulgarian and Romania experience affected the development of the Union's strategy towards Turkey and the countries from the Western Balkans, the examination of the second phase of the fifth enlargement not only highlights important novel developments but also allows us to test the impact of institutional and external factors on key evolutionary developments of EU enlargement conditionality.

The chapter is structured into two parts. On the basis of the *stage-structured conditionality model*, the first part traces the transformation of EU conditionality between the stages of the accession process. The second part of the chapter examines the relationship between the developments of EU conditionality and the following factors (1) *EU member states*, (2) *EU inter-institutional dynamics*, (3) *public opinion in the EU*, (4) *enlargement countries* and (5) *external pressures caused by economic or security shocks and crises.*

Tracing the evolution of EU conditionality towards Bulgaria and Romania

Romania was the first and, for more than a decade, the only CEEC to have contractual relations with the EC, it signed a Generalised System of Preferences Agreement in 1974 and an Agreement on Industrial Products in 1980, whereas the diplomatic relations between Bulgaria and the EC were established in 1988 (European Commission, 1997). In order to contextualise the analysis of the EU enlargement conditionality, this section briefly accounts for the development of the relations between the EU and Sofia and Bucharest prior to the establishment of their membership perspective.

Bulgaria and Romania were among the first CEECs[1] with which the EC signed TCAs. The relations between the EC and Sofia and Bucharest entered a new phase with the signature of EAs, respectively on 8 March and 1 February 1993. The Agreements not only provided a new legal framework for the development of bilateral relations but also recognised that 'the ultimate objective' of the associated countries was 'to become a member of the Community' (*Official Journal*, 1994d, 1994e). Unlike, the first EAs signed with the Visegrád countries, the agreements with Bulgaria and Romania included a 'human rights clause' which stated that 'Respect for the democratic principles and human rights established by the Helsinki Final Act and the Charter of Paris for New Europe' and also 'the principles of market economy' (only in the case of Romania) 'constitute essential elements of the present association' (*Official Journal*, 1994d, 1994e). Membership was officially established as a common objective at the Copenhagen European Council in June 1993. This decision marked the beginning of the pre-negotiation stage for all CEECs, including Bulgaria and Romania.

Pre-negotiation stage

Conditions

As the previous chapter discussed in detail the *conditions for applying for membership* with which all CEECs had to comply and the EU did not introduce any new developments in the case of Bulgaria and Romania, the analysis focuses on the *conditions for opening of accession negotiations* which Sofia and Bucharest had to meet.

Following the conclusion of the Copenhagen and the Madrid European Councils which laid down the membership criteria, Agenda 2000 marked the EU's first steps towards clarifying and specifying the scope of the conditions. The Commission stated that respect of the political criteria 'is a necessary, but not a sufficient condition for opening accession negotiations' and confirmed that the recommendations for the opening of the membership talks were to be based on applicants' sufficient progress in satisfying the conditions of membership defined by the European Council in Copenhagen and their preparedness to satisfy the conditions for membership in the medium term (European Commission, 1997: 38). However, in 1999, following a recommendation from the Commission to start 'negotiations with all countries which meet the Copenhagen political criteria' the Union amended the *conditions for opening of accession negotiations* and stressed the absolute priority of the political criteria (European Commission, 1999). The EU introduced another important development by establishing additional country-specific conditions. The Commission stated that:

> the opening of negotiations with Bulgaria should be conditional on a decision by the Bulgarian authorities before the end of 1999 on acceptable closure dates for units 1–4 in the Kozloduy nuclear plant and upon a confirmation of a significant progress accomplished in the economic reform process.
>
> (European Commission, 1999)

It also specified that:

> the opening of the negotiations with Romania should be conditional on the confirmation of effective action announced by the Romania authorities to provide adequate budgetary resources and to implement structural reform of child care institutions before the end of 1999. It is also conditional upon a further assessment of the economic situation before negotiations are formally opened, in the expectation that appropriate measures will have been taken to address the macro-economic situation.
>
> (European Commission, 1999)

The analysis of the conditions set out by the EU with which Sofia and Bucharest had to comply during the pre-negotiation stage illustrates an important shift in the EU's approach to establishing the scope of its requirements. The Union not only took a U-turn by 'reducing' the *conditions for opening accession negotiations* to compliance with the political criteria but also introduced for the first time individual country-specific conditions. Although both developments were intricately linked and influenced by the profile of the candidate countries (see section

'Enlargement countries' in this chapter), their implications were not confined to the fifth enlargement round.

Incentives structure

This subsection explores the evolution of the second element of EU conditionality – the incentives structure, which examines the *reward–threat balance*. On the basis of the *stage-structured conditionality model*, the analysis traces the developments in two categories of rewards: *accession advancement rewards* and *financial rewards* (or financial assistance) and two categories of threats: *implicit threats*, which sanction non-compliance by delaying the receiving of the accession advancement rewards and *explicit threats*, which introduce specific penalising measures.

In the first half of 1993, Bulgaria and Romania received two *accession advancement rewards* – just few months after the signing of their respective AAs, the European Council confirmed their membership perspective in June 1993 (Council of the European Union, 1993). The Madrid European Council took the first steps to establishing a credible membership perspective by setting a timetable for the accession process, it linked the preliminary stage of negotiations with the CEECs to the start of negotiations with Cyprus and Malta, which had already been scheduled to begin 'six months after the conclusion of the 1996 Intergovernmental Conference' (Council of the European Union, 1995a, 1995b). The timetable was confirmed at the Dublin European Council in December 1996.

The Luxembourg European Council in July 1997 provided Sofia and Bucharest with another accession *advancement reward* by confirming their candidate country status. However, as the Union did not consider the progress towards complying with the membership conditions sufficient, it did not recommend the start of accession negotiations with them, thus using an *implicit threat* rather than another *accession advancement reward*. Two years later, the Helsinki European Council decided to launch the accession negotiations with Bulgaria and Romania, Latvia, Lithuania, Slovakia, and Malta in February 2000. The summit not only provided the next *accession advancement reward* for the countries which were not included in first group, but it reinforced the credibility of the membership perspective by introducing the EU's commitment to 'to welcome new Member States from the end of 2002 as soon as they have demonstrated their ability to assume the obligations of membership and once the negotiating process has been successfully completed' (Council of the European Union, 1999b).

The investigation of the second element of the incentives structure – the threats during the pre-accession stage indicates that the EU used mainly *implicit threats* to induce compliance with its conditions. The advancement of the accession process, in particular the decisions for the start of the accession negotiations were conditional on sufficient progress in meeting the membership conditions. The application of *explicit threats* was limited to financial sanctions. As in the case of the other candidate countries, the EU confirmed that 'if the commitments contained in the Europe Agreement are not respected and/or progress towards fulfilment of the Copenhagen criteria is insufficient', the Council could suspend any pre-accession financial assistance (*Official Journal*, 1998).

The review of the pre-negotiation incentive structure shows that Bulgaria and Romania were slower than the Visegrád three to advance their relationship with the EU. Although the Union introduced more *implicit threats* (such as the possibility to suspend unilaterally the application of the EAs), they were not exclusive to Sofia and Bucharest, but also included in the agreement with the other CEECs. Therefore, the early developments of the incentive structure followed a linear trajectory rather than a targeted approach. Although the EU applied an *implicit threat* (by delaying the start of the accession negotiations), the *reward–threat balance* was still dominated by a range of *accession advancement rewards* and *financial rewards*.

Monitoring

The Luxembourg European Council not only established two groups of candidate countries but also integrated monitoring as an essential part of the accession process by confirming that the Commission would make regular reports, reviewing the progress of each applicant state from CEE (Council of the European Union, 1997a). The Union followed a uniform approach and did not introduce separate monitoring instruments for the 'ins' and 'pre-ins'. Nevertheless, the first two sets of Progress Reports[2] were more significant for Bulgaria, Romania, Latvia, Lithuania and Slovakia rather than the Luxembourg group of countries, as they provided the basis for the Council's decision to extend the accession negotiations to Sofia, Bucharest, Riga, Vilnius and Bratislava.

The analysis confirms that the early developments of the monitoring instruments followed a consistent pattern which provided firm foundations for tracking yearly progress. Furthermore, the Opinions and the reports of the Commission were based on a homogenous framework which allowed the EU to comparatively evaluate progress across the candidate countries.

Conclusions

The study highlights important developments of the evolution of EU enlargement conditionality. The EU not only amended the *conditions for opening accession negotiations* by confirming that compliance with the political criteria laid down at the Copenhagen European Council was a prerequisite for the opening of the membership talks but also introduced individual country-specific conditions. This shift in the EU's approach to setting conditions marks the beginning of a transition from uniform to differentiated conditionality. The review of the *reward–threat balance* shows that the Union preferred the use of carrots to sticks to induce compliance with its conditions. Although the Council sanctioned Bulgaria's and Romania's insufficient progress by delaying the start of the accession negotiations, the EU provided both countries with positive pre-negotiation incentive structures, which were dominated by a range of *accession advancement* and *financial rewards*. Furthermore, the annual publication and increasing sophistication of the progress reports confirms the growing significance of monitoring for the enlargement process. The developments during the pre-negotiation stage shows that the EU introduced the application of differentiated, positive conditionality towards Bulgaria and Romania.

Negotiation stage

Conditions

The section discusses the developments of the scope and range of the EU conditions during the negotiation stage. Although Bulgaria and Romania (together with Latvia, Lithuania, Slovakia and Malta) advanced their relationship with the Union and joined the group of negotiating countries in February 2000, the accession negotiations with Sofia and particularly Bucharest endured a much bumpier ride. As the aim of the research is not to examine in detail the developments in each of the negotiation chapters, the analysis is limited to the implications of the ever-growing *acquis* and the conditions which Bulgaria and Romania had to accept in order to close the accession negotiations.

One of the key characteristics of the European integration project is its evolving nature, which is also reflected by the growing body of EU laws. Therefore, it was only natural that at a later stage the Balkan states had to comply with more conditions. One senior EU official reflected on the developments in one of the most challenging chapters – Justice and Home Affairs – by noting that:

[w]hen we opened accession negotiations in 2000 with Hungary on chapter 24, it was like a walkover in a couple of months. It was a

very theoretical exercise, information was sent and the information was assessed here (Brussels) by nine different units at that time. There were a couple of peer-reviews compared to Bulgaria and Romania, we were there every three months with a team of ten experts.

(Interview 21, 2009)

The Commission official also pointed out that 'the acquis has doubled in size between the day we started negotiating with Hungary and the day we closed accession negotiations with Romania' (Interview 21, 2009). The increasing number of conditions in various negotiation chapters made the membership talks with Sofia and Bucharest more demanding. However, it was the Union's position to make the closure of the accession negotiations conditional on the acceptance of unprecedented safeguard clauses which illustrates the more stringent approach of the EU towards the two Balkan countries.

Bulgaria completed the membership talks in June 2004 after agreeing to the inclusion of the 'super' safeguard clause which allowed the Council to postpone the accession of the country by one year (*Agence Europe*, 2004; Council of the European Union, 2004b). One senior EU official highlighted the political significance of the new clause by reflecting on its development:

We finished with Bulgaria before we finished with Romania. There was a strong push for the Bulgarians by the Irish, who were at that time at the Presidency and at some stage I still remember discussing [the conclusion of the negotiations] at Rond Point Schuman with the Irish Ambassador. Basically I said to her: we will never be able to convince the member states if we don't have some kind of insurance after completing the enlargement negotiations. That was why we invented the super safeguard clause [...] if we had not done that we would not have been able to complete the accession negotiations with Bulgaria, that was very clear.

(Interview 18, 2009)

The Romanian Foreign Minister Mircea Genoana 'was "surprised" at the "speed" with which Bulgaria agreed, without seeking to negotiate to lessen the "extremely strong" language' (*Agence Europe*, 2004). However, Romania's insufficient commitment to reform its system of state subsidies, particularly in the steel sector and long-standing problems of corruption made the completion of the membership talks with Bucharest not only much more difficult but also conditional on an even stricter set of requirements (*Financial Times*, 2004b; *EurActiv*, 2004).

One senior EU reflected on the twists and turns leading to the closure of the chapter on Justice and Home Affairs (one of the last two outstanding chapters) by pointing out:

> 'Clearly the recommendation to close accession negotiations with Romania was negative on our side, but we have been overruled by our Commissioner. Again – it is really important to bear this in mind – you had the Socialist government in Romania, Social Democrat Enlargement Commissioner and you had a Social Democrat Commissioner for Justice, Freedom and Security, all part of the European socialist family, that certainly helped to push through [a decision] that the recommendation should be positive.
>
> (Interview 21, 2009)

However, the Commission official highlighted the link between the closure of the chapter the establishment of additional country-specific condition by noting that:

> [t]he answer we got was that the final decision was positive, but we had carte blanche to draft the positions for closing, so I went back to my office and started together with my colleagues and we drafted sixty-six conditions that Romania should meet between the closing the accession negotiations and the accession to the EU. Seven of these conditions were particularly important and were singled out. One member state in the Council, namely Finland, was opposed and wanted to follow the initial Commission line of not closing the accession negotiations, and therefore negotiated a deal with the other member states that they would attach a suspension close to not fulfilling those seven conditionalities.
>
> (Interview 21, 2009)

It is important to note that the 'super' safeguard clause allowed the Council to decide by qualified majority whether to postpone the accession of Romania by one year. Furthermore, Annex IX of the Accession Treaty linked the activation of the clause not only to insufficient progress in addressing the seven commitments[3] in the area of Justice and Home Affairs, but also to the requirements in the area of Competition policy.[4]

The scope of the conditions which Sofia and Bucharest had to accept in order to complete the accession negotiations illustrates the evolutionary nature of EU enlargement policy. In addition to highlighting the expansive nature of the EU rules and regulations and respectively the widening range of conditions, Bulgaria's and Romania's experience confirms the increasing application of targeted and differentiated conditionality. Furthermore, the final common position for closing the negations on chapter 24 'Justice and Home Affairs' with Bucharest shows the growing relevance not only of the closing benchmarks but also of the skilful entrepreneurship of the Commission at navigating through competing pressures.

Incentives structure

Although the Helsinki European Council decided to begin accession negotiations with Bulgaria, Romania, Latvia, Lithuania, Slovakia and Malta, the Union also noted:

It emerges that some candidates will not be in a position to meet all the Copenhagen criteria in the medium term. The Commission's intention is to report in early 2000 to the Council on progress by certain candidate States on fulfilling the Copenhagen economic criteria.

(Council of the European Union, 1999b)

The official start of the accession negotiations on 15 February 2000 marked an important step in the relations between the EU and the six candidate countries. In addition to opening and closing negotiation chapters (see Table 3.1), the EU provided Sofia and Bucharest with another important *accession advancement reward* by setting a target date for the completion of the negotiations. The Nice European Council presented a road map based on the Helsinki timetable that the EU would be 'in a position to welcome those new Member States which are ready as from the end of 2002' (Council of the European Union, 2000b). The Göteborg European Council in June 2001 confirmed that 'the road map has proved to be an ambitious and realistic framework for the negotiations' (Council of the European Union, 2001a).

However, six months later the EU noted the growing gap between Bulgaria and Romania and the other ten candidate countries by stating that:

Table 3.1 Accession negotiations: Opening and closing chapters

Chapters	Bulgaria		Romania	
	Opened	Closed	Opened	Closed
1. Free Movement of Goods	May 2001	June 2002	March 2002	June 2003
2. Free Movement for Persons	October 2001	June 2002	March 2002	December 2003
3. Freedom to Provide Services	March 2001	November 2001	December 2002	September 2004
4. Free Movement of Capital	November 2000	July 2001	June 2001	June 2003
5. Company Law	November 2000	June 2001	March 2001	December 2001
6. Completion Policy	March 2001	June 2004	November 2000	December 2004
7. Agriculture	March 2002	June 2004	November 2002	June 2004
8. Fisheries	March 2001	June 2001	May 2001	June 2001
9. Transport Policy	June 2001	June 2003	June 2001	December 2003
10. Taxation	July 2001	June 2002	October 2001	June 2003
11. EMU	March 2002	April 2002	June 2002	June 2002
12. Statistics	October 2000	November 2000	October 2000	December 2000
13. Employment and Social Policy	October 2001	April 2002	October 2001	April 2002
14. Energy	November 2001	November 2002	March 2002	June 2004
15. Industrial Policy	December 2001	December 2001	July 2002	July 2002
16. SMEs	March 2000	June 2000	May 2000	May 2000
17. Science and Research	March 2000	June 2000	May 2000	May 2000
18. Education and Training	March 2000	June 2000	March 2000	May 2000
19. Telecommunications and Information Technologies	October 2000	October 2001	November 2000	November 2002

Table 3.1 (Continued)

Chapters	Bulgaria		Romania	
	Opened	Closed	Opened	Closed
20. Culture and Audiovisional Policy	March 2000	November 2000	October 2000	December 2002
21. Regional Policy and Coordination and Structural Instruments	November 2001	June 2004	March 2001	September 2004
22. Environment	July 2001	June 2003	March 2002	November 2004
23. Consumers and Health Protection	October 2000	November 2000	July 2001	July 2001
24. Justice and Home Affairs	June 2001	October 2003	April 2002	December 2004
25. Customs Union	June 2001	July 2002	May 2001	November 2002
26. External Relations	March 2000	November 2000	June 2000	June 2000
27. CFSP	March 2000	June 2000	June 2000	June 2000
28. Financial Control	May 2001	October 2001	July 2002	October 2003
29. Finance and Budgetary Provisions	November 2001	June 2004	December 2002	June 2004
30. Institutions	April 2002	April 2004	April 2002	December 2004
31. Others	June 2004	June 2004	December 2004	December 2004

Source: European Commission (2004c; 2012); Papadimitriou and Phinnemore (2009).

[t]he European Union is determined to bring the accession negotiations with the candidate countries that are ready to a successful
conclusion by the end of 2002, so that those countries can take
part in the European Parliament elections in 2004 as members [...]
if the present rate of progress of the negotiations and reforms in
the candidate States is maintained, Cyprus, Estonia, Hungary, Latvia,
Lithuania, Malta, Poland, the Slovak Republic, the Czech Republic and Slovenia could be ready. It appreciates the efforts made by
Bulgaria and Romania and would encourage them to continue on
that course.

(Council of the European Union, 2001a)

The historic European Copenhagen Council in December 2002 officially
decoupled the two Balkan states from the other CEECs, Cyprus and
Malta. However, it should be noted that there was a virtual agreement
among the EU and national officials that the Union's decision was not
unexpected, as Bulgaria and Romania had previously set 2007 as their
target entry date. Although the European Council did not complete
the accession negotiations with Sofia and Bucharest in 2002, the EU
reaffirmed its strong commitment to the countries by increasing their
pre-accession assistance and declaring 'its objective to welcome Bulgaria
and Romania as member of the European Union in 2007' (Council of
the European Union, 2002).

The European Council not only reiterated its support for concluding
the negotiations in 2004 and noted that 'Accession Treaty can be signed
as early as 2005' but also underlined 'the determination of the Union to
facilitate this timeline' (Council of the European Union, 2003b). However, a couple of weeks before the target date – the end of the 2004 –
the Commission's position to put the negotiations with Bucharest on
hold sent shock waves through the political elites in Romania and EU
member states (*Financial Times*, 2004a). One senior Commission official
recollected the dramatic turn of events:

The conditions to conclude the negotiations at the end of 2004 were
not there [...] so what Olli Rehn did in his first week in office
was quite drastic. Under Verheugen's leadership DG Enlargement
had already prepared the draft common positions for Competition Policy and Justice and Home Affairs foreseeing the closure of
the negotiations on these chapters and the Dutch presidency had
already planned concluding the negotiations in December. Olli Rehn
reversed the instructions, withdrew the draft common positions

proposing provisional closure and we wrote it again, not proposing provisional closure.

(Interview 9, 2009)

The EU official elaborated further on the complexity of the situation by reflecting on member states' reactions and their determination to meet the repeatedly reaffirmed target dates:

The Dutch were very unhappy and a number of other member states as well. Verheugen in the house was absolutely furious, some others were a little surprised [...] in the end what happened was then that we had all sorts of emergency meetings [...] So [we] quickly came around to find a way, in which the Commission could in the end agree to actually propose the closure of the negotiations [...] but that needs to be done based on certain meaningful conditions and monitoring mechanism, which allows us to keep a part of the leverage to keep the pressure on, even after the negotiations have been concluded.

(Interview 9, 2009)

The analysis of the incentive structure shows that the accession negotiations with the two Balkan states followed a more complex trajectory compared to the 'Laeken Ten'. However, the EU's decision to decouple Bulgaria and Romania from the other candidate countries should not be interpreted as a punishment, but as an expected consequence of Bulgaria's and Romania's commitments to becoming members of the Union in 2007. Furthermore, despite remaining issues in the areas of Justice and Home Affairs and Competition, the Union did not delay the completion of the accession negotiations with Romania.

Monitoring

The developments of the monitoring instruments during the accession stage highlight the continuity in EU enlargement policy. In order to trace and evaluate the progress made by Bulgaria and Romania towards accession the Commission prepared four sets of Regular Report in the period between 2000 and 2004. They followed the structure of the first reports published in 1998 and reflected on the relations between the candidate country and the EU; and assessed the compliance of the candidate country with the three Copenhagen criteria. As the EU was scheduled to take key decisions regarding the advancement of the enlargement process in December 2002 and December 2004, the Regular out lists of individual country-specific benchmarks in some of the challenging policy areas. The 2005 Comprehensive Monitoring Reports highlighted 'the remaining gaps in policies, legislation and its implementation' and identified 16 areas of serious concern which required 'immediate and decisive action' for Sofia and 14 areas for Bucharest (European Commission, 2005a, 2005f).

The May 2006 Monitoring Reports focused exclusively on 'the areas in need of further improvement in the light of the three Copenhagen accession criteria' and outlined six areas of serious concern which required 'urgent action' for Bulgaria and four areas for Romania (European Commission, 2006a, 2006i). The September 2006 Monitoring Report highlighted some problematic issues in the areas of food safety, air safety, EU agricultural funds and established individual country-specific lists of benchmarks in the areas of judiciary and the fight against corruption, which Bulgaria and Romania had to address. Some of the issues which required immediate attention included public administration reform; the justice system reform; fight against corruption; fight against trafficking in human beings; ill-treatment in custody and prison conditions; children protection; the disabled and mental healthcare system; and the protection and integration of the minorities (European Commission, 2005a, 2005f).

The analysis highlights the importance of benchmarking for the development of EU enlargement policy during the accession stage. The establishment and the regular modification of the sets of country-specific conditions which Bulgaria and Romania needed to address (prior to their accession to the Union) confirm the emergence of three intertwined trends – the application of increasingly differentiated, targeted and detailed conditionality. The fact that the Commission used the monitoring reports to present specific policy items and requirements illustrates another element of the evolution of the policy – the growing multi-functionality and relevance of the monitoring instruments.

Incentive structure

The examination of the accession incentive structure reveals significant changes in the *reward–threat balance* after the signing of the Accession Treaty. The rewards provided by the Union were mainly *financial rewards*, as the only *accession advancement reward* was the actual accession of the countries to the Union. Although the EU did not introduce any *implicit threats*, it established a wide range of *explicit threats* by specifying, for the first time in the accession process with Sofia and Bucharest, *preventive or remedial sanctions* in the form of safeguard clauses.

Reports published in these years included evaluations of the ca
countries' track record since the 1997 Opinions on their appl
(European Commission, 2002b, 2002c, 2004e, 2004f). Furthern
Commission increased significantly the relevance of monitorin;
as it started to use them not only as a basis for its recon
tions (whether to grant a reward or impose a sanction), but al
instrument for prioritising conditions.

Conclusions

The study highlights the rapidly evolving nature of EU enl;
policy. Although the Union did not change the structure of t!
sion negotiations, the instrumental approach of the Comm
setting the range and the scope of the closing benchmarks i
the increasing application of detailed and differentiated condi
The analysis of the *reward–threat balance* shows that the Union
one *implicit threat* by decoupling Bulgaria and Romania from
ten candidate countries which completed the membership talk
However, the significance of the decision should not be ex
as neither Sofia nor Bucharest envisaged that they would be
join the EU before 2007. It is important to focus on the deve
after the 2002 Copenhagen European Council: not only did t
increase the financial assistance for the two countries, but a
cemented and delivered on its commitment to complete the
negotiations with them by the end of 2004, despite growi
tainty about the states of preparedness of countries. As the *rev*
balance was dominated by *accession advancement rewards* an
rewards, the incentive structure during the negotiation stage
tive. The Commission developed the scope of the Regular R
increased significantly the relevance of monitoring for the ad\
of the accession process. The analysis of the developments
negotiation stage shows the growing application of differen
targeted conditionality towards Bulgaria and Romania.

Accession stage

Conditions

Following the completion of the accession negotiations, th
countries were expected to finalise their preparations for as:
responsibilities of membership, which included complianc
Copenhagen criteria and the specific arrangement for eacl
acquis chapters. However, the Commission provided Sofia an
with further guidance on the scope of the membership criteri

Following the completion of the membership talks, the EU confirmed that '[f]or cases of serious shortcomings, the Accession Treaty will contain three safeguard clauses as a last resort mechanism (general economic, internal market and justice and home affairs)' and announced that:

> as the period between the end of the negotiations and Bulgaria's and Romania's accession is likely to be long, and given the large number of commitments that still need to be fulfilled, the Commission considers that the Accession Treaty should as a precautionary measure contain a specific safeguard clause [...] It would allow the Commission to recommend to the Council at any time before the entry into force of the Accession Treaty to postpone the envisaged date of accession by one year to January 2008 if there is clear risk that Bulgaria and Romania will be manifestly unprepared to meet the requirements of membership by 1 January in a number of important areas.
>
> (European Commission, 2004b)

The safeguard clauses, specified in Articles 36, 37 and 38 of the Act of Accession, were the same as the ones provided for the eight CEECs, Cyprus and Malta in the 2003 Accession Treaty. The general economic safeguard clause[5] allowed member states to apply for authorisation to take protective measure with regard to Bulgaria and Romania in the event of serious economic difficulties.[6] The two specific safeguard clauses stated that the Commission may establish appropriate measures if the acceding countries caused, or risked causing, a serious breach of the functioning of the internal market (Article 37) or if there were serious shortcomings or any imminent risk of such shortcoming in the transposition and implementation of the *acquis* in the area of justice and home affairs (Article 38) (*Official Journal*, 2005a). Although all three safeguard clauses could be activated 'until the end of a period of up to three years after accession', the Treaty specified that the internal market and the JHA safeguard clause 'may be invoked even before accession' (*Official Journal*, 2005a).

The introduction of the additional 'super' safeguard clause set an important precedent, as the EU established for the first time the possibility of postponing the accession of a country by stipulating that:

> if ... there is clear evidence that the state of the state of preparation for the adoption and implementation of the acquis in Bulgaria and Romania is such that there is serious risk of either of those States

being manifestly unprepared to meet the requirements of membership by the date of accession of 1 January 2007 in a number of
important areas, the Council may, acting unanimously on the basis
of a Commission recommendation, decide that the date of accession
of that State is postponed by one year to 1 January 2008.

(*Official Journal*, 2005a)

However, the policy changes were not limited to the 'super' safeguard
clause, as the EU applied a differentiated approach to establishing the
scope of the *explicit threats* by introducing stricter additional *preventive or
remedial sanctions* for Bucharest. Article 39 (paragraphs 2 and 3) specified
that the Council may decide by a qualified majority vote to postpone the
accession of Romania in the case of serious shortcomings in the fulfilment of any of the 11 requirements listed in Annex IX of the Accession
Treaty.

The review of the incentive structure confirms the observation from
the previous chapter that the completion of the accession negotiations
marks the transformation from positive to negative incentive structure. In contrast to the earlier stages of the process, the *reward–threat
balance* during the accession stage is dominated by a wide range of *preventive and remedial sanctions*. In addition to confirming the continuity
of enlargement policy, Bulgaria's and Romania's experience highlights
two unprecedented developments in the EU's approach. Not only did
the Union established a safeguard clause allowing the postponement of
the accession, but it also differentiated between two Balkan states by
providing for the use of majority voting in the case of Romania.

Monitoring

Although the 2004 Enlargement Strategy confirmed that 'the Commission will issue yearly comprehensive monitoring reports, covering
all *acquis* chapters, public administration, judiciary and fight against
corruption as well as the track record in economic reforms', the EU
stepped up the monitoring and prepared two reports in 2006 (European
Commission, 2004b).

The first set of Comprehensive Monitoring Reports, which was published in 2005, assessed Bulgaria's and Romania's preparations for membership and not only flagged the remaining gaps 'in policies, legislation
and its implementation' but also identified the steps that needed to
be taken (European Commission, 2005a, 2005f). Although the second
monitoring report provided even more specific measures by establishing two sets of benchmarks, the Commission refrained from making a

recommendation regarding the accession date. As one EU official recollected '[w]e were postponing the final decision on the effective date of accession, as much as it was feasible until early autumn of 2006' and noted that '[i]deally we would have pushed and kept the constructive uncertainty until December 2006 but in practice you cannot do that' (Interview 9, 2009). The Commission confirmed that

> [t]he Commission will report on Bulgaria's and Romania's progress in addressing the outstanding issues no later than early October. On this basis, the Commission will consider whether the date of their accession to the European Union on 1 January 2007 can be maintained. This report will also specify any areas where safeguards or other remedial measures may be needed upon accession.
>
> (European Commission, 2006f)

Furthermore, the Commission acknowledged for the first time the possibility of introducing additional measures by noting that

> if the implementation of reforms in the justice system is not sufficiently advanced in either country before accession, or the fight against corruption in the judiciary has not yielded sufficient tangible results, the Commission will establish on the basis of Article 38 of the Act of Accession a mechanism for further monitoring in this area.
>
> (European Commission, 2006a)

The third report, which was published in September 2006, stated that 'Bulgaria and Romania are sufficiently prepared to meet the political, economic and acquis criteria by 1 January 2007' (European Commission, 2006h). However, it identified 'issues which require further work' and confirmed that 'the Commission, after consulting with the Member States, will set up a mechanism for cooperation and verification of progress in the areas of judicial reform and fight against corruption, money-laundering and organised crime' and established two lists of benchmarks which Sofia and Bucharest needed to address (European Commission, 2006h).

The assessment of the monitoring instruments used by the Commission to report on Bulgaria's and Romania's progress towards membership during the accession stage highlights the growing significance of monitoring for the enlargement process, which is reflected not only by the frequency of the reports but also by their increasing multi-functionality.

The analysis shows that after the completion of the accession negotiations, in addition to providing a basis for the Commission's recommendations regarding the advancement of the accession process, the
reports acted as an instrument for political pressure by introducing new
conditions and threats.

Conclusions

This stage confirms the growing application of differentiated and targeted conditionality, as the EU's approach to setting out conditions
for Sofia and Bucharest is characterised by the wide use of individual
and country-specific benchmarks. The review of the incentive structure
shows that the EU, in an unprecedented move, expanded and differentiated the scope of the *explicit threats* by introducing a new 'super
safeguard' clause which allowed for the postponement of the accession of the countries by one year. As the *reward–threat balance* was
dominated by a wide range of *preventive and remedial sanctions*, the
incentive structure during the accession stage was negative. The Commission prepared very detailed *advanced reports* which reinforced the
relevance of monitoring not only for the advancement of the accession process but also for the establishment of the conditions which the
acceding countries needed to address. The analysis of the developments
during the accession stage shows that the EU applied differentiated, negative conditionality towards Bulgaria and Romania and confirms the
evolutionary nature of EU enlargement conditionality.

Post-accession stage

Conditions

Although the September 2006 Monitoring report concluded that
'Bulgaria and Romania will be in a position to take on the rights and
obligations of EU membership on 1 January 2007', the Commission
stressed the need for 'further tangible results' in the areas of judicial
reform, the fight against corruption and organised crime[7] and set up
the Cooperation and Verification Mechanism (CVM) in order to monitor progress in these areas after their accession (European Commission,
2006a). Thus, the EU set another precedent by introducing for the very
first time a special mechanism for monitoring new member states' compliance with set criteria. The Commission stated that Bulgaria needs to
address the following six benchmarks:

1. Adopt constitutional amendments removing any ambiguity regarding the independence and accountability of the judicial system.

2. Ensure a more transparent and efficient judicial process by adopting and implementing a new judicial system act and the new civil procedure code. Report on the impact of these new laws and of the penal and administrative procedure codes, notably on the pre-trial phase.
3. Continue the reform of the judiciary in order to enhance professionalism, accountability and efficiency. Evaluate the impact of this reform and publish the results annually.
4. Conduct and report on professional, non-partisan investigations into allegations of high-level corruption. Report on internal inspections of public institutions and on the publication of assets of high-level officials.
5. Take further measures to prevent and fight corruption, in particular at the borders and within local government.
6. Implement a strategy to fight organized crime, focusing on serious crime, money laundering as well as on the systematic confiscation of assets of criminals. Report on new and ongoing investigations, indictments and convictions in these areas.

(European Commission, 2006b)

The Commission laid down the following four benchmarks for Romania:

1. Ensure a more transparent and efficient judicial process notably by enhancing the capacity and accountability of the Superior Council of Magistracy. Report and monitor the impact of the new civil and penal procedures codes.
2. Establish, as foreseen, an integrity agency with responsibilities for verifying assets, incompatibilities and potential conflicts of interest, and for issuing mandatory decisions on the basis of which dissuasive sanctions can be taken.
3. Building on progress already made, continue to conduct professional, non-partisan investigations into allegations of high – level corruption.
4. Take further measures to prevent and fight against corruption, in particular within the local government.

(European Commission, 2006c)

In 2009, the EU further specified the scope of the conditions by setting out two lists of recommendations. The Commission identified 21 tasks for Sofia in the areas of the fight against corruption and organised crime and the efficiency of judiciary; and 18 tasks for Bucharest in the following areas: new codes, reform of the judiciary, unification of jurisprudence, the fight against high-level corruption, the activities of the National Integrity Agency and the fight against corruption at local level (European Commission, 2009f, 2009g). In July 2010, the Union 'while recalling the outstanding recommendations' further clarified the CVM benchmarks by establishing additional ten recommendations for each country (European Commission, 2010h, 2010i). The set of reports published in July 2011 also provided two lists of recommendations 22 for Bulgaria and 17 for Romania (European Commission, 2011d, 2011e). In 2012 the Commission presented an overall assessment of the progress made towards fulfilling the objectives of the mechanism. However, the recent political events in Bucharest overshadowed the positive developments in the country. The President of the European Commission used extremely critical language:

> Events in Romania have shaken our trust. Challenging judicial decisions, undermining the constitutional court, overturning established procedures and removing key checks and balances have called into question the Government's commitment to respect the rule of law. Party political strife cannot justify overriding core democratic principles. Politicians must not try to intimidate judges ahead of decisions or attack judges when they take decisions they do not like. The competences of a Constitutional Court cannot be changed overnight.
>
> (Barroso, 2012)

As a result, in addition to the existing CVM benchmarks, the Commission issued ten specific recommendations aimed at resolving the controversies on the rule of law and judicial independence (European Commission, 2012b). This unprecedented move in an area with very limited *acquis* highlights the broadening range of the CVM conditionality. The January 2014 monitoring reports provided new lists of recommendations for Sofia and Bucharest (see European Commission, 2014c, 2014d).

The analysis of the CVM conditions reveals the expansive nature of post-accession conditionality. The monitoring reports demonstrate that over the last eight years the EU has elaborated significantly on the scope of the initial benchmarks. The introduction of a new dimension aimed at restoring the rule of law and judicial independence in Romania presents further evidence for this pronounced trend. Furthermore, the distinguishing approach of the Commission to addressing similar issues, particularly the establishment of different benchmarks in order to remedy similar shortcomings in the efficiency of the judicial process, highlights the increasing application of targeted and differentiated conditionality.

Incentive structure

As highlighted in the previous chapter there are two key differences in the *reward–threat balance* after the accession of the new member state. The EU is 'stripped' of its strongest 'tool' for inducing compliance – the membership perspective and the rewards provided by the Union are limited to *financial rewards* (part of financial assistance previously agreed in the framework of pre-accession programmes). During the post-accession stage, the Union relies on a wide range of *explicit threats*. However, it is essential that we distinguish between the *preventive and remedial sanctions* established in the framework of post-accession conditionality and the sanctions which are applicable to all member states.

The EU took the first steps to establishing the scope of the *explicit threats* applicable to Sofia and Bucharest by confirming that the *preventive and remedial sanctions*, introduced by the three safeguard clauses,[8] included in the Accession Treaty could be invoked 'until the end of a period of up to three years after accession' (*Official Journal*, 2005a). Although the Commission took *preventive and remedial sanctions* in the areas of food safety, air safety and agricultural funds, it was the introduction of the CVM which significantly expanded the scope of the *explicit threats* by specifying that if Bulgaria and/or Romania:

> fail to address the benchmarks adequately, the Commission may apply safeguard measures based on articles 37 and 38 of the Act of Accession, including the suspension of Member States' obligation to recognise and execute, under the conditions laid down in Community law, Bulgarian judgments and judicial decisions, such as European arrest warrants.
> (European Commission, 2006b: 3; 2006c: 3)

The EU established the CVM for an unspecified period of time by confirming that it 'should be repealed when all the benchmarks have been satisfactory fulfilled' (European Commission, 2006b, 2006c). However, even when the monitoring report confirmed that '[t]he assessment points to the serious difficulties which the Bulgarian authorities are facing in making real headway in judicial reform and the fight against corruption and organized crime' and that 'there are few results to demonstrate that the system is actually functioning correctly', the

Commission concluded that it 'considers support to be more effective than sanctions and will not invoke the safeguard provisions set out in the Accession Treaty' (European Commission, 2008c). The Commission's decision not to activate any of the safeguard measures is directly related to the scope of the *explicit threats* and more precisely to the penalising power of the *remedial and preventive sanctions* established by the safeguard clauses. Although the *remedial and preventive sanction* introduced by the JHA safeguard clause is considered limited and inadequate, some member states have pushed for its activation. Not only the Commission, but also the member states have used the CVM to put political pressure on Bulgaria and Romania. In an unprecedented move, the Dutch Minister of EU affairs, Frans Timmermans sent a letter to the Justice Commissioner Jacques Barrot asking the Commission to consider activating the JHA safeguard clause should the reports fail to register sufficient progress (*EurActiv*, 2009a). Timmermans' letter was the first and the last attempt at imposing the safeguard clauses. The July 2009 Progress Reports concluded that 'the conditions for invoking the safeguard clauses are not fulfilled' and confirmed that the Mechanism 'needs to be maintained until the reforms are achieved' (European Commission, 2009c, 2009d).

However, unlike the mechanism, the applicability of the safeguard clauses expired on 1 January 2010, leaving the EU without any formal incentives to induce compliance with its conditions. Although the Commission considered introducing new *explicit threats* by linking the removal of the mechanism with Bulgaria's and Romania's accession to the Schengen area, the opinions in the college diverged and the idea was abandoned (*EurActiv*, 2009b). Nevertheless, some member states, particularly the Netherlands and Germany, insisted that both issue were related and postponed the enlargement of the border-free travel area, despite the two countries' compliance with the technical requirements for accession (*EUObserver*, 2011a; *EurActiv*, 2011c). The Netherlands has insisted that they would lift their veto after two consecutive positive CVM reports (*EurActiv*, 2014). It is interesting to note that one of the priorities of Timmermans in his new capacity as First Vice-Presidentof the European Commission is the co-ordination of the CVM (European Parliament, 2014a). As one national official noted he 'is someone who knows that file, has been actively involved in the file, actively contributed with interpretation of how this file should be managed in relations with other files like Schengen' (Interview 25, 2014).

The Commission neither invoked any of the remedial and preventive sanctions included in the safeguard provisions nor established new sanctions in the framework of the CVM. However, *general financial sanctions*, based on standard policy procedures, have been imposed against both Bulgaria and Romania. The analysis of the post-accession incentive-structure is also complicated by the fact that the CVM has been linked politically to the Schengen enlargement. Furthermore, there is an overwhelming consensus among EU and national officials that the mechanism has inflicted a strong reputational damage on Sofia and Bucharest. The study illustrates that the application of EU enlargement conditionality is not confined to the applicability of the safeguard clauses. Three years after the Commission' recommendation, Bulgaria and Romania's accession to border-free travel zone remains blocked.

Monitoring

In January 2015, the Commission published the 14th set[9] of monitoring reports under the CVM. As evidenced by the discussion in the previous sections, similarly to the accession stage, but much more often, the EU has used the monitoring instruments to establish new conditions by further specifying the scope of the CVM benchmarks. Furthermore, the Commission has significantly intensified the monitoring process not only by reporting 'as and when required at least every six months' but also by introducing additional monitoring instruments such as technical updates, thus dramatically enhancing the detailisation of its assessments (European Commission, 2006b, 2006c). By establishing a comprehensive framework for rigorous post-accession monitoring, the CVM provides the EU with an instrument for continuous political pressure. As national officials from the Permanent Representations of the members states to the EU pointed out, the publication of the Progress or Interim Reports attracts a lot of media attention not only in Bulgaria and Romania, but also in old member states like the Netherlands and Germany.

The examination of the unprecedented monitoring mechanism set for Sofia and Bucharest exemplifies the complex evolutionary nature of the monitoring process, which is reflected not only by the frequency of the reports and their increasing multi-functionality, but also by their political impact. The analysis confirms that in addition to fulfilling the functions of assessment tools, the monitoring reports provide the basis for further recommendations; establish new conditions or introduce new threats; act as a means of communication between the EU and the two member states; and last but not least provide an instrument for continuous political pressure.

Conclusions

The study of the post-accession conditionality towards Bulgaria and Romania highlights important new developments. This stage marks a turning point for EU enlargement conditionality, as it shows that its application is not confined to the accession process and continues after the candidate countries have become fully-fledged member states. Furthermore, the establishment of the CVM set a precedent by introducing a monitoring mechanism aimed exclusively at the two member states. The mechanism exemplifies the transformation of the monitoring reports from assessment tools into instruments for political pressure.

Conclusions

The chapter highlights important evolutionary developments in the application of EU enlargement conditionality towards Bulgaria and Romania. The EU gradually elaborated and clarified the scope and the range of the membership requirements during the early stages. However, the introduction of additional country-specific conditions for the start of the accession negotiations with Sofia and Bucharest marked the beginning of a transition from highly uniform to differentiated conditionality, which culminated during the post-accession stage with the establishment of the CVM. Furthermore, the Commission's approach to addressing similar shortcomings in the efficiency of the judicial process by introducing different benchmarks highlights the increasing application of targeted conditionality.

The incentive structure also underwent a significant transformation. Although the EU used two *implicit threats* (by delaying the start and the conclusion of the accession negotiations), the *reward–threat balance* during the pre-negotiation and negotiation stage was still dominated by a range of *accession advancement rewards* and *financial rewards*. The Union favoured the use of carrots over sticks to induce compliance with its conditions. After the completion of the accession negotiations, the EU introduced unprecedented *explicit threats* by providing for an additional 'super' safeguard clause in the Accession Treaty and setting out a rigorous post-accession monitoring framework. The alteration in the balance between rewards and threats illustrates the transformation from *positive* incentive structure to *negative* incentive structure, which in turn reflects the gradual shift from positive to negative conditionality. The unprecedented post-accession monitoring exemplifies the complex evolutionary nature of the monitoring instruments, which is reflected not only by the frequency of the reports and their increasing multi-functionality, but also by their political impact.

The two-level analysis on the basis of the *stage-structured conditionality model* confirms that the evolution of the EU enlargement conditionality towards Bulgaria and Romania is characterised by three distinct trends. Firstly, examination of the developments of the EU conditions illustrates a shift from broad uniform conditionality to targeted and differentiated conditionality. Secondly, the alternation in the *reward–threat balance* indicates another important change: from positive to negative conditionality. Last but not least, the study highlights the growing relevance and multi-functionality of the monitoring reports.

Explaining EU conditionality towards Bulgaria and Romania

With a view to analysing the evolution of EU enlargement conditionality, the book specifies that *EU enlargement policy is a function of differentiated influences from multiple actors and external pressures.* The definition highlights the complex constellations of actors involved in the accession process and emphasises their relevance by focusing on the influence which they can exert rather than their competences. Although the book stresses the leading role of the main EU institutions, it delves deeper into policy dynamics by analysing key policy developments with reference to the following factors: (1) *EU member states*, (2) *EU inter-institutional dynamics*, (3) *public opinion in the EU*, (4) *enlargement countries* and (5) *external pressures caused by economic or security shocks and crises*.

EU member states

This section discusses the impact the Council of the EU on the development of EU enlargement conditionality by looking into the influence of individual member states. The analysis follows a selective approach and focuses on the debates which informed the decisions of the Luxembourg and the Helsinki European Council.

As all the key decisions regarding granting the *accession advancement rewards* are taken unanimously by the Council of the EU, the preferences of the member states are of crucial importance for the second element of EU enlargement conditionality – the incentive structure. EU and national officials agree that good and particularly strong relations between a member state or a group of member states and a candidate country or a group of candidate countries have a positive impact on the advancement of the accession process. However, the examination of news reports on the position of EU member states leading to the Luxembourg and Helsinki decisions reveals the lack of strong patronage for the two Balkan states. Although most applicant countries were supported strongly by one or more member states (for a detailed discussion see Chapter 2), there were not any vocal proponents for Bulgaria and Romania. Following the publication of the Commission's Progress reports in November 1998, member states' preferences did not shift dramatically:

> On one side, the Nordic countries (Denmark, Sweden and Finland) expressed themselves in favour of a 'more positive and more encouraging' treatment of Latvia and Lithuania, while others called upon the EU to send a more positive sign to Slovakia in order to honour the change that has taken place in this country since the elections in September. On the other side, several delegations (a majority according to some) felt one should definitively encourage the applicant countries to continue along the road towards reform and preparation for membership but that precise perspectives should not be indicated at this stage regarding the opening of negotiations with any of the countries of the 'second group'.
>
> (*Agence Europe*, 1998b)

France, but also Italy and Greece warned against the risk of markedly isolating Bulgaria and Romania (*Agence Europe*, 1998a). However, Tony Blair was the first to speak strongly in favour of Romania's membership:

> Britain wants the European Union to enlarge, and to do so soon. I want Romania to be part of that process. Let me emphasise that the British Government is committed to the earliest possible accession for Romania. We have already made clear in public that the level of EU assistance to Romania will take account of the burden created by the Kosovo crisis. We will resist any attempt to slow down the enlargement process because of Kosovo. Today I want to make a further commitment. At the Helsinki European Council in December, Britain will support an invitation to Romania to begin negotiations to accede to the European Union.
>
> (Blair, 1999)

One senior Commission official recollected that 'Blair's briefing when he went to Bucharest was to be much more reserved on opening negotiations' and noted that 'Blair certainly was the first EU head of government to come out publicly and say: yes, we believe, we should open accession negotiations with Romania' (Interview 20, 2009). Another senior EU official highlighted the significance of the member states' preferences with regard to the EU's decision not to decouple Bulgaria and Romania from the second group of candidate countries by saying, 'I think in a way, it was also very clear that these two countries had also very important friends in the EU and so they could not be left behind' (Interview 11, 2009). However, another EU official stressed that 'Bulgaria did not have a strong sponsor like Poland or the Baltic states' (Interview 3, 2009).

The evaluation of the role of the Council for the development of the first phase of the EU enlargement shows that the influence of the member states on the accession process is not confined to their veto powers in the accession process. As evidenced by the decisions of the Luxembourg Summit, member states' preferences are highly relevant for EU enlargement conditionality and strong support for a candidate or a group of candidate countries can significantly improve the incentive structure. Although it is difficult to identify particularly strong voices for Bulgaria and Romania (with the exception of the UK and France), both Balkans states benefited from the lack of strong opposition to their accession to the Union.

Inter-institutional dynamics

As this chapter highlights the novel features of the accession process with Bulgaria and Romania, the analysis focuses on the entrepreneurship of the Commission for the opening of the membership talks, the introduction of enhanced accession monitoring and the establishment the CVM. This section also looks at the impact of the EP on shaping the Union's enlargement policy and incorporates the reflections and the comments of senior EU officials on the significance of their respective institutions for the accession of two Balkan states.

The Commission's recommendation, which provided the basis for the Helsinki European Council decision to open accession negotiations with all candidate countries that fulfilled the Copenhagen political criteria (Bulgaria, Latvia, Lithuania, Malta, Romania and Slovakia), shows a significant change in the EU's enlargement policy. Although it is difficult to establish whether the shift was a result of the growing commitment to reunifying Europe or the strong vision of the new Commission College, it illustrates the crucial role of the Commission for managing and engineering the key modalities of the enlargement process. The President of the Commission justified the loosening of the Luxembourg conditions for launching membership talks by stressing that:

[i]f we apply this recommendation to the letter, it rules out opening negotiations with most of the remaining applicant countries since they do not fully meet the economic criteria. The risk in taking this 'hard line' approach is that the countries concerned, having already made great efforts and sacrifices, will become disillusioned and turn their backs on us. Their economic policies will begin to diverge, and an historic opportunity will have been lost – perhaps forever.

(Prodi, 1999)

His comments were echoed by the Commissioner of the newly established DG Enlargement (see Appendix II for a list of all Commissioners in charge of Enlargement), who noted that:

[t]he Commission is proposing a change of strategy on political grounds. If we further subdivide the second group or put them on a back burner, we risk losing some countries along the way by depriving their reforms of a tangible, credible objective. Because the political consequences of this cannot be measured, no risk should be taken.

(Verheugen, 1999)

One senior EU official reflected on the nature of the recommendations by saying that:

[i]n 1999, it was certainly political, on the other hand at that time, it would not have been very easy to suggest seriously that there is a huge difference between a country like Latvia and a country like Bulgaria and Romania.

(Interview 10, 2009)

Another senior Commission official confirmed that:

there was a strong political push also to have Bulgaria and Romania in it [the Helsinki group] and I have the impression that there also a clear link between the debate on the three Baltic countries and Bulgaria and Romania.

(Interview 18, 2009)

However, it is important to note that the compromise on modifying the uniform *conditions for opening accession negotiations* was balanced out by the introduction of specific conditions for Bulgaria and Romania.

As Verheugen pointed out 'we also have to uphold the credibility of our own criteria, the Copenhagen criteria. This is why we are imposing conditions in two cases' (Verheugen, 1999).

The role of the Commission was also essential for other *accession advancement rewards* such as the establishment of the credibility of the membership perspective. Both the President of the Commission and the Commissioner for Enlargement were passionate supporters and promoters of the accession process with the CEECs:

> I have repeatedly stressed that enlargement is the single most important task that this Commission is committed to set on track. There is a need to achieve this new page of history for the Union, as soon as possible, in accordance with the objectives set by the European Council and the Commission itself.
>
> (Prodi, 2000)

Prodi's ambitious vision was matched by Verheugen's fierce determination:

> The current round of enlargement negotiations, the largest in the history of European unification, is morally imperative, strategically necessary and politically feasible. The project is already well advanced and there is no turning back. Over the whole range of these negotiations; the question now is not whether, but how and when.
>
> (Verheugen, 2000)

The Commission was quick to translate the strong rhetoric into action. The 2000 Strategy Paper established a detailed roadmap 'providing a clear sequence for tackling these issues in the course of 2001 and 2002' and confirmed that:

> [t]his approach should permit the conclusion of negotiations in the course of 2002 with those candidate countries who fulfill all the criteria for membership, thus putting the Union in a position to welcome new Member States from the end of 2002.
>
> (European Commission, 2000a)

One senior EU official highlighted the crucial role of the Commissioner in resolving the highly sensitive and thorny issue of setting target dates by noting that:

> [t]his was a big discussion between the member states and the Commission but clearly in the driving seat at the time was the Commissioner Günter Verheugen and it was quite a difficult debate.
>
> (Interview 18, 2009)

Bulgaria and Romania's separation from the first group of candidate countries to join the Union was not surprising. As one senior EU official pointed out, 'I think it was meant that they would not come in, in 2004, but I think there was general agreement they were not ready' (Interview 3, 2009). The 2004 enlargement did not lead to a decrease in the Commission's activism in engineering the modalities of the accession process; on the contrary, the Commission introduced three novel developments to the EU's enlargement policy: the super safeguard clause; enhanced accession monitoring; and post-accession monitoring mechanism (the CVM). One senior EU official confirmed the leading role of the Commission for the introduction of an additional safeguard clause by noting that '[i]t was not something by which the member states were totally surprised. But the idea of the clause itself was pretty much the Commission's' (Interview 20, 2009).

Tightening the screws on Bulgaria and Romania was not limited to the possibility of postponing accession. The Commission also enhanced the monitoring process by publishing three rather than the previously agreed two reports, thus delaying the confirmation of the accession date. One senior EU official highlighted the role of the Commission by pointing out that:

> [s]o there was a conscious effort to try to keep, to engineer a little bit of suspense around this, by having this cycle of, the Commission would come up with its views in spring and then postponing the final verdict again [...] I think it helped to achieve certain things, but as evident in the present problems, it is certainly not effective in achieving all the things that we would have hoped.
>
> (Interview 10, 2009)

He also confirmed that the Commission was responsible for breathing life into another novel development – the CVM:

> The member states were not pushing for it, the idea was generated and the product development took place in fact here [in the Commission]. We did it together – Olli Rehn's Cabinet and Frattini's Cabinet,

together with the two DGs. And then, of course, it was discussed at length with the member states as well. But the proposal came from the Commission.

(Interview 10, 2009)

The new shifts in the inter-institutional dynamics with regard to Bulgaria's and Romania's accession process were not limited to the role of the Commission and the Council, as the engagement and relevance of the Parliament also increased. It was the 2004 Report prepared by Baroness Emma Nicholson, calling for the suspension of the accession negotiations with Romania, which showcased the growing potential of the EP to influence the Union's enlargement policy. One senior official reflected on the role of the country rapporteurs in comparative perspective:

The rapporteurs in Foreign Affairs Committee saw their role a bit differently. Curiously enough, they were both British. One was Jeffery Van Orden, who was conservative. He was the rapporteur for Bulgaria for most of the time. He saw his role as basically being a cheerleader for Bulgaria [...]. Emma Nicholson was the rapporteur for Romania [...] She saw her role much more, as a nanny or governess, basically, saying like it was and it was tough love. She was very, very involved with the Romanian adoption issue, which was a very big Romanian scandal, not much better with Bulgaria, but you know it did not get noticed. In early 2004, she produced a draft report following the Commission's 2003 November regular report on Romania, which basically said Romania is not delivering and we should postpone Romania's accession.

(Interview 20, 2009)

He also highlighted the consequences of the report:

Essentially, the challenge the Romanian government had to do was to restore their credibility because [...] And so they produced a list of short-term deliverables – a to-do list. Năstase and Geoană came to Brussels and they saw Verheugen and Prodi and the EP and said we will deliver by the end of June these various things which included reforming and improving the judicial reform and a certain number of financial measures [...] and they managed on the basis of that to get a provisional maybe.

(Interview 20, 2009)

The discussion of the role and the significance of the key EU institutions for the 2007 enlargement provides interesting insights into the inter-institutional dynamics of the Union. The analysis illustrates the crucial role of Commission for engineering the key modalities of the enlargement process and highlights the impact of the EP on shaping (to the extent of potentially threatening) the accession of Bulgaria and Romania.

Although the Council is ultimately in charge of the incentive structure as it decides if and when to grant the *accession advancement rewards*, the analysis of the inter-institutional dynamics demonstrates the strong entrepreneurship of the Commission. The study provides interesting examples how the Commission and its leadership could significantly influence the incentive structure by building a strong case for *accession advancement rewards* or by inventing new *explicit threats*. The chapter also confirms the key role of the Commission for establishing and shaping the scope of the EU conditions. Last but not least, it highlights the growing potential of the EP to influence the advancement of the accession process, especially when MEPs are determined to pursue specific issues.

Public opinion

This section investigates the variation in EU public support for enlargement and analyses the attitudes towards the accession of Bulgaria and Romania in comparative perspective and draws on the data from the Standard Eurobarometer surveys. As questions regarding enlargement were not included in all of the Eurobarometer reports since 1990, the analysis of the public attitudes briefly comments on the early developments and focuses primarily on the period between the spring of 1996 and the autumn of 2006. The wide range of the data allows us to identify the key trends in EU public opinion and reflect on their relevance and implication for the development of EU enlargement policy.

The Spring 1991 Eurobarometer survey differentiated between the former communist countries (despite the fact that the EC had established contractual relationships with only five of them: Hungary, Poland, Czechoslovakia, Bulgaria and Romania) by asking the respondents if certain CEECs, specifically referring to 'Poland, Hungary and Czechoslovakia' would have become members of the EC in the year 2000 (Eurobarometer, 1991a).

The findings of a co-operative venture of 24 leading European newspapers,[10] which revealed that absolute majorities of EC citizens wanted only three of the soon-to-be applicants – Poland, Hungary and Malta – to be members by 2000, confirmed the variation in the public support (Eurobarometer, 1992). The survey showed that more respondents were in favour of the Czech Republic (47:34) and Cyprus (44:36) than Romania (43:39), Estonia (42:36), Lithuania (41:38) Bulgaria (41:40), and Latvia (40:38), while more interviewees were opposed to than supportive of the membership of Slovakia (36:42) and Slovenia (33:44) (Eurobarometer, 1992). Following the establishment of the membership perspective of the CEECs, the 1994 Autumn Eurobarometer confirmed that many EC citizens differentiated between the Visegrád three and Bulgaria, Slovakia, Slovenia and Romania. Unfavourable opinions about the membership of the latter four countries outweighed the favourable ones in Belgium, France and Luxembourg.

The comparative examination of the public attitudes towards enlargement and particularly towards the accession of Bulgaria and Romania to the EU, in the period between the spring of 1996 and the autumn of 2006 (see Appendix IV) provides more evidence for the three distinct trends which were outlined in the second chapter. Again, we can see that the support for enlargement varied and varied greatly depending on which country the respondents come from. In some of the member states, particularly in Sweden, Denmark and Greece attitudes towards enlargement were quite favourable and support was generally above the EU average. In other countries like France, Austria and Belgium levels of support were consistently below the EU average for all applicant countries. The analysis also highlights a new development – the ten member states which joined the Union in May 2004 were much more enthusiastic about further enlargement. The support in the EU10 was significantly[11] higher (ranging from 61% to 78%) than in the old member states.

The study also confirms the second trend, outlined in the previous chapter, that attitudes towards enlargement also varied depending on the candidate country in question (see Appendix IV). Support for Bulgaria and Romania was never as high as support for the forerunners – Hungary, Poland and the Czech Republic.

However, most of the other candidate countries did not manage to secure the approval of the EU public. More people were opposed to than favoured the membership of Bulgaria, Lithuania, Romania and Slovenia in autumn of 1997, the spring of 1999, the spring and the autumn of 2000, autumn of 2001 and in the spring of 2002 (with only exception of Lithuania then its membership was supported by 40% and opposed by 37%). Support for Bulgaria was almost identical

Table 3.2   EU public attitudes to candidate and potential candidate countries: 2005–2006

Candidate and potential candidate countries	Spring 2005				Autumn 2005				Autumn 2006			
	EU Member states				EU Member states				EU Member states			
	EU 25	EU 25	EU 15	EU 10	EU 25	EU 25	EU 15	EU 10	EU 25	EU 25	EU 15	EU 10
±	+	−	+	+	+	−	+	+	+	−	+	+
BG	50	36	46	70	48	37	45	64	46	40	42	68
RO	45	41	43	58	43	42	41	53	41	46	38	55
TU	35	52	32	48	31	55	32	40	28	59	26	37
HR	52	34	48	72	51	35	47	70	50	36	46	74
FY	43	41	40	57	41	42	39	51	40	44	37	57
BH	42	43	39	56	40	43	39	50	39	46	36	54
AL	36	50	33	47	33	50	32	40	32	53	30	45

Source: Eurobarometer (2005a, 2006a, 2006b).

to that of the Baltic countries and slightly higher than support for Romania (see Appendix IV) Support for Slovenia and Romania was the least widespread ranging from 33% to 39%. Furthermore, it was only in the spring of 1999 that the people opposed to Slovenia's and Romania's membership were less than those in favour of it. As illustrated in Table 3.2, after the 2004 enlargement, support for both Bulgaria and Romania increased, but this development is attributed to the strong pro-enlargement attitude of the EU10 rather than a sudden change in the attitudes of the citizens of the old member states.

The analysis also confirms that the average support for the EU enlargement was not particularly high. Although, it peaked twice above 50% in the autumn of 2001 (51%) and in the spring of 2005 (53%), the high levels of support in 2005 were a result of the strong pro-enlargement attitudes of the citizens of the EU10. The Standard Spring 2005 report shows that only 37% of the respondents in the old member states were in favour of further enlargement while 43% were against it (Eurobarometer, 2005a). Table 3.2 illustrates further the divide between 'Old' and 'New' Europe with regard to support for candidate and potential candidate countries.

The chapter confirms that public opinion did not have any substantial positive or negative effect on the advancement of the accession process with Sofia and Bucharest. Even though support for both Balkan countries was not significantly higher or lower than the support for the Baltic

States and Slovenia, Bulgaria and Romania neither joined the first group of six countries to start accession negotiations, nor could make the cut for the 2004 enlargement. The comparative analysis of the implications of the public opinion on the development of EU enlargement policy confirms that it was not a decisive factor in the case of the fifth enlargement, as it did not influence any of the decisions of the Union regarding the advancement of the process.

Enlargement countries

This section discusses the relationship between the group dynamics generated by Bulgaria and Romania and the evolution of the EU enlargement conditionality, by focusing on the following two aspects:

- the impact of the problematic issues and reform challenges (the applicants need to address); and
- the implications of the existence or lack of group dynamics (which is examined with reference to the number of applicant states at the same stage of the accession process).

The previous chapter highlighted the links between the purpose and the range of the Copenhagen criteria and the issues which the CEECs needed to address urgently. In the early 1990s, both Bulgaria and Romania were faced with the same challenges as the other associated countries (Hungary, Poland, Czechoslovakia) – carrying out major political and economic reforms. Therefore, we can confirm that the membership conditions also reflect the demanding tasks which Sofia and Bucharest had to tackle. However, both Balkan states offer more insights into the relationship between the profile of the candidate countries and the nature of EU conditions. First, the introduction of additional country-specific conditions for the start of accession negotiations highlights the strong link between sensitive issues such as nuclear safety (Bulgaria), economic reform, childcare reform (Romania) and the formalisation and extension of conditions with which applicants needed to comply in order to join the Union. Furthermore, the establishment of the CVM which has introduced several sets of country-specific benchmarks reinforces the significance of the profile of the candidates for the development of the EU conditions even after accession. As one senior EU Commission official pointed out with reference to the introduction of the CVM:

> what happened was that we thought that the critical mass was there and we could make a decent case that the countries had not

completed the reforms, it was obvious, but the critical mass was there that they could be taken in, in 2007 and there were wider geopolitical considerations, but at the same time, we had to be open for the facts that the situations was not satisfactory and therefore, we decided to take some exceptional measures.

(Interview 9, 2009)

The comments were echoed by another senior EU official who also confirmed that '[t]he reason for the special mechanism was that many felt that Bulgaria and Romania were not ready yet, especially institutionally' (Interview 12, 2009).

In addition to the nature of the issues which the applicants needed to address, it is also important to examine the impact of the number of candidate countries on the advancement of the accession process. Although Bulgaria and Romania acceded to the Union together in 2007, they were also part of other group configurations throughout the fifth enlargement of the EU. Initially, Bulgaria and Romania were grouped together with the Visegrád countries, as all five of them signed the TCAs with the EC in 1989/90. Although Hungary, Poland and Czechoslovakia ascended on the ladder of contractual relations by signing EAs in 1991, it was not until 1993 that Bulgaria and Romania were also granted a status of associate country. However, by 1997 the situation had changed as the Commissioner for External Relations pointed out:

It is scarcely surprising that some applicants are more advanced than others in satisfying the conditions for membership which were established by the Copenhagen and Madrid European Councils. Some began the transition to systems based on political and economic freedom earlier than others. Some chose more rapid and more far reaching reform strategies than others. Some have been more resolute and more robust in implementing reforms. This is no reproach but simply a reflection of different historical, political, economic and social situations.

(Van den Broek, 1997b)

Although the Commission recommendations, which provided the basis for the Luxembourg conclusions, divided the applicants into two groups, the Commissioner stressed that '[w]e never think in terms of "ins" and "outs" but rather of "ins" and "pre-ins"'(Van den Broek, 1997b). The Progress reports in 1998 confirmed that Bulgaria and Romania were lagging behind the other 'pre-ins' (Latvia, Lithuania and Slovakia), however, the Helsinki European Council introduced a significant policy shift by inviting all the countries from the 'second group' to start accession negotiations. The existence of group dynamics had important implications for key EU's decisions to grant one of the key *accession advancement rewards* – opening accession negotiations – to Bulgaria and Romania. As one senior EU official pointed out:

> I think the feeling then was that there was not much to be gained by leaving Bulgaria and Romania out, because in Romania, although the economic situation was very bad, we were in 1999 seeing the first signs of a government which was trying to get things in hand. And we saw already the proof of that in 2000, in terms of the first positive economic growth, since 1995–1996. And I think for Bulgaria, it was party political but also there was also a sense that Bulgaria was starting to organise itself.
>
> (Interview 20, 2009)

Another senior EU official also highlighted the relevance of group dynamics for the advancement of the accession process and commented that:

> [t]here was a strong political push also to have Bulgaria and Romania in it [the Helsinki group] and I have the impression that there also a clear link between the debate on the three Baltic countries and Bulgaria and Romania. In a sense that the three Baltic countries were considered not to be really in a state to join the EU but there was a very strong pressure coming more from the Northern member states. So a number of others also said, then, it does not make a lot of sense: three Baltic states come in, but Bulgaria and Romania do not come in, and there was the whole of question of the stabilisation of the Balkans which played a big role. Although it was rapidly clear that Bulgaria and Romania would not be able to join at the same time as the other ten, it was also very clear that they should be part of the fifth enlargement.
>
> (Interview 18, 2009)

Despite being 'reunited' with the other negotiating countries, both Balkan states again managed to form a group within the group of candidate countries. Neither Sofia nor Bucharest set 2003 or 2004 as their own target date for accession to the Union. Another senior Commission official also acknowledged the existence of dividing lines and recollected that 'it was meant that they would not come in, in 2004, I think there was general agreement they were not ready' and commented that '2007 was something that was picked as a time, they [Bulgarians] knew that would not be as advanced as the other countries but they could not have known that they would be ready in 2007' (Interview 3, 2009).

There is also evidence for the significance of the group dynamics for another *accession advancement reward* – the credibility of the membership perspective – particularly with reference to the establishment of timetables for the completion of the accession process and setting target dates. The Thessaloniki European Council provides evidence that this was also the case for Bulgaria and Romania. Although they were separated from the 'Laeken ten' which became members of the EU in 2004, the Council confirmed that:

> Bulgaria and Romania are part of the same inclusive and irreversible enlargement process. Following the conclusions of the European Council in Copenhagen and depending on further progress in complying with the membership criteria, the objective is to welcome Bulgaria and Romania as members in 2007.
>
> (Council of the European Union, 2003a)

The link between the significance of the group dynamics and the EU's commitment to 2007 as a target date was also highlighted by a senior EU official who commented that when 'a big decision is made for some [candidate countries] then there is also a message for the others [...] you cannot avoid it. It is a moment when the other country feels totally left out' (Interview 5, 2009). The official noted that 'it is unavoidable because when you decide to let some in, you will also have to give the message to the others' (Interview 5, 2009).

The comparative assessment of the profile of Bulgaria and Romania provides more evidence for the impact of applicant states on the development of EU enlargement conditionality. The research findings highlight the strong links between the challenging issues which Sofia and Bucharest had to address and several novel developments (establishment of addition country-specific *conditions for opening accession negotiations* and the introduction of post-accession monitoring mechanism), which illustrate the growing application of differentiated and targeted conditionality. Furthermore, the analysis confirms the influence of group dynamics on the advancement of the accession process.

External pressures

In order to examine the relationship between external pressures and the evolution of EU enlargement policy, particularly towards Bulgaria and Romania, this section follows a selective approach. As the second chapter has illustrated the significance of the end of the Cold War and the Yugoslav wars for the early development of the EU enlargement, this section focuses on two other pivotal events – the Kosovo crisis and the enlargement of the North Atlantic Treaty Organization (NATO).

The Kosovo crisis in the late 1990s had a significant impact on shaping the priorities, strategies and policies of the EU. In addition, to strengthening the EU's external policies by the establishment of the CFSP, the volatility of the Balkan region also lent a new momentum to the accession process, especially to the advancement of the accession process with Bulgaria and Romania. The key conclusion of the Helsinki European Council to open accession negotiations with all candidate countries that fulfilled the Copenhagen political criteria – Bulgaria, Latvia, Lithuania, Malta, Romania and Slovakia – although motivated by a wide range of factors, was inextricably linked to the volatility of the Balkan region. The Commissioner for enlargement Günter Verheugen highlighted the implications of the Kosovo crisis for the enlargement process by confirming that:

> [t]he strategic recommendations [to open accession negotiations] are based on the assumption that we need a strong political signal in Helsinki. This is what the Member States want too. Like us, they have learned a fundamental lesson from the Kosovo crisis. Peace and stability across Europe are not yet a matter of fact: they must be maintained in some areas and achieved in others. This is a situation where the Commission has chosen to act as initiator and guardian. It is a matter of using and enhancing political momentum.
>
> (Verheugen, 1999)

The President of the Commission Romano Prodi also acknowledged the geostrategic relevance of the Balkans and warned against the risk of excluding some of the applicant countries:

> In the changed political landscape of Europe, especially in the Balkan region, some countries may also let slip the progress they have made towards democracy and human rights, and the European Union will have seriously failed the people of those countries. I and my

Commission colleagues believe we need to take a bold step forward to prevent this happening and to inject vital new momentum into the enlargement process.

(Prodi, 1999)

Similar concerns were raised by the Enlargement Commissioner, who also drew attention to the risks of excluding Bulgaria and Romania from the second group of applicants:

The Commission is proposing a change of strategy on political grounds. If we further subdivide the second group or put them on a back burner, we risk losing some countries along the way by depriving their reforms of a tangible, credible objective. Because the political consequences of this cannot be measured, no risk should be taken.

(Verheugen, 1999)

Another process which had a significant impact on the political landscape in Europe was the post-Cold War enlargement of NATO. It is worth noting that key decisions regarding both the NATO and the EU enlargement were made in 1997 and 1999. Although both enlargements were often analysed comparatively, speculation about linking the then future conclusions of the Luxembourg European Council to the decision of the Alliance's Madrid Summit to invite Poland, Hungary and the Czech Republic to begin accession talks, provoked a strong response from the President of the Commission Jacques Santer:

I often hear comments to the effect that, for certain eastern countries, joining the European Union would be some form of compensation for not joining NATO. This kind of 'easy fix' may well be attractive from an intellectual point of view. But things are different in real life. The European Union is a club which a country joins when it is ready to do so – and when the Union is ready as well.

(Santer, 1997)

The Commissioner for External Relations Hans van den Broek also rejected the assumption that the EU enlargement could be conditioned by the NATO enlargement and clearly separated both accessions by highlighting their key differences:

The enlargement of the European Union is both in terms of timing and nature very different from that of NATO. The enlargement of both institutions are mutually reinforcing when it comes to peace and stability in Europe, but are taking place on the basis of different criteria. The timing of the accession of new members to the European Union should, therefore, not be influenced by the timing or selection of candidates for the accession to NATO.

(Van den Broek, 1997a)

Furthermore, the Commissioner established the superiority of the EU enlargement by stressing that it 'will be a time consuming and complex exercise. A lot more complicated than joining, for example, NATO' (Van den Broek, 1998). His comments were echoed by a senior EU official who also highlighted the complexity of the EU accession process:

The organisations are completely different, I think with NATO, you can do a lot after you have joined and develop military capabilities and capacities, but there were certain things in common in the way the government functions, having a military and civilian hand, so there are things which mutually support developments in both processes but joining the Union is a whole lot more complex.

(Interview 3, 2009)

The analysis of the implications of the Kosovo crisis and the post-Cold War enlargement of NATO for the development of EU enlargement policy highlights the variation in the impact of external factors on the internal dynamics of the Union. The Kosovo crisis had a significant impact on the political landscape of Europe, which the EU quickly translated into 'new momentum' for the enlargement process by opening accession negotiations with all the candidate countries which fulfilled the Copenhagen political criteria. The Helsinki European Council, which confirmed that compliance with the Copenhagen political criteria is sufficient for the start of the accession negotiations, marked a significant policy shift in EU enlargement policy. More importantly, it did not decouple Bulgaria and Romania which were lagging behind from the other candidate countries.

The collapse of communism and the Yugoslav conflicts had a significant impact on EU enlargement policy. It is important to note their role particularly for the EU's crucial decision to establish accession of the CEECs as a shared objective in June 1993, which marks the beginning of a new approach to the EU's enlargement policy. Unlike the Balkan crisis, the impact of the NATO enlargement on the accession process of the Union was very limited. The EU systematically rejected the speculation that its enlargement process could be conditioned by the expansion of the Alliance by highlighting the parallel trajectories of both processes.

Conclusions

This chapter demonstrates that EU enlargement conditionality towards Bulgaria and Romania is characterised by three distinct trends. Firstly, the development of the EU conditions illustrates a shift from broad, uniform conditionality to targeted and differentiated conditionality. Secondly, the alteration in the *reward–threat balance* indicates another important change: from positive to negative conditionality. Last but not least, the findings highlight the growing relevance and multi-functionality of the monitoring reports. In order to explain these developments, the multi-level analysis dissects the influence of institutional and external factors.

The study confirms the essential relevance of EU institutions for the development of the scope and range of EU requirements. Furthermore, it illustrates the impressive entrepreneurship of the Commission for the introduction of individual country-specific conditions for Sofia and Bucharest, which in turn led to the increasing application of detailed, targeted conditionality. The analysis also highlights the growing influence of the Parliament which managed to establish adoption legislation and judiciary reform as key priorities. However, the research findings reveal that the profile of the candidate countries can influence the scope of the requirements. Although neither the additional *conditions for opening accession negotiations* nor the benchmarks set out by the CVM were actively engineered by Bulgaria and Romania, these novelties reflect the Union's acknowledgement of the specific challenges which the applicants need to address and points to the growing relevance of external actors.

The examination of the factors affecting the developments of the incentive structure reveals a very complex picture. Similarly to the discussion of the evolution of EU conditions, the analysis confirms the crucial role of the institutional factors – member states' preferences and inter-institutional dynamics. The study also points to the growing influence of the Commission over shaping the development of the accession process. It firmly cemented its position as a policy driver, which is reflected not only by its responsibilities for the preparation of the Union's enlargement strategies and the introduction of novel developments such the CVM but also by its impact on the Council.

Despite the similarities in the EU's approach to Sofia and Bucharest and the other candidate countries, the Union introduced significant changes to the range and the scope of the conditions with which both Balkan states had to comply and dramatically intensified the monitoring process. The developments provide more evidence for the evolutionary nature of EU enlargement policy. The comprehensive examination on the basis of *stage-structured conditionality model* illustrates the increasing application of differentiated, targeted and detailed conditionality, which confirms the linear trajectory of development of EU requirements. Similarly, the intensification and specification of detail in the reports shows that evolution of monitoring represents a natural progression; whereas the evolution of the incentive structure was characterised by a shift from positive to negative conditionality.

The analysis confirms the leading role of the Commission and the Council for the development of the policy, but also points to the relevance of actors, which are not directly involved in the decision-making process. The research findings show that the impact of candidate countries is not a direct result of their bargaining power and that they can shape both the scope of EU conditions and the incentive structure. Furthermore, the examination illustrates the catalysing effects of the external pressures caused by security crises on the advancement of the accession process. The study confirms that a single factor cannot account for the evolution of EU enlargement conditionality and highlights the advantages of a comprehensive approach, which allows us to examine the impact of a dense constellation of factors.

4
EU Conditionality in the Context of the South-Eastern Enlargements

This chapter contributes to the examination of the evolution of EU enlargement conditionality by focusing on Turkey and the Western Balkans. The study notes the similarities in the EU's approach towards South-Eastern Europe but concentrates on the scope and the implication of four far-reaching changes: the chapterisation of the political criteria; the introduction of opening and interim benchmarks; the transformation of the accession negotiations into 'an open-ended process'; and the introduction of disequilibrium clauses. It also reflects on relevance of EU's integration capacity. The chapter analyses the EU's approach towards Croatia and Turkey, FYROM, Montenegro, Serbia, Bosnia and Herzegovina, Albania and Kosovo. The case study selection, which includes the newest member of the Union and candidate and potential candidate countries at different stages of the enlargement process, moving at different speed, facing a wide range of complex problems, allows us not only to highlight the latest developments but also to rigorously test the impact of institutional and external factors on EU conditionality.

The chapter is structured into two parts. On the basis of the *stage-structured conditionality model*, the first part traces the transformation of EU conditionality between the stages of the accession process. The second part of the chapter examines the relationship between the developments of EU conditionality and the following factors: (1) *EU member states*, (2) *EU inter-institutional dynamics*, (3) *public opinion in the EU*, (4) *enlargement countries* and (5) *external pressures caused by economic or security shocks and crises*.

Tracing the evolution of EU conditionality towards Turkey and the Western Balkans

Unlike the CEECs, whose relations with the Union were established almost simultaneously in the late 1980s and early 1990s, the European journeys of Turkey and the Western Balkan countries have followed different paths. In order to contextualise the analysis of the EU enlargement conditionality, this section briefly accounts for the development of the relations between the EU and Turkey, Croatia, FYROM, Montenegro, Serbia, Bosnia and Herzegovina, Albania and Kosovo prior to the establishment of their membership perspective.

The relations between Turkey and the EU go back to 1959, when Turkey applied for associate membership of what was then the EEC. On 12 September 1963, the Association Agreement (also known as the Ankara Agreement), aimed at the establishment of a customs union between Turkey and the EEC, was signed. It was supplemented by an Additional Protocol in 1970. The military coup of 1980 led to a temporary freeze in the EEC–Turkey relations until 1983. On 14 April 1987, Turkey submitted its application for full membership to the EEC. Although the Commission's opinion confirmed Turkey's eligibility for membership, it recommended only 'a series of substantial measures [...] which would enable both partners to enter now on the road towards increased interdependence and integration' (Commission of the European Communities, 1989). One of the measures was the completion of the customs union, which was established in 1995. Two years later, the Luxembourg European Council virtually brought the relations between Turkey and the EU to a halt, as Turkey was not included in the enlargement process with the CEECs. The Helsinki European Council in December 1999 marked the beginning of a new era as the EU concluded that Turkey was a candidate country (Council of the European Union, 1999b).

The EU established relations with Albania in 1991 and signed a Trade and Cooperation Agreement (TCA) one year later (European Commission, 2010c). Although Croatia, Serbia, Montenegro, FYROM, Bosnia and Herzegovina and Kosovo had contractual relations with the EC before 1991 through the EC–Yugoslavia co-operation agreement, its application was abolished when the Yugoslav federation fell apart. The violent disintegration of the country sparked a series of armed conflicts in Slovenia (1991), Croatia (1991–1995), Bosnia and Herzegovina (1992–1995), Kosovo (1998–1999) and FYROM (2001). The Yugoslav wars in the 1990s took thousands of lives and destabilised the region.

The EC established diplomatic relations with Croatia in 1992. Three years later, the Council agreed to open negotiations with Zagreb on a TCA. However, due to military offensives the negotiations were suspended (Europa Press Release, 1996). The EU initiated diplomatic relations with FYROM in December 1995; the following year it nego-tiated a co-operation agreement with Skopje. In addition to a human rights clause similar to those included in the Europe Agreements, it contained an evolutionary clause 'expressing the Contracting Parties' desire to strengthen their relationship and making reference to FYROM's aspirations towards an association' (*Official Journal*, 1997a).

On 29 April 1997, the EU's adoption of a regional approach, aimed at strengthening stability in South-Eastern Europe and promoting co-operation between the counties in the region. It marked an important development in the relations between the Union and Croatia, FYROM, Bosnia and Herzegovina, Federal Republic Yugoslavia (FRY) and Albania, as the approach established political and economic conditionality for the development of bilateral relations. The relations between the EU and Sarajevo were launched in 1998 with the establishment of the EU–Bosnia and Herzegovina Consultative Task Force. In 1999, the EU introduced a new dimension to its policy towards the region by chang-ing the nature of the contractual relationships – replacing the prospect of a Cooperation agreement with that of a more advanced tailor-made SAAs (Council of the European Union, 1999c). The relations between the EU and Serbia were established formally in 1999 when the country was included in the Stabilisation and Association process. The Cologne European Council reaffirmed 'the readiness of the European Union to draw the countries of this region closer to the prospect of full integration into its structures', but it was the Feira European Coun-cil of June 2000 which established the membership perspective of the countries included in the SAP by declaring that '[a]ll the countries concerned are potential candidates for EU membership' (Council of the European Union, 1999a, 2000a). Following the independence of Montenegro from the state union with Serbia, the EU initiated formal relations with the country in June 2006. Since 1999 the EU has been actively involved in the reconstruction of Kosovo, in 2003 the Union stressed that 'the people of a multiethnic and a democratic Kosovo will have their place in Europe' (Council of the European Union, 2003c). The relations between the EU and the region have also been devel-oped under its Common Defence and Security Policy (CDSP), and the Union has deployed missions in Bosnia and Herzegovina, Kosovo and FYROM. However, the chapter focuses only on relations between the

EU and the region in the framework of the SAP and the accession process.

Pre-negotiation stage

Conditions

In 1999 the Amsterdam Treaty amended the *conditions for applying for membership*, specified in Article 49 (ex Article O) of the TEU. It modi-fied Article 49 and included the constitutional principle, enshrined in Article 6 (ex Article F), that 'the Union is founded on the principles of liberty, democracy, respect for human rights and fundamental freedoms and the rule of law',[1] thus making respect for the founding principles of the Union an explicit *condition for applying for membership*. The Lisbon Treaty, which came into force on 1 December 2009, further modified the conditions by confirming that any European state 'which respects the values referred to in Article 1a and is committed to promoting them may apply', the treaty also expanded the range of prerequisites (previ-ously referred to in Article 6(1) by including human dignity and equality and specifically emphasising the significance of the rights of persons belonging to minorities (*Official Journal*, 2007).

The Helsinki European Council confirmed that 'Turkey is a candi-date State destined to join the Union on the basis of the same criteria as applied to the other candidate States' (Council of the European Union, 1999b). However, the extension of the membership perspective to the Western Balkans significantly expanded the scope of *conditions for opening of accession negotiations*. The EU stressed that:

> the pace of further movement of the Western Balkan countries towards the EU lies in their own hands and will depend on each country's performance in implementing reforms, thus respecting the criteria set by the Copenhagen European Council of 1993 and the Stabilisation and Association Process conditionality.
> (Council of the European Union, 2003c)

The SAP conditionality, which integrated the conditions initially estab-lished in the framework of the EU regional approach towards South-Eastern Europe by the Council on 29 April 1997, included (among other requirements) co-operation with the International Criminal Tribunal for the Former Yugoslavia (ICTY) and regional co-operation, return of refugees and displaced persons, democratic reforms, and free and fair elections. In addition to the general requirements, the Council

Conclusions set out country-specific conditions for Croatia, Bosnia and Herzegovina and FRY (see Council of the European Union, 1997b).

The EU 2005 Enlargement Strategy confirmed the significance of the SAP for the accession process by noting that the SAAs 'help to prepare Western Balkan countries for future membership by introducing EU rules in various fields' (European Commission, 2005c). Furthermore, the Commission outlined the stages leading to and the conditions for the conclusion of the SAAs. The road map for the Western Balkans specified that before opening SAA negotiations 'the EU examines whether the basic conditions are in place. A sufficient degree of stabilisation is a pre-condition for opening negotiations' (European Commission, 2005c). The EU agreed that '[o]nce stabilisation is sufficiently ensured, the Commission can recommend to the Council in a Feasibility Report **whether** and **under what conditions** SAA negotiations can start' [bold emphasis added] and decided that 'SAA negotiations can be concluded once the country has made sufficient overall progress in the reform areas essential for implementation of the agreement' (European Commission, 2005c). Furthermore, the Union built on the existing *conditions for applying for membership* by specifying that '[a] country's satisfactory track-record in implementing its SAA obligations (including the trade-related provisions) will therefore be **an essential element for the EU to consider any membership application**' [bold emphasis added] (European Commission, 2005c).

The European Council in December 2004 elaborated on the *conditions for opening of accession negotiations*. The EU stressed that the start of the membership talks with Croatia was conditional on full co-operation with ICTY and urged the country to 'take all necessary steps to ensure that the remaining indictee is located and transferred to The Hague' (Council of the European Union, 2004b). Furthermore, the Union decided to open accession negotiations with Turkey 'provided that it brings into force [these] specific[2] pieces of legislation' (Council of the European Union, 2004b).

The Commission incorporated full compliance with the ICTY into the Copenhagen political criteria by stating that:

> [b]efore accession negotiations can be opened, the country needs to reach a sufficient degree of general compliance with the Copenhagen criteria. The political criteria must be met,[3] including full cooperation with the International Criminal Tribunal for the Former Yugoslavia (ICTY) where relevant.
>
> (European Commission, 2005c)

However, it specified further the *conditions for opening of accession negotiations* with FYROM by noting that:

> [t]he Accession Partnership identifies eight key priorities for progress in the accession process by the former Yugoslav Republic of Macedonia. The Commission assesses these key priorities as benchmarks in this Progress Report. A recommendation on the start of accession negotiations will depend on the results achieved.
>
> (European Commission, 2009c)

A senior Commission official underlined the significance of the benchmarks (including proper implementation of the SAA; constructive political dialogue; implementation of the law on police; judiciary reform; implementation of anti-corruption legislation; political independence of public administration; reduction of youth and long-term unemployment; improvement of the business climate) by noting that:

> I go to Skopje every month to meet with the deputy Prime Minister. We sit down around a table with excel sheets [...]. The eight key reform benchmarks, we have subdivided into more specific indicators and we go through all of these once a month systematically to see what progress has been made.
>
> (Interview 10, 2009)

Furthermore, the Commissioner for Enlargement identified a ninth benchmark – the conduct of free and fair elections (Crisis Group, 2009).

The Commission also established detailed sets of *conditions for opening of accession negotiations* with Albania, Montenegro and Serbia. In November 2010, the Commission identified 12 key priorities for the start of the accession negotiations with Tirana, including:

- proper functioning of Parliament;
- adoption of pending laws requiring a reinforced majority in Parliament;
- appointment of Ombudsman;
- modification of the legislative framework for elections in line with OSCE-ODIHR;[4, 5]
- conduct of free and fair elections;
- completion of essential steps in public administration reform;
- strengthening the rule of law through;

- effective implementation of the government's anti-corruption strategy and action plan;
- strengthening the fight against organised crime;
- preparation, adoption and implementation of a national strategy and action plan on property rights;
- reinforcement of the human rights protection and implementation of anti-discrimination; and
- improved treatment of detainees in police stations, pre-trial detention and prisons.

(European Commission, 2010c)

One year later, the EU made the opening of the membership talks with Montenegro conditional on the following seven key priorities:

- the improvement of the legislative framework for elections and strengthening of the Parliament's legislative and oversight role;
- completion of essential steps in the public administration reform;
- strengthening the rule of law through de-politicised and merit-based appointments of members of the judicial and prosecutorial councils and of state prosecutors;
- improvement of the anti-corruption legal framework and the implementation of the government's anti-corruption strategy and action plan;
- strengthening the fight against organised crime;
- enhancement of media freedom; and
- implementation of the legal and policy framework on anti-discrimination in line with European and international standards.

(European Commission, 2010e)

In 2012 the Commission recommended that the EU should open accession negotiations with Serbia when it reaches 'further significant progress' in the normalisation of relations with Kosovo in line of the conditions of the SAP by:

> fully respecting the principles of inclusive regional cooperation; fully respecting the provisions of the Energy Community Treaty; finding solutions for telecommunications and mutual acceptance of diplomas; by continuing to implement in good faith all agreements reached; and by cooperating actively with EULEX in order for it to exercise its functions in all parts of Kosovo.

(European Commission, 2011a)

The review of the conditions set by the EU during the pre-negotiation stage indicates three important developments. The Union significantly expanded on the scope of the *conditions for applying for membership* by linking the evaluation of the membership applications to the progress in the SAP. Although the Copenhagen criteria were institutionalised as uniform membership conditions, the EU has differentiated between the enlargement countries by establishing additional country-specific *conditions for opening accession negotiations*. Furthermore, the EU's approach towards the candidates underlines the firm focus of EU enlargement conditionality on the rule of law, judicial reform and fight against corruption.

Incentives structure

During the pre-negotiation stage, the EU can use a wide range of *accession advancement rewards*: granting a membership perspective, signing an AA, implementing an AA, granting candidate status, agreeing to open accession negotiations and committing to a credible membership perspective. As the confirmation of the membership perspective is the first *accession advancement reward*, it marks the beginning of the pre-negotiation stage. However, the establishment of the exact date of Turkey's membership perspective is a particularly challenging task. Article 28 of the Ankara Agreement stated that:

> [a]s soon as the operation of this Agreement has advanced far enough to justify envisaging full acceptance by Turkey of the obligations arising out of the Treaty establishing the Community, the Contracting Parties shall examine the possibility of the accession of Turkey to the Community.
>
> (*Official Journal*, 1964)

Nevertheless, there have been discussions whether the reference to the accession of Turkey to the EEC (an organisation for economic integration) in 1963 should be regarded as a confirmation for its membership to the EU, which is both a political and economic union. The Luxembourg European Council marked a turning point. Although it confirmed 'Turkey's eligibility for accession to the European Union', it led to a sharp rift in the relations between Union and Turkey because the country was not included in the group of 11 applicants with which the enlargement process was launched (Council of the European Union, 1997a). As the Helsinki European Council unreservedly confirmed Turkey's membership perspective by recognising it as a candidate country, this chapter examines the developments of EU enlargement conditionality towards Turkey since December 1999.

Several months after the advancement of the relationship between Ankara and Brussels, the EU not only confirmed the membership perspective of the Western Balkan countries but also introduced a new milestone on the way to full membership – the status of potential candidate (Council of the European Union, 2000a). In 2001 the EU signed an Accession Partnership with Turkey, and SAAs with Croatia and FYROM, thus granting the countries another accession advancement reward (see Table 4.1). Five years later the Union established an SAA with Albania, with Montenegro in 2007 and with Serbia and Bosnia and Herzegovina in 2008. The EU turned a new page in the relationship with Kosovo with the start of the SAA negotiations in October 2013.

Although the EU did not make a commitment to a timetable for the advancement of the accession process, in December 2002 the Copenhagen Summit concluded that 'if the European Council in December 2004, on the basis of a report and a recommendation from the Commission, decides that Turkey fulfils the Copenhagen political criteria, the European Union will open accession negotiations with Turkey without delay' (Council of the European Union, 2002). In a similar vein, the Union 'reiterated its determination to fully and effectively support the European perspective of the Western Balkan countries' but insisted that 'the speed of movement ahead lies in the hands of the countries of the region' (Council of the European Union, 2003b).

In June 2004, the EU granted Zagreb *another accession advancement reward* when it 'decided that Croatia is a candidate country for membership' (Council of the European Union, 2004a). Six months later, the European Council agreed to open accession negotiations with Croatia and Turkey. In December 2005 Skopje also received an important *accession advancement reward* when the EU decided 'to grant candidate country status to the Former Yugoslav Republic of Macedonia' (Council of the European Union, 2005b). Five years later, the Union recognised Montenegro as a candidate country. Serbia was given the key *accession advancement reward* in 2012. Although the Commission recommended that Tirana should be granted a candidate status in 2013, the member states confirmed Albania as a candidate country in June 2014 (European Commission, 2014a).

The analysis of the credibility of membership perspective demonstrates that the EU has been opposed to setting target dates for the advancement of the relations between the Union and candidate and potential candidate countries. Furthermore, the reluctance of member

Table 4.1 State of play: EU enlargement process with Turkey and the Western Balkans (January 2015)

First steps to EU membership	Turkey	Croatia	Montenegro	Serbia	FYROM	Albania	Bosnia and Herzegovina	Kosovo
SAA signed	NA	29.10.2001	15.10.2007	29.04.2008	09.04.2001	12.06.2006	16.06.2008	
SAA enforced	NA	01.02.2005	01.05.2010	01.09.2013	01.04.2004	01.04.2009		
Membership application	14.04.1987	21.02.2003	15.12.2008	22.12.2009	22.03.2004	24.04.2009		
Commission opinion	20.12.1989	20.04.2004	15.12.2008	14.10.2011	09.11.2005	09.11.2010		
Candidate country status	11.12.1999	01.06.2004	17.12.2010	01.03.2012	16.12.2005	27.06.2014		
Council decision to open accession negotiations	16.12.2004	16.12.2004	26.06.2012	28.06.2013				
Start of accession negotiations	03.10.2005	03.10.2005	29.06.2012	21.01.2014				
Progress (January 2015)	Chapters open: 14 Chapters closed: 1	Member state since 01.07.2013	Chapters open: 16 Chapters closed: 2	Preparing to open Chapters 23 and 24	Start of the accession negotiations blocked	Addressing key priorities for opening accession negotiations	Lack of progress	Negotiating SAA

states to follow the Commission's recommendations has significantly shaken the credibility of the process. Since 2009 the Commission has recommended six consecutive times the opening of the accession negotiations with FYROM. However, the Council of the EU has failed to act on the recommendation due to lack of consensus. The delay of the Council to recognise Albania as a candidate country caused some frustration in Tirana. Furthermore, the statement of new President of the Commission Jean-Claude Juncker that negotiations should continue, but 'no further enlargement will take place over the next five years' raised concerns about the EU's commitment to the ongoing accession process. The outgoing Enlargement Commissioner Füle remarked that '[i]t was a wrong message to the Western Balkans at a wrong time' (*Economist*, 2014).

However, it is also important to note that DG Enlargement has introduced a number of initiatives to counteract the negative impact of stalemates. In May 2012 the Commission launched Positive EU–Turkey agenda with aim to 'keep the accession process of Turkey alive and put it properly back on track after a period of stagnation' (Europa Press Releases, 2012). The Commission also established High Level Dialogue on the Accession Process of Bosnia and Herzegovina, High Level Accession dialogue with FYROM and High Level Dialogue on Key priorities with Albania. The Commission has also actively contributed to the visa-liberalisation process with the candidate and potential candidate countries. After the fulfilment of specific conditions (in the areas of document security, migration management, public order and security and fundamental rights), the EU granted visa free travel to FYROM, Serbia and Montenegro, Albania and Bosnia and Herzegovina. The Commission launched a visa liberalisation dialogue with Kosovo in 2012 and with Turkey in 2013. Although the visa-free schemes provided impetus for reform, some member states have raised concerns about growing number of asylum applications from the Western Balkans.

The review of the second element of the incentives structure – the threats during the pre-accession stage – indicates that the EU used mainly *implicit threats* to induce compliance with its conditions. As evidenced by the previous section, the advancement of the accession process has been conditional on meeting country-specific conditions. The EU sanctioned Croatia's failure to fully co-operate with ICTY by postponing the opening of the accession negotiations, which was scheduled for 17 March 2005 (Council of the European Union, 2004b, 2005c). Following a positive report from the ICTY Chief Prosecutor in October

2005, '[t]he Council concluded that Croatia had met the outstanding condition for the start of accession negotiations, and that negotiations should therefore begin as soon as possible' (Council of the European Union, 2005d). After Turkey 'brought into force the six outstanding pieces of legislations it was required to' on 1 June 2005, the EU decided to open accession negotiations with Ankara on 3 October 2005 (European Parliament, 2005). The Union has also sanctioned Bosnia and Herzegovina for its failure to implement Sejdić-Finci ruling[6] of the European Court of Human Rights. Although the SAA was ratified in June 2008, 'the Council has refrained from taking a decision on its entering into force' (European Commission, 2014a).

The analysis of the second category of threats – *explicit threats* – shows that the EU has provided for the application of *financial sanctions*, but also applied *preventive or remedial sanctions*. According to Article 5 of Council Regulation (EC) No 2666/2000 of 5 December 2000 on Assistance for Albania, Bosnia and Herzegovina, Croatia, FRY and FYROM:

1. Respect for the principles of democracy and the rule of law and for human and minority rights and fundamental freedoms is an essential element for the application of this Regulation and a precondition of eligibility for Community assistance. If these principles are not respected, the Council, acting by qualified majority on a proposal from the Commission, may take appropriate measures.
2. Community assistance shall also be subject to the conditions defined by the Council in its Conclusions of 29 April 1997, in particular as regards the recipients' undertaking to carry out democratic, economic and institutional reforms.

(*Official Journal*, 2000)

Similarly the Council Decision of 8 March 2001 on the principles, priorities, intermediate objectives and conditions contained in the Accession Partnership with Turkey, confirmed that:

Community assistance is conditional on the fulfilment of essential elements, and in particular on progress towards fulfilment of the Copenhagen criteria. Where an essential element is lacking, the Council, acting by a qualified majority on a proposal from the Commission, may take appropriate steps with regard to any pre-accession assistance.

(*Official Journal*, 2001)

The EU applied *preventive or remedial sanctions* to Serbia several times. The Union abandoned the SAA negotiations as Belgrade did not fully comply with ICTY conditionality. The Union resumed the negotiations with Serbia in June 2007. Although SAA was signed in 2008, its implementation was 'repeatedly blocked or postponed by the Netherlands due to its insistence that war criminals Ratko Mladić and Goran Hadžić were arrested first' (*EurActiv*, 2014). Belgrade started applying the agreement unilaterally on 1 January 2009. It entered into force in September 2013.

The investigation of the pre-negotiation incentive structure shows that the EU used a wide range of *accession advancement rewards* and introduced new instruments such as High Level Dialogues, aimed at helping the countries move forward in the accession process. The Union not only was reluctant to make a commitment to a timetable for the progress of the accession process with Turkey and the Western Balkans, but has also set a date before which no further enlargement would take place. In addition to transforming the range of the rewards, granted during the initial stage of the accession process, the EU has changed the parameters of the incentive structure by extending the spectrum of threats. Furthermore, the Union has applied *implicit threats* and *preventive and remedial sanctions* when countries failed to comply with its conditions.

Monitoring

During the pre-negotiation stage, the EU has used a wide range of instruments to monitor compliance with its conditions. Annual Progress Reports (in 1998 and 1999) and Regular Reports evaluated Turkey's progress. Furthermore, the Union relied on three separate monitoring frameworks in order to assess the progress of the Western Balkan countries.

Following the establishment of the Regional Approach towards the countries from South-Eastern Europe, the EU started publishing Conditionality Reports to measure their compliance. Although the reports were presented prior to the establishment of the membership perspective of the region, they confirmed the high relevance attached to monitoring by noting that: 'The next *possible* steps in relations with the various countries [...] will be assessed on the basis of this present report' (European Commission, 1998a). In April 2002, the EU introduced a new monitoring framework: Annual SAP Reports, which evaluated the progress of the Western Balkan countries in terms of political and economic development and the implementation of the SAP. Unlike the Regular Reports, the SAP Reports included separate subsections which outlined the priority areas that needed to be addressed in the next 12 months. The third (and last) series of SAP reports were published in 2004. In November 2005, the EU extended the application of Progress Reports to all candidate and potential candidate countries.

The Commission prepared six annual reports on Turkey's progress between 1998 and 2004. Despite their different names (Regular Reports and Progress Reports), they followed a similar structure. The 2002 and 2004 Regular Reports provided a detailed examination of Turkey's track record. As the 2004 Regular Report was set to provide 'the basis on which the Commission formulated its recommendation as to whether Turkey fulfils the Copenhagen political criteria', it included an assessment of Turkey's compliance with the political criteria since it became a candidate country in December 1999 (European Commission, 2004g).

The assessment of the EU's monitoring instruments illustrates that SAP Reports and Progress Reports shared a lot of similarities, as both reflected on the political and economic development of the countries. However, the Progress Reports, which initially monitored only the progress of the candidate countries, focused more on the accession process, as they evaluated compliance with all of the Copenhagen membership criteria. The reports prepared by the Commission provided the detailed assessment, which was of crucial importance for the advancement of the relations between the EU and candidate and potential candidate countries. A senior EU official summarised the key developments by noting that: 'we have imposed a very strict discipline, even closer monitoring than we had ever with Bulgaria and Romania at a much, much earlier stage of the process' (Interview 10, 2009).

Conclusions

The analysis of the pre-negotiation conditionality towards Turkey and the Western Balkans highlights new important developments of the evolution of EU enlargement conditionality. The extension of the application of the Copenhagen criteria to the Western Balkan countries institutionalised them as uniform membership conditions. However, the establishment of additional country-specific *conditions for opening accession negotiations* indicates the growing application of differentiated conditionality. Furthermore, the EU introduced a range of *preventive and remedial sanctions*, which establish specific penalising measures such as the suspension of the application of the AAs and weakened the positivity of the incentive structures. The Union used *evaluation reports* which highlighted key priority areas and expanded into detailed assessments of crucial significance for the of the enlargement process.

Negotiation stage

Conditions

This section concentrates on the key changes introduced by the renewed consensus on enlargement in 2006 and the New Approach to the accession negation in 2012. The membership talks with Turkey and Croatia illustrate important developments in the EU's approach to setting out conditions with which the candidate country need to comply. The first novelty was the increase in the number of negotiation chapters from 31 to 35 (see Appendix I). However, the constantly evolving *acquis* is not the only reason for the introduction of new chapters. The Commission remarked on the significance of one of the new chapters by stressing that 'the current negotiating framework provides for a chapter on Judiciary and Fundamental Rights, under which the political issues are to be addressed. This permits progress in crucial areas to be kept under close scrutiny' (European Commission, 2006g). Whereas, some of the big chapters such as Energy and Agriculture were split into two smaller chapters[7] for more practical reasons.

The second novel development was the introduction of benchmarks for the opening of chapters (opening benchmarks). The EU confirmed that:

> Benchmarks are measurable and linked to key elements of the acquis chapter. In general, opening benchmarks concern key preparatory steps for future alignment (such as strategies or action plans), and the fulfilment of contractual obligations that mirror acquis requirements. Closing benchmarks primarily concern legislative measures, administrative or judicial bodies, and a track record of implementation of the acquis. For chapters in the economic field, they also include the criterion of being a functioning market economy.
>
> (European Commission, 2006g)

In the accession negotiations with Zagreb, the EU laid down opening benchmarks for 11 chapters and closing benchmarks for all the chapters with the exception of Science and Research; Education and Culture and the two non-*acquis* chapters: Institutions and Other Issues (Government of Croatia, 2011). One Croatian official contextualised the extensive benchmarking by noting that 'Croatia had 134 benchmarks for opening chapters, and around 400 measures, that are parts of benchmarks' (Kujundžić, 2011).

In 2012 the EU brought about two important changes to the accession negotiations. Firstly, the Union confirmed that: 'the chapters Judiciary and fundamental rights and Justice, freedom and security will be tackled early in the negotiations to allow maximum time to establish the necessary legislation, institutions, and solid track records of implementation before the negotiations are closed' (European Commission, 2012a). Secondly, the EU introduced interim benchmarks and specified that:

> Depending on the chapter, precise benchmarks will refer in particular to legislative alignment with the acquis and to a satisfactory track record in the implementation of key elements of the acquis demonstrating the existence of an adequate administrative and judicial capacity. Where relevant, benchmarks will also include the fulfilment of commitments under the Stabilisation and Association Agreement, in particular those that mirror requirements under the acquis.
>
> (European Commission, 2014b)

The Union introduced another important development by outlining the set of requirements against which Turkey's, Croatia's, Montenegro's and Serbia's progress would be measured. In addition to the Copenhagen criteria, the negotiating frameworks included country-specific conditions. The list of conditions for Zagreb included full co-operation with ICTY; commitment to good neighbourly relations and strong contribution to the development of closer regional co-operation; Croatia's undertaking to resolve any border disputes; fulfilment of Croatia's obligations under the SAA; and the implementation of the European Partnership. The conditions for Ankara included:

- unequivocal commitment to good neighbourly relations (and its undertaking to resolve any outstanding border issues);
- support for efforts to achieve a comprehensive settlement of the Cyprus problem (including steps to contribute to a favourable climate for a comprehensive settlement, and progress in the normalisation of bilateral relations between Turkey and all EU member states); and
- fulfilment of Turkey's obligations under the AA and its Additional Protocol extending the AA to all new EU member states as well as the implementation of the Accession Partnership.

In the negotiating framework with Montenegro, the Union stressed the significance of the SAP conditionality and the need to resolve any border disputes, as well as addressing the 'areas of weakness identified in the Commission's Opinion (European Commission, 2012c). In the case of

Serbia, the Union underlined 'Serbia's continued engagement, in line with the Stabilisation and Association process conditionality, towards a visible and sustainable improvement in relations with Kosovo*' and noted that:

> This process shall ensure that both can continue on their respective European paths, while avoiding that either can block the other in these efforts and should gradually lead to the comprehensive normalisation of relations between Serbia and Kosovo, in the form of a legally binding agreement by the end of Serbia's accession negotiations, with the prospect of both being able to fully exercise their rights and fulfil their responsibilities.
>
> (European Commission, 2014b)

The EU also reflected and elaborated on its absorption capacity by confirming that:

> the Union's capacity to absorb Turkey, while maintaining the momentum of European integration is an important consideration in the general interest of both the Union and Turkey. The Commission shall monitor this capacity during the negotiations, encompassing the whole range of issues set out in its October 2004 paper on issues arising from Turkey's membership perspective, in order to inform an assessment by the Council as to **whether this condition of membership has been met** [bold emphasis added].
>
> (European Commission, 2005e)

However, this was not the case with Croatia, Montenegro and Serbia, as the EU's capacity to absorb the countries was not referred to as a condition to be observed. In response to a request from the Council, the Commission provided the first detailed definition for absorption capacity (since it was included in the Copenhagen Council Conclusion in June 1993) by stating that:

> [t]he EU's absorption capacity, or rather integration capacity, is determined by the development of the EU's policies and institutions, and by the transformation of applicants into well-prepared Member States. The capacity of would-be members to accede to the Union is rigorously assessed by the Commission on the basis of strict conditionality. Integration capacity is about whether the EU can take in new members at a given moment or in a given

period, without jeopardizing the political and policy objectives established by the Treaties. Hence, it is first and foremost a functional concept.

(European Commission, 2006g)

The Commission further specified that:

[t]he capacity of the Union to maintain the momentum of European integration as it enlarges has three main components: institutions, common policies, and budget. The Union needs to ensure that its institutions continue to act effectively, that its policies meet their goals, and that its budget is commensurate with its objectives and with its financial resources.

(European Commission, 2006g)

The review of the scope and the range of the conditions set out by the EU during the negotiation stage illustrates several important developments. Firstly, the very clear prioritisation of Chapter 23 (Judiciary and Fundamental Rights) and Chapter 24 (Justice, Freedom and Security) emphasises the growing significance of compliance with the political criteria for the advancement of the accession negotiations. Secondly, intensified benchmarking reflects the increasing application of targeted conditionality and the high level of specification of the EU conditions. Last but not least, the analysis illustrates that the EU followed a differentiated approach even when defining the scope of its (now) integration (previously) absorption capacity.

Incentives structure

The official start of the accession negotiations with Zagreb and Ankara on 3 October 2005 marked an important step in the relations between the EU and Croatia and Turkey. However, the Union did not provide the countries with another *accession advancement reward* by setting a timetable for the completion of the process. It is interesting to note that the EU decided on a point of time before which accession negotiations with Turkey cannot be finalised by noting that they 'can only be concluded after the establishment of the Financial Framework for the period from 2014 together with possible consequential financial reforms' (European Commission, 2005e). The EU not only imposed restrictions on the earliest date for the conclusion of the accessions with Ankara, but also introduced for the very first time the possibility of applying of permanent safeguard clauses 'in areas such as freedom of movement of persons, structural policies or agriculture' (European Commission, 2005e).

In December 2006, shortly after the completion of the first stage of the negotiations – the analytical examination of the *acquis*,

> the Council decided that negotiations will not be opened on eight chapters relevant to Turkey's restrictions regarding the Republic of Cyprus and that no chapter will be provisionally closed until the Commission confirms that Turkey has fully implemented the Additional Protocol to the Association Agreement.
>
> (European Commission, 2007b)

Nevertheless, the negotiations with Turkey moved forward and the EU provided Ankara with *accession advancement rewards* by opening chapters. At the same time Croatia managed to achieve a good overall progress and in November 2008, the Commission presented a road map for reaching the final stage of the accession negotiations. However, the EU insisted that it would 'refrain from setting any target dates for accession until the negotiations are close to completion' and provided an indicative timetable only for the technical conclusions of the negotiations (which was affected by the Slovenian blockade and was not met) (Council of the European Union, 2006a). Despite the border dispute with Slovenia, which put the membership talks with Croatia on hold for almost a year, Zagreb completed the accession negotiations with the EU on 30 June 2011.

The advancement of the membership talks with Ankara remains limited. By the end of 2014 Turkey has managed to open 14 chapters and provisionally close only one. In addition to the restrictions introduced due to Turkey's failure to fully implement the Ankara Protocol, individual member states have blocked the opening of 17 chapters; and thus only three (particularly demanding) chapters remain that can be open: Chapter 5 – Public Procurement; Chapter 8 – Competition Policy; and Chapter 19 – Social Policy and Employment (Interview 24, 2014).

The evaluation of the second element of the incentives structure – threats – indicates that during the negotiation stage the EU used both *implicit* and *explicit threats* to induce compliance with its conditions. The *implicit threats*, which sanction non-compliance by delaying the receiving of the *accession advancement rewards*, were incorporated in the negotiating frameworks, which confirmed that the pace of the negotiations would depend on progress in meeting the requirements for membership. Unlike *implicit threats*, *explicit threats* introduce specific penalising measures. In addition to the already established *financial sanctions*, the EU introduced the possibility of applying *preventive or remedial sanctions* on Turkey Croatia, Serbia and Montenegro by stating that:

[i]n the case of a serious and persistent breach in a candidate State of the principles of liberty, democracy, respect for human rights and fundamental freedoms and the rule of law on which the Union is founded, the Commission will, on its own initiative or on the request of one third of the Member States, recommend the suspension of negotiations and propose the conditions for eventual resumption.

(Council of the European Union, 2004b; European Commission, 2012c, 2014b)

After the launch of the New Approach to the accession negotiations in 2012, the EU stresses that if the progress under chapters 23 and 24 significantly lags behind the overall progress in the negotiations:

after having exhausted all other available measures, the Commission will on its own initiative or on the request of one third of the Member States propose to withhold its recommendations to open and/or close other negotiating chapters, and adapt the associated preparatory work, as appropriate, until this imbalance is addressed. The Council will decide by qualified majority on such a proposal and on the conditions for lifting the measures taken.

(European Commission, 2012c)

Furthermore, in the case of Serbia, the Union established an additional disequilibrium clause which confirmed that the membership talks will be put on hold 'in case progress in the normalisation of relations with Kosovo, dealt with under Chapter 35, significantly lags behind progress in the negotiations overall, due to Serbia failing to act in good faith, in particular in the implementation of agreements reached between Serbia and Kosovo' (European Commission, 2014b).

The assesment of the incentive structure illustrates that the negotiation stage has undergone an impressive transformation. Firstly, the EU did not use all of the *accession advancement rewards* at its disposal, as it was reluctant to make a commitment to a timetable for the progress of the accession process with Turkey, Croatia, Montenegro and Serbia. Secondly, the Union altered the incentive structure by introducing new threats. The negotiating framework for Turkey and Croatia provided for the suspension of the membership talks, thus establishing for the first time during the negotiation stage *preventive and remedial sanctions*. The partial suspension of negotiations with Turkey illustrates the EU's determination not only to expand the scope of *explicit threats* but also to apply them to sanction non-compliance. Furthermore, the Union established disequilibrium clauses linked to progress in key areas. Last but not least, the EU applied a differentiated approach to specifying the scope of the threats applicable to Zagreb, Ankara, Podgorica and Belgrade.

Monitoring

This subsection discusses the range and the scope of the monitoring instruments during the negotiation stage. The analysis is limited to the reports reflecting on the progress of the membership talks with Croatia, Turkey, Montenegro and Serbia. The Progress Reports followed the same structure, each of them included: a brief description of the relations between the candidate country and the EU; an analysis of the situation with regard to the political criteria; an assessment of the compliance with the economic criteria; and an examination of the candidate country's ability to meet the third Copenhagen criteria (the capacity to assume the obligations of membership). It is noteworthy that the 2005 reports were the last to provide a general evaluation. Since 2006, the Commission draws detailed conclusions on the progress of all candidate and potential candidate countries in its annual Enlargement Strategies.[8] The Progress Reports did not include country-specific lists of conditions. However, the Union has used the Enlargement strategies and the opening EU Common Positions respectively to flag the areas which required further efforts from Zagreb,[9] Ankara,[10] Podgorica and Belgrade; and establish benchmarks for the opening and the provisional closure of the negotiations on individual chapters.

The Commission's decision to prepare an Interim Report for Croatia underlines the great importance attached to the establishment of convincing and credible track records in the field of judiciary and fundamental rights and illustrates the increasing intensification of the monitoring process. The ongoing membership talks with Montenegro and Serbia provide more evidence for the political significance of these areas. The negotiating frameworks confirm that the Commission will keep the Council informed and report to it twice a year on the progress under Chapter 23 and Chapter 24 (European Commission, 2014b).

The review of the monitoring reports not only confirms the high relevance of monitoring for the advancement of the accession process but also provides further evidence for its evolutionary nature. In addition to the Annual Progress Reports, which the EU has cemented as integral part of its enlargement strategies, the Union enhanced the range of monitoring instruments by preparing for the first time an additional Interim Report during the negotiation stage.

Conclusions

The study identifies new important developments of the evolution of EU enlargement conditionality. The Union emphasised the growing relevance of the political criteria for the advancement of the accession negotiations by introducing a new chapter on Judiciary and Fundamental Rights and linking the progress of the membership talks to progress under Chapters 23 and 24. Furthermore, the EU's approach to setting conditions with which the candidate countries need to apply is characterised by extensive benchmarking, which reflects the growing application of targeted and differentiated conditionality. The assessment of the incentive structure shows that the EU not only refrained from setting any target dates for the accession of Turkey and Croatia but also, for the first time in the case of Turkey and Croatia, described the negotiations as an opened-ended process. Furthermore, the Union introduced *explicit threats* by providing for the suspension of the membership talks. The Commission developed the scope of the Regular Reports and increased significantly the relevance of monitoring for the advancement of the accession process.

Accession stage

As Croatia is the only country, from the case studies, to have completed the accession stage, this section focuses on the development of EU conditionality towards Zagreb. Following the completion of the accession negotiations, the acceding countries were expected to finalise their preparations for assuming the responsibilities of membership, which included compliance with the Copenhagen criteria and the specific arrangement for each of the *acquis* chapters. It is important to note that the Accession Treaty identified three areas which required intensified efforts from Croatia: the judiciary and fundamental rights; freedom, security and justice, and competition policy. The EU outlined a list of ten priorities in the area of the judiciary and fundamental rights:

- effective implementation of the Judicial Reform Strategy and Action Plan;
- strengthening the independence;
- accountability, impartiality and professionalism of the judiciary;

- improvement of the efficiency of the judiciary;
- improved handling of domestic war crimes cases;
- a sustained track record of substantial results based on efficient;
- effective and unbiased investigation, prosecution and court rulings in organised crime and corruption cases at all levels including high level corruption;
- improved track record of strengthened prevention measures in the fight against corruption and conflict of interest;
- strengthening the protection of minorities, dealing with outstanding refugee return issues; enhanced protection of human rights; and
- full co-operation with the ICTY.

(Official Journal, 2012)

The Union also stressed that Croatia needs to implement and enforce the EU requirements with regard to external border management, police co-operation, the fight against organised crime, and judicial co-operation in civil and criminal matters. Furthermore, the Accession treaty specified that Zagreb's commitments in the area of competition policy included the restructuring of the ship-building industry and the steel sector (*Official Journal*, 2012). The Comprehensive Monitoring Report on Croatia's state of preparedness for EU membership published in October 2012 urged Zagreb to intensify its efforts in the following five areas: preparations for future EU structural funds, shipbuilding industry, the rule of law, fight against corruption and external border management and provided the country with a list of ten very specific priority actions (European Commission, 2012b).

The review of the incentive structure confirms the observation from the previous chapters that the *reward–threat balance* during the accession stage is dominated by a wide range of preventive and remedial sanctions. The Accession Treaty did not contain a postponement clause as in the case of Bulgaria and Romania, however it confirmed that The Council, acting by qualified majority on a proposal from the Commission, may take all appropriate measures if issues of concern are identified during the monitoring process (Official Journal, 2012). The safeguard clauses, specified in Articles 37, 38 and 39 were the same as the ones provided for the eight CEECs, Cyprus and Malta in the 2003 Accession Treaty and Bulgaria and Romania in 2005.

The general economic safeguard clause[11] allowed member states to apply for authorisation to take protective measure with regard to Croatia in the event of serious economic difficulties.[12] The two specific safeguard clauses stated that the Commission may establish appropriate measures if Zagreb caused, or risked causing, a serious breach of the functioning of the internal market (Article 38) or if there were serious shortcomings or any imminent risk of such shortcoming in the transposition and implementation of the *acquis* in the area of justice and home affairs (Article 39) (*Official Journal*, 2012).

Following the signing of the Accession Treaty, the Commission prepared three monitoring reports. The first report Monitoring Report on Croatia's Accession preparations was issued in April 2012, six months later the Commission presented Comprehensive Monitoring Report on Croatia's state of preparedness for EU membership. The final monitoring report was presented in March 2013. The evaluation of the progress was based on the findings of half-yearly monitoring tables – a new instrument, which the Commission introduced with the aim of providing a detailed update on the commitments undertaken by Zagreb. The tables listed 78 commitments analysed with reference to: (1) Croatia's commitments under the EU Common Positions; (2) Actions taken (during the monitoring period); (3) Commission's assessment, overall level and remaining issues; and (4) Future actions. The study confirms the significance of monitoring for both assessing the progress and clarifying the scope of the conditions. However, the level of detail in case of Croatia was particularly impressive. As one senior Commission official recollected:

> I could have told you at every point in time where we were on the exact cycle of fight against corruption, how many indictments we have had, which of those indictments have moved to the prosecution state, which of the prosecution state have led to conviction state, what happened on the appeal what happened to the sentences, we had incredible level of details which allowed us to make an assessment as to whether we believe that the trends are being established unequivocally.
>
> (Interview 23, 2014)

The study reveals the very detailed nature of the EU requirements, which has also been matched by intensified monitoring instruments including the introduction of rigorous monitoring tables. The examination identifies another interesting development – although the Accession Treaty did not include a postponement clause, it did provide for the application of corrective measures. The analysis illustrates the ongoing evolution of EU enlargement conditionality and highlights the strong entrepreneurship of the Commission.

Post-accession stage

Although the Netherlands insisted that Croatia should be subject to post-accession monitoring, the Commission and most the member states firmly opposed the establishment of an additional monitoring mechanism similar to the CVM for Bulgaria and Romania (*EUObserver*, 2011b). One senior Commission official noted that Štefan Füle the Commissioner for Enlargement and Neighbourhood policy 'was very clear it was not going to be closed under his watch with a CVM, so it was either going to be: yes we believe that Croatia is ready or we believe that Croatia is not ready and there is further work to do, so it was going to be a green traffic light or a red traffic light, it was not going be an orange traffic light under his watch' (Interview 23, 2014). The scope of EU post-accession conditionality towards Croatia is limited to the three safeguard clauses established by the Accession Treaty, which could be evoked 'until the end of a period of up to three years after accession' (*Official Journal*, 2012).

Conclusions

Although Croatia is the only country to have completed the accession process since the establishment of the renewed consensus on enlargement in 2006, the study outlines a number of important policy changes. Over the last ten years, the EU has not only elaborated and further specified the scope of the membership requirements, but also firmly cemented the cardinal significance of the rule of law and fundamental rights. Benchmarking has emerged as an essential element of EU enlargement strategy. The introduction of opening and interim benchmarks has transformed the dynamics of the membership talks.

The ongoing enlargement process highlights the relevance of the early stages for the establishment of solid track records in challenging areas such as judicial reform and fight against corruption. These developments demonstrate an important progression in the EU demands: from the adoption of the *acquis* and the alignment with the Union's policies to ensuring the sustainability of the reforms through credible track records of implementation. The comparative analysis of the negotiating frameworks for Turkey, Croatia, Montenegro and Serbia illustrates another key development – the growing application of differentiated conditionality. Furthermore, the introduction of a range of *preventive and remedial sanctions* combined with the eroded credibility of the accession process (particularly in the case of FYROM and Turkey) has weakened the positivity of the incentive structure. The extensive application of benchmarks has also contributed to the further development of EU monitoring instruments. The research findings confirm that the Union has continued to strategically utilise monitoring reports in order to evaluate compliance, clarify the scope of EU requirements and apply political pressure.

Although it is too early to evaluate the impact of the New Approach to the accession negotiations, it has already transformed the dynamics of the accession process. It is interesting to see if the EU will extend the application of the approach to Turkey. The new Commissioner for Neighbourhood Policy and Enlargement Negotiations Johannes Hahn stressed the significance of the rule of law and fundamental rights for the advancement of the accession process with Ankara. However, conditioning the progress of the membership talks on progress in Chapters 23 and 24 seems unlikely not only because the 2005 Negotiating framework did not include the disequilibrium clause, but also because the opening of the chapters continues to be blocked by Cyprus. As the candidate and potential candidate countries have a long way to go before they join the Union, it is clear that EU enlargement conditionality will continue to evolve and we should expect even more extensive application of country-specific conditionality.

Explaining EU conditionality towards Turkey and the Western Balkans

With a view to analysing the evolution of EU enlargement conditionality, the book specifies that *EU enlargement policy is a function of differentiated influences from multiple actors and external pressures.* The definition highlights the complex constellations of actors involved in the accession process and emphasises their relevance by focusing on the influence which they can exert rather than their competences. Although the book stresses the leading role of the main EU institutions, it delves deeper into policy dynamics by analysing key policy developments with reference to the following factors: (1) *EU member states*, (2) *EU inter-institutional dynamics*, (3) *public opinion in the EU*, (4) *enlargement countries* and (5) *external pressures caused by economic or security shocks and crises*.

EU member states

This section discusses the impact the Council of the EU on the development of EU enlargement conditionality by looking into the influence of individual member states. The analysis follows a selective approach and focuses on three key aspects: (1) bilateral issues between candidate countries and member states, (2) shifts in member states' attitudes towards enlargement and (3) member states' impact on benchmarks. The first part examines the implications of bilateral problems for the advancement of the accession process by looking at most serious cases: the border dispute between Croatia and Slovenia; the issues between Turkey and Cyprus and Greece; and the name issue between FYROM and Greece. The second part reflects on member states preferences, focusing particularly on France's and Germany's attitudes towards Turkey and the divisions between member states regarding the Union's enlargement policy. The third part analyses the increasing application of opening and interim benchmarks and their impact on member states' veto powers in the accession negotiations.

Although bilateral issues were present in the fifth round of enlargement, none of them had such a detrimental effect on the accession process, as in the case of Croatia, Turkey and FYROM. One senior official commented that:

Bilateral issues between current member states and candidate countries or bilateral issues between candidate countries, these have now become the biggest obstacles for progress in enlargement and I don't think this was really the case with the previous rounds.

(Interview 12, 2009)

The Commissioner for Enlargement Olli Rehn noted that: 'Each of the problems has its own historical and contextual background. We cannot put them all into the same basket; they have different characteristics' (*Agence Europe*, 2009b). However, the aim of the section is not to examine in detail the nature of disputes but to analyse their impact on EU enlargement conditionality, particularly with reference to the incentive structure and the range and the scope of the conditions set out by the EU.

Shortly after the Commission presented an indicative roadmap for the completion of the technical part of the accession negotiations with Croatia, a long-standing border dispute between Croatia and Slovenia put the accession negotiations on hold for almost a year. The dispute, which had persisted since the breakup of the former Yugoslavia, escalated in December 2008 when Slovenia decided to effectively block the accession negotiations with Croatia 'on the grounds that some of the material that Croatia has submitted to the EU, including documents on fisheries, prejudged the resolution of the dispute over their border in the Bay of Piran' (*European Voice*, 2009). The Commission consistently maintained the view that 'the border issue is a bilateral issue that should not be brought to the table of the accession negotiations' and encouraged both states to solve the open border dispute 'in the spirit of good neighbourly relations' and actively participated in intense consultations (European Commission, 2009e). One Commission official stressed the far-reaching implication of the dispute by noting that: 'Slovenia does harm even the other countries from the Western Balkans. People say if already Slovenia is blocking Croatia, how much will Croatia block Serbia and [how much will] Serbia block the other countries?' (Interview 4, 2009).

The advancement of the accession process with another candidate country has also been put on hold because of a long-running bilateral dispute. The name issue between FYROM and Greece has prevented FYROM from receiving two *accession advancement rewards*: opening accession negotiations and moving to the second phase of the SAA implementation. Despite six consecutive recommendations from the Commission recommendations, the Council has not yet reached a unanimous decision. In December 2010 the Greek Foreign Minister Droutsas reiterated the Greek stance:

> Our position on Skopje's accession perspective is clear and well known to everyone. We sincerely want the opening of FYROM's accession negotiations with the EU. We support the accession of this country, but with full respect for the rules and obligations FYROM has undertaken to the EU and all of its member states. One basic rule is respect for good neighbourly relations. This is stressed once again. And a basic demand for our being able to talk about the opening of accession negotiations with FYROM is the resolution of the name issue. Like last year, all of this is reiterated in a clear manner, in clear language.
>
> (Droutsas, 2010)

Although the resolution of the bilateral problem between FYROM and Greece was not included as a formal condition for the start of the accession negotiations, the Commission confirmed that it was 'essential' (European Commission, 2014a). One senior EU official stressed that:

> The fact of the matter is Greece as a member state of the European Union is in a far stronger position than FYROM. If they are serious about their European perspective about joining the EU, then they

need to recognise that and accept that they will have to make certain compromises if they want the next step.

(Interview 22, 2013)

However, the name issue is not the only bilateral issue between a candidate country and Greece. The Aegean Sea Continental Shelf dispute has strained the relations between Turkey and Greece and the EU. The high degree of importance attached to the enlargement process by Greece was confirmed by Droutsas who stressed that 'the enlargement process is interwoven with Greece's foreign policy. This enlargement policy is very important to us, and it is obvious that we want to have – and do have – a strong voice in the development of the discussion in the EU on this subject' (Droutsas, 2010).

One senior Commission official pointed out that although the dispute between Greece and Turkey 'is a very old and difficult bilateral problem', the issue between Cyprus and Turkey 'is quite unusual bilateral problem, I mean, there are Turkish tanks and Turkish soldiers in Cyprus' (Interview 8, 2009). Turkey's failure to extend the implementation of the Ankara Protocol to Cyprus virtually brought the accession negotiations to a halt as the General Affairs Council agreed not to open the following eight chapters: Chapter 1: Free Movement of Goods; Chapter 3: Right of Establishment and Freedom to Provide Services; Chapter 9: Financial Services; Chapter 11: Agriculture and Rural Development; Chapter 13: Fisheries; Chapter 14: Transport Policy; Chapter 29: Customs Union; and Chapter 30: External Relations. It also decided not to provisionally close any chapter 'until the Commission verifies that Turkey has fulfilled its commitments related to the Additional Protocol' (Council of the European Union, 2006b).

The impact of individual member states on the ongoing enlargement process has not been limited to blockages related to bilateral issues. Some member states have shaped significantly EU enlargement policy. The negotiating frameworks with Turkey and Croatia introduced a new development by declaring that 'the accession negotiations are an open-ended process, the outcome of which cannot be guaranteed' (European Commission, 2005d; 2005e). One senior official confirmed that:

> [t]his was a hook given to Schüssel to convince him to start the accession negotiations. In 2005, when they [member states] discussed the negotiating framework with Turkey, Plassnik – the Austrian Foreign Minister – she fought for having mentioned the privileged partnership also as a possibility, but she did not manage.
>
> (Interview 8, 2009)

The official further reflected on the relevance of the member states' preferences for the start of the accession negotiations with Turkey by pointing out that:

at that time it was Austria in December 2004 and in October 2005, [but] you still had this [favourable] constellation in the Council. Austria was the main opponent. All the others, Italy was in favour, Spain was in favour, the Netherlands had the presidency in December 2004, then these other countries took the wait-and-see approach [...] so this was the political environment which helped for the start of the accession negotiations with Turkey. Had you had the current balance of power in the Council, probably we would not have started the accession negotiations with Turkey.

(Interview 8, 2009)

However, in the case of Turkey, controversy and disagreement between member states have not been limited to start of the accession negations, as Turkey's chief EU negotiator Volkan Bozkir noted, 'Unfortunately, the negotiation process is not proceeding as it ought to be. The accession process has been facing resistance particularly led by certain member states. 17 chapters are still blocked on political grounds' (Anadolu Agency, 2014). One Turkish official further explained that:

for some of the chapters the screening process has been completed and we have been given the benchmarks, but the screening process for some of the chapters has not been completed yet, because the discussions on the screening process to agree on the opening benchmarks could not be completed because of the member states' positions in the Council enlargement group... They are all unilateral positions of member states and the French ones are totally unacceptable, they are arguing that the chapters are directly related to full membership, to the accession of Turkey, so they will not let these chapters go, but the whole process is about membership, we are negotiating for membership, we are not negotiating for something else.

(Interview 2, 2009)

A senior EU official summarised the French position on Turkey's bid for membership by saying that: 'The French approach to the negotiations with Turkey is that we want a privileged partnership and all the chapters which can be compatible with a possible future privileged partnership, we open them, not a problem, but block those chapters which prejudge accession' (Interview 8, 2009). However, France is not the only member state opposed to Turkey's accession. The Commissioner for Enlargement remarked that:

> [m]any European politicians have advocated the idea of a privileged partnership for Turkey rather than full membership. This takes place despite the fact that the EU and its leaders in the European Council unanimously decided to open accession negotiations, while underlining that the negotiations are by their very nature an open-ended process with no predetermined outcome.
>
> (Rehn, 2006b)

A senior Commission official commented on the opposition to Turkey's membership by saying that:

> several other countries are very happy that France and Germany take the lead, so they can hide their position, it's true, not just France and Germany, Austria and others that sometimes do not dare to say, there are several countries.
>
> (Interview 15, 2009)

However, Turkey has also received a lot of support from some member states. In December 2010, the foreign ministers of Britain, Sweden, Finland and Italy published a joint letter in the International Herald Tribune and warned Europe against 'turning its back on Turkey' (*EUObserver*, 2010).

One senior EU official reflected on the shifts in the member states' preferences regarding the ongoing enlargement by stating that: 'Out of the original EU six, Italy is a strong enlargement supporter, but the five other are not that strong in supporting enlargement as they were until 2004' (Interview 12, 2009). Another official also commented on the divisions in the Council noting that 'Italy supports Albania, the New members states from Central and Eastern Europe are very much supporting all the Western Balkans countries, the UK supports Kosovo, but you don't have the same overall support' (Interview 24, 2014).

Against the background of divisions between the member states, the growing application of closing benchmarks and the introduction of opening and interim benchmarks have significant implications not only for the veto power of individual member states, but also for the scope and the range of the EU conditions. As the Greek foreign minister pointed out following the start of the accession negotiations with

Turkey: 'We have passed from the time when we did not set conditions to a time when we set conditions, a great many conditions, that Turkey is obliged to accept' (*Agence Europe*, 2005).

One Turkish national official outlined some of the implication of benchmarking by saying that:

> sometimes, it is difficult to understand what the benchmark means, because it is a product of 27 member states and the Commission is preparing the draft and they submit it to the Council and it's discussed in the Council enlargement group and 27 member states come up with creative ideas to improve these draft benchmarks in line with their own interests. Some of them don't touch it at all, but some of them would like to make it as much difficult as possible for Turkey.
>
> (Interview 2, 2009)

One senior member of the Commission also reflected on the application of opening benchmarks by noting that:

> [t]he idea is that, first a good implementation of pre-existing bilateral relations and then in the case of Turkey, proper strategy of alignment with the calendar, roadmap. It helps better streamline the negotiations afterwards. If it is conducted in good faith, now, the reality is that maybe a number of countries use the opening benchmarks as a leverage to impose more conditions.
>
> (Interview 8, 2009)

Following the completion of the accession negotiations with Croatia, the Commissioner for Enlargement Füle emphasised the fact that benchmarks multiply the veto power of member states by noting that the 138 benchmarks which Croatia had to meet represented '138 possibilities for any member state to veto' (*European Voice*, 2011).

The study confirms the crucial role of the member states for the second element of EU enlargement conditionality – the incentive structure. Furthermore, the analysis highlights the detrimental impact of open bilateral issues between candidate countries and member states on the accession process. As one senior Council official noted: 'If a country wants to join and the issues is with a member state, you can stay to the country sort it out before you come in, because the country that is already in the EU, will make it a condition for them to give their agreement' (Interview 22, 2013). The section also notes the lack of strong consensus among member states and growing divisions regarding both the scope and the speed of the EU enlargement process. Last but not least, the discussion illustrates how the growing application of opening and closing benchmarks not only multiplies the veto power of member states, but also allows them to shape the scope and the range of the conditions that enlargement countries need to satisfy.

Inter-institutional dynamics

This section investigates the influence of the inter-institutional dynamics of the Union on the development of its enlargement policy towards Turkey and the Western Balkans. Although the EP continued to actively support and monitor the accession process, the Commission's activism intensified significantly after the completion of the accession negotiations with Bulgaria and Romania. Consequently, the analysis focuses on the role of the Commission in keeping enlargement firmly on the EU agenda against the background of growing divisions among the member states about the direction and the speed of the enlargement process. It reflects on the growing entrepreneurship of the Commission by looking into its impact on: the opening of the accession negotiations with Ankara and Zagreb; the establishment of renewed consensus on enlargement and the mediation of bilateral disputes between candidate countries and member states.

Although the Union recognised Turkey as a candidate country in 1999, the advancement of the accession process with Ankara proved to be highly controversial. In the midst of growing opposition to Turkey's application, the Commission actively pursued a viable solution. Although the Negotiating framework confirmed that 'the shared objective of these negotiations is accession', it also for the first time specified that 'these negotiations are an open-ended process the outcome of which cannot be guaranteed beforehand' (European Commission, 2005e). One senior EU official confirmed that new development was the result of a negotiated compromise and highlighted the Commission's role by noting that:

> We had to find a formula accepted by all member states, so we had to find a text which was acceptable to those countries which were not happy about it. Austria was until the very end blocking the opening of the accession negotiations with Turkey. Austria was very negative on Turkey, but Austria was not the only one, you can imagine other countries: Cyprus, France, so we had to find a text that the countries being negative on Turkey can live with – one aim – and the second was we did not want the mandates [for negotiations] between

Croatia and Turkey to be very different. They had to be somewhat similar and that was the end result, but it was proposed by the Commission.

(Interview 4, 2009)

It should be noted that the reference to the accession negotiations as an open-ended process has become a characteristic feature of the ongoing enlargement of the Union as it was also included in the negotiating frameworks with Croatia and Iceland (European Commission, 2005d, 2010g). However, a senior EU official highlighted another new development which was engineered in order to launch the negotiations with Ankara by pointing out that the Commission included only for Turkey the possibility of applying permanent safeguard clauses (European Commission, 2005e; Interview 15, 2009).

The role of the Commission for the development of EU enlargement policy was not limited to facilitating the agreement on the start of the membership talks with Ankara and Zagreb. It also reaffirmed the political significance of the ongoing accession process by establishing the key principles of the EU's enlargement policy towards Turkey and the Western Balkans and reorganising the structure of the accession negotiations. One senior EU official reflected on the link between the declining enthusiasm for further enlargement and the growing entrepreneurship of the Commission and commented that: 'The situation for Verheugen was a lot easier because everybody supported it [enlargement], now Olli Rehn invented the sense of the carefully managed enlargement policy' (Interview 14, 2009). Another EU official noted that:

Olli Rehn thought that in order to enhance the credibility of the Commission, leading the process, in a changed context, we needed to go back to the basics, be more orthodox. Verheugen acted in a different context, from his own convictions, but Verheugen had gotten used , from 1998 to 2002, to getting away with many things, because there was this large historical mission, still carrying the process, this was certainly not the case in 2004.

(Interview 9, 2009)

Commissioner Rehn justified the new approach of the Commission by pointing out that:

The virtue of the renewed consensus on enlargement is that it both emphasises the strategic value of enlargement, i.e. the EU's soft power and, at the same time, identifies the ways and means to ensure our capacity to function, while gradually integrating new members.

(Rehn, 2008b)

The reaffirmed commitment of the Union towards South-Eastern Europe was accompanied by practical measures aimed at improving the quality of the accession process. Olli Rehn highlighted one of the key aspects of the new approach by noting that 'We now use benchmarks more systematically' (Rehn, 2008b). One senior EU official outlined the advantages of this new development and commented that:

> to make a number of short closing conditions on which they can focus and deliver is a much more realistic process than what we had with the fifth enlargement. As a principle it is very good and it adds to the credibility of the Commission and also helps the countries to focus better, to better prepare at very important stage of the pre-accession progress.
>
> (Interview 21, 2009)

Although there is a virtual agreement among the EU officials that the systematic use of benchmarks has significantly improved the accession negotiations, it is difficult to establish whether the new approach has strengthened the position of the Commission vis-à-vis the Council. A senior member of the Council Secretariat reflected on the new inter-institutional dynamics by noting that:

> At the beginning I thought that this [benchmarking] gives an enormous power to the Commission, but then I noticed that at least some members look very carefully, of course, it depends on the strength of your administration, your administrative capacity. If you take France, we all know, they have a very efficient public administration they look very carefully; they come regularly with questions, comments, proposals.
>
> (Interview 19, 2009)

However, a senior official from one of the candidate countries insisted that the extensive use of benchmarks has shifted the inter-institutional balance and commented that:

> Now when they [the conditions] are spelled out you cannot do anything, now you cannot lobby [member states] to close a chapter if you

don't fulfil the benchmarks, previously, chapters were closed based on some political decisions [...]. Now because it is less political, more technical and the Commission has more power in a way to decide. If it is more technical, they [Commission officials] tend to be more objective than the member states.

(Interview 1, 2009)

Although it is difficult to argue that the Commission has become more influential than the Council, as the Council is the institution which decides unanimously on the opening and closing of the negotiation chapters, most interviewees highlighted the Commission's potential to influence the development of the accession process. One national official reflected on the reorganisation of the accession negotiations and stressed that: 'this time around, deliberately, I think the concentration, the discussion is now in the Commission and then Commission suggests to the Council' (Interview 1, 2009). These comments were echoed by an EU official who noted that 'the debate is structured by what the Commission proposes and it is a way of having the debate in a certain direction' (Interview 19, 2009).

The Commission's commitment to strengthening the credibility of the accession process is also reflected by its involvement in mediating bilateral issues between candidate countries and member states. Following the escalation of the Croatia-Slovenia border dispute, Rehn actively sought to facilitate the dialogue between the two countries and help them find a solution (*EUObserver*, 2009). In June 2009 one senior EU official reflected on the Commission's efforts to unblock the membership talks with Zagreb and noted that:

Commissioner Rehn is very much involved in trying to solve this bilateral dispute between Croatia and Slovenia and we see some progress, so we are trying our best to ensure that the negotiations progress goes according to the road map.

(Interview 14, 2009)

A national official acknowledged the complexity of the situation and insisted that 'in a sense the Commissioner is the only one who can do that [mediate] because no member state can take it up' (Interview 13, 2009). Although the Commission has not intervened in the name dispute between Greece and FYROM, it has tried to mitigate its impact. In March 2012, with a view to lending a new momentum to the accession process with FYROM, the Commission launched a High Level

Accession Dialogue with Skopje (European Commission, 2012a). The Commissioner for Enlargement pointed out that the new initiative 'is by no means a substitute for actual negotiations' and commented that the 'aim is to support the reform process, to inject new dynamism into it and to boost the European perspective for the country' (Füle, 2012). The Commission also boosted the accession process with some of the other candidates with a series of High level dialogues and the EU Positive Agenda for Turkey.

The assessment of the impact of the inter-institutional dynamics on the evolution of EU enlargement policy towards Turkey and the Western Balkans reaffirms the crucial significance of the Council for the advancement of the accession process. The analysis also shows that against the background of declining enthusiasm for further enlargement, the Commission's activism has intensified significantly. In addition to steering the accession negotiations into a more technical direction, the Commission has pursued a very active role in counteracting the damaging effects of bilateral disputes between candidate countries and member states. The growing influence of the Commission on shaping the parameters of the accession process highlights its crucial role as a driving force for the development of EU enlargement policy.

Public opinion

This section reflects on the variation in EU public support for enlargement and analyses the attitudes towards the accession of Turkey and the Western Balkan countries in comparative perspective. It draws on the data from the Standard Eurobarometer surveys and focuses primarily on the period between the autumn of 2000 (following the establishment of the membership perspective of the Western Balkans in June 2000) and the autumn of 2014. The wide range of the data allows us to identify the key trends in EU public opinion and reflect on their relevance and implication for the development of EU enlargement policy.

The comparative review of public opinion (see Appendices III and V) confirms that the support for enlargement varied and varied greatly depending on which country the respondents come from. In some of the member states, particularly in Poland, Latvia and Romania, attitudes towards enlargement were very favourable and support was significantly above the EU average. In other countries such as France, Austria and Germany and Luxembourg, the levels of support were consistently below the EU average.

Although the support for EU enlargement varied over time, it is evident that the public opinion in the countries which joined the Union in 2004, 2007 and 2013 was much more enthusiastic about further enlargement. However, it is worth noting that since 2011 Cyprus and the Czech Republic are the only two new members where more people are against further expansion of the EU. Furthermore, the examination of public opinion highlights another interesting development – growing opposition to enlargement. Since 2011 more EU citizens have been opposed to rather in favour of further expansion. This trend has been very pronounced in the EU15, Spain has been the only 'old' member state where the people supporting enlargement outnumbered those against it. The public opinion in Sweden has also been largely in favour. The anti-enlargement mood has been persistently prominent in Austria and France and Luxembourg (see Appendices III and V). However, there has also been growing opposition to enlargement in the CEECs. Although this trend can be detected in Romania, with only 14% against new expansions and 72% in favour, it is the most pro-enlargement country in 2014 (Eurobarometer, 2014b).

The analysis also confirms the second trend outlined in the previous two chapters that the attitudes towards enlargement varied also depending on the candidate country in question. Public opinion in the majority of the old member states has consistently been against Turkey's accession. It is worth noting that while strong opposition to Turkish membership has been prominent in France, Greece, Cyprus and Luxembourg, it reached a record high of 91% in Austria in the autumn of 2010. On the other side of the spectrum, Romania has been the only outstanding supporter with 61% of the public opinion in favour of Turkey.

There has been a significant shift in the attitudes towards Croatia. Although initially public opinion in most of the old member states was opposed to Croatia's accession since 2005 the trend has been reversed. Spain, Greece, Ireland and, in recent years, Sweden have been among the strongest supporters of Croatia's membership. Public opinion in EU12 has been in favour of Croatia, with the highest levels of support in the Czech Republic, Hungary and Slovakia.

The EU citizens have been predominantly against the accession of FYROM, with the highest levels of opposition in Austria, Luxembourg and France. Although initially Greece was in favour, the opposition to FYROM reached a record high of 76% in the autumn of 2008. Spain, Sweden and most of the EU10 have continuously supported the Western Balkan candidate. Slovenia and Bulgaria, where more than 63% of the public opinion has been in favour, are the strongest supporters for FYROM membership.

It is interesting to note that the EU citizens in favour of the accession of Serbia, Montenegro, Bosnia and Herzegovina, Albania and Kosovo were always outnumbered by those against their membership. The support for Tirana and Pristina has been particularly low. In 2010, 58% of the EU citizens opposed the membership of Albania and 57% – the membership of Kosovo, whereas the EU citizens in favour of their accession were only 29% (Eurobarometer, 2010b).

Although the declining public support for enlargement did not have a direct negative effect on the EU's incentive structure such as blocking the granting of *accession advancement rewards*, it could have and has the potential to do so. Following the escalation of the border dispute between Slovenia and Croatia, the Slovenian Foreign Affairs Minister Samuel Zbogar announced that Croatia's accession to the EU may be put to a referendum (*EurActiv*, 2009a). Although both countries managed to reach an agreement on a settlement mechanism, Slovenia decided to call a referendum on the border arbitration deal (*EurActiv*, 2010b). It was narrowly approved by Slovenians, with 51.5% in favour, but a 'No' vote could have had a detrimental impact on Zagreb's membership talks (*Financial Times*, 2010). Furthermore, the outcome of the accession negotiations with Turkey is expected to be dependent on public support. In this respect, the strong opposition to Turkish membership in France and Austria, where about 60% of the citizens have been consistently against it, is a serious concern, as both countries are committed to holding referendums. France amended its Constitution to impose 'an automatic referendum for ratification of any new accession, after that of Croatia', whereas Austria has promised to hold a referendum on Turkey's accession, but its commitment is not yet legally binding (*Agence Europe*, 2008; *EurActiv*, 2011a). The increasing significance of public opinion for the enlargement policy of the Union was noted by Commissioner Rehn who made Communication one of the cornerstones of his three C's enlargement strategy.

Enlargement countries

This section discusses the relationship between the profile of Turkey Croatia, FYROM, Montenegro, Serbia, and Bosnia and Herzegovina, Albania and Kosovo and the evolution of the EU enlargement conditionality, by focusing on the following two aspects:

- the impact of the problematic issues and reform challenges (the applicants need to address) on the scope and range of the EU conditions; and
- the implications of the existence or lack of group dynamics (which is examined with reference to the number of applicant states at

the same stage of the accession process) for the development of the incentive structure, particularly with reference to the *accession advancement rewards*.

The previous two chapters underlined the links between the range of the Copenhagen criteria and the issues which the CEECs needed to address urgently. The development of EU enlargement policy towards Turkey, Montenegro, Serbia, FYROM, Albania, Bosnia and Herzegovina and Kosovo provides more evidence for the strong relationship between the profile of the candidate countries and the nature of EU conditions. The breakup of Socialist Federal Republic of Yugoslavia led to the emergence of new independent states amid series of violent ethnic conflicts, damaging both the economies and the social fabric of the region. Commissioner Rehn acknowledged the complexity of the situation and noted that:

> [t]he Western Balkans is a particular challenge for the EU. The region contains small countries that are at different stages on their road towards membership. Consequently, the enlargement policy needs to transform itself into the specific needs of these weak states and divided societies.
>
> (Rehn, 2006a)

A member of Croatia's Permanent Mission to the EU reflected on the new developments and pointed out that:

> we belong to a different process, in terms of the political name that was given to it – the Stabilisation and Association process – a policy invented by the EU to develop inter-regional policy. So we belong to that group of countries which were given the European perspective especially after the Thessaloniki summit [...]. The regional approach and then the SAP took a look at the specificity of the countries and one of the specificities was that they had the war situation during the 1990s – out of which you have the ICTY cooperation; out of which you have the obligation for the refugee return; out of which of you have to settle all these questions considered to be necessary so the countries could progress further.
>
> (Interview 1, 2009)

In addition to building strong democracies and functioning market economies, the Union has repeatedly underlined the importance of regional co-operation for long-term stability, economic development and reconciliation in the Western Balkans and called on the countries to take stronger ownership of the process. Although the EU confirmed that the SAP 'is at the heart of the Union's policy' towards region, it also stressed that 'it takes account of the situation of each country' and 'proposes an individualized approach to each of the countries' (Zagreb Declaration, 2000). The introduction of additional country-specific conditions for the start of accession negotiations with Croatia, Turkey, Montenegro, Serbia and FYROM illustrates the increasing application of differentiated conditionality and highlights the growing significance of the profile of the candidate countries. The negotiating frameworks for Podgorica and Belgrade provide more evidence for this trend. Although both frameworks were developed on the basis of the new approach to the rule of law, the Commission introduced an additional disequilibrium clause for Serbia linking the advancement of the membership talks to the progress in the normalisations process with Kosovo.

The simultaneous start of the negotiations with Zagreb and Ankara emphasises the strong link between the group dynamics generated by candidate countries and the evolution of EU enlargement policy. A Croatian national official pointed up the similarities in the EU's approach towards both countries and commented that:

> the negotiating frameworks were discussed at the same time and there is always this balancing act the EU is doing. They say it's individual and Turkey is a special case, but you still have two documents on the table, one for Turkey, one for Croatia and when you think about Croatia's negotiating framework, of course the discussion on Turkey influences, of course the discussion on the what will happen on the Western Balkans influences it, because the EU is not drafting only a document for Croatia [...] The negotiating frameworks say that the negotiations are an open-ended process. What does it mean for Turkey? We know it was there because of Turkey, they wanted to emphasise this sentence that it was open-ended process, no guarantee that Turkey will become a member but that sentence is still in Croatia's negotiation framework.
>
> (Interview 1, 2009)

Furthermore, the group dynamics generated by Zagreb and Ankara has also had an impact on another aspect of EU enlargement policy – the range of the conditions for opening and closing individual chapters. A national official reflected on the similarities in the EU Common positions and observed that:

because we had the screening together with Turkey, we had a feeling that the benchmarks, sometimes, if you compare the benchmarks, opening and closing benchmarks for Croatia and Turkey, they were informed by the Turkish case in Croatia's case and vice versa, they are similar, sometimes.

(Interview 1, 2009)

However, the impact of the applicant states is not limited to the scope and the range of EU conditions, the accession process with Croatia, and the ongoing enlargement stress the relevance of the group dynamics among the EU hopefuls for the advancement of the accession process. A Croatian national official reflected on Zagreb's application for membership by discussing how being excluded from the fifth enlargement round made it more difficult to generate momentum for their candidacy:

[W]e had to lobby hard when we applied for membership, because we were discouraged to apply. Actually, it was an effort of six months. We talked to all the member states, the Commission. They were very reluctant. They actually discouraged Croatia from applying because they still did not know what will happen with negotiations from the fifth enlargement [...] at that time, the negotiations were in the final stage with the ten, so after a while it became easier, but we really worked very closely with the Commission trying to convince them to consider our application.

(Interview 1, 2009)

The official further pointed out that:

there was much bigger drive in the fifth enlargement [...] in our case, every step that we went through was not more difficult, but there were more obstacles in political sense: to get the application for membership accepted; to convince that we are a good candidate; to start accession negotiations. Every step took more time in procedural terms and more months for the EU to decide to take every step along the way.

(Interview 1, 2009)

Although the launch of the membership talks with Zagreb and Ankara marked a historical milestone for the EU's enlargement policy, the lack of strong group dynamics among the two countries prevented them from boosting their positions in the negotiations with the Union. A

Croatian national official noted the implications of the wide range of differences between Turkey and Croatia and commented that:

[i]n the beginning we tried [working together] but then we realised that we are so different, and their approach is so different [...] even if we talk about education and culture, we still found differences in the approaches of the two countries. We exchanged information, we have very good cooperation with them, both in Turkey and here (Brussels) and it has worked, but in term of having a joint effort they are such different cases, we cannot lobby further for such different cases, we don't have such close ties as they had in the fifth enlargement.

(Interview 1, 2009)

Although Zagreb and Ankara completed together the screening of the *acquis*, their paths diverged: Turkey progressed at a modest pace, while the negotiations with Croatia reached an advanced stage. The Commission for Enlargement acknowledged that 'the next country likely to join is Croatia, with others at different points along the road' (Rehn, 2006c). However, as Zagreb emerged at the finishing line, the lack of strong group dynamics influenced another step of the accession process – the conclusion of the negotiations. A Commission official confirmed that the border dispute between Croatia and Slovenia delayed the finalisation of the membership talks and noted that:

the political pressure on completing the enlargement with Croatia is by far not the same as it was with the twelve. The accession of the fifth enlargement countries was a clear priority for the EU, for the Commission and for the member states.

(Interview 7, 2009)

The lack of strong group dynamics among Turkey Croatia as well as the other Western Balkan countries has had an impact on another *accession advancement reward* – the credibility of the membership perspective. A senior Commission official highlighted the link between the number of applicant states at the same stage of the accession process and the EU's approach to establishing timetables and target dates and pointed out that:

[w]e are also in a situation where the candidates and possible candidates are at such different stages of the process that it would be impossible to set out any unanimous common schedules and then set

out differentiating schedules. I am not sure that that would be helpful because that would result immediately in rows between the candidate countries and then comparing timetables [...] So the usefulness of the target dates at this stage is quite questionable, and maybe at some point later but at this point – no.

(Interview 12, 2009)

The analysis of the impact of the candidate countries on EU enlargement conditionality confirms that although applicant states have a narrow scope for manoeuvring in the accession process, they do indirectly shape the development of EU enlargement policy. The findings reveal that the profile of the Western Balkan countries and Turkey, particularly the problematic issues and the deficiencies that they need to address, has influenced significantly the range and scope of EU conditions. Furthermore, the study illustrates that the lack of strong group dynamics among the candidate countries can have a detrimental impact on the advancement of the accession process. The slow pace of the enlargement with the countries of South-Eastern Europe cannot be solely attributed to the lack of a large group of candidates at the same stage of the process. However, the European journey of Croatia illustrates that it has become increasing more difficult for individual countries to build up and keep the momentum for their membership aspirations.

External pressures

In order to assess the relationship between external factors and the evolution of EU enlargement policy, this section follows a selective approach. As the previous two chapters have illustrated the significance of the end of the Cold War and the Balkan conflicts for the early development of EU enlargement towards the CEECs, this section focuses on the implications of the Yugoslav wars for the establishment of the EU enlargement strategy towards the Western Balkans and Turkey. It also analyses the impact of the 'European paralysis' following the rejection of the Constitutional Treaty in 2005 and the Eurozone crisis on the development of EU enlargement policy.

The President of the Commission Romano Prodi was one of the first to highlight the implications of the Balkan conflicts for the membership perspective of the countries from the region. In October 1999, he noted that '[r]ecent developments such as the Kosovo crisis raise broader geopolitical questions. Questions about the prospect of membership for European countries which are not yet part of the enlargement process' and stressed that '[n]ow, as we plan our enlargement strategy, is the time to address these questions seriously' (Prodi, 1999). The President of the Commission insisted that 'we should hold out to these countries the prospect of eventual EU accession provided certain conditions are met' and suggested that:

> we should devise new and innovative forms of co-operation with these countries, in the form of what I have called 'virtual membership'. By this I mean giving them access to the stimulus and advantages of close co-operation even before they are ready for full membership. In this way, we should make it clear to Albania and the countries of the former Yugoslavia that we see them as members of the European family of nations, and that once they have met the criteria for membership we shall welcome them into the EU, provided certain important steps are taken beforehand.
>
> (Prodi, 1999)

The link between the troubled past of the Western Balkans and the membership perspective of the countries of the region was also emphasised by Commissioners responsible for enlargement who noted that:

> [i]t was in Sarajevo that we were reminded of the fury that can be unleashed by the dark forces of division. Suddenly we had war again in Europe. Millions were forced to flee. The Balkan war also reminded us that conflicts in Europe always spill over, that the destabilisation of any part of the continent inevitably becomes a threat to the whole. The lesson for us was that there is no alternative in order to create peace and stability in this large area of Europe but to extend towards the East, the Northeast and the Southeast the structures of European integration. This is what the enlargement of the EU is all about.
>
> (Verheugen, 2003)

His successor, Olli Rehn, recalled the EU's failures at dealing with the troubled region:

> In 1991–92, Europe also pondered a new Treaty, pre-occupied and fragmented. On our southern borders, the Balkans was on the brink of war. We succeeded at Maastricht, but failed in Yugoslavia. And neither are the European leaders about to forget the Union's dramatic inability to act when war broke out in Bosnia in 1992. Who does not remember how vehemently civil society called for European intervention at the time?
>
> (Rehn, 2007)

Rehn highlighted the positive impact of the membership perspective by confirming that '[t]his prospect is acting as a powerful factor of peace in a region long referred to as the "powderkeg" of Europe' (Rehn, 2007). On a similar note, a Member of the European Parliament noted that:

> [w]hat happened in the 90s was an alarm signal and we did not react at the beginning correctly. We tried to catch up in the end but it is clear that without the stability in this region, the Union would not have any stability and everybody knows that.
>
> (Interview 16, 2009)

Another senior EU official also commented that:

> [t]he main reason for the European perspective of the Western Balkans is the stabilisation of the region. That's the reason why stabilisation policy was supported in the Council, completion of the reunifying Europe in a way, but the mere reason is that they need to have a European perspective because of certain things that happened recently.
>
> (Interview 7, 2009)

Another crisis which has had a significant impact on the development of EU enlargement policy was the failure of the ratification of the Constitutional treaty. As the Commissioner for Enlargement pointed out:

> The climate at the time was marked by uncertainty about the EU's commitment to the Balkans. France and the Netherlands had voted 'no' in the referenda in 2005, and 'absorption capacity' was top of the agenda.
>
> (Rehn, 2008a)

Moreover, Rehn warned, 'We face a serious situation. The EU's enlargement fatigue started and became a scapegoat in June 2005, after the two failed referenda on the Constitutional Treaty' (Rehn, 2006d). Some member states, and particularly France, voiced their concerns about granting FYROM a candidate status by stating that 'this is perhaps not a particularly well chosen time to launch a further wave of expansion', the French Foreign Minister Philippe Douste-Blazy insisted:

> Granting candidate country status sends out an important signal, and we must ask ourselves whether all of the conditions have been

met, whether this is the right time to send the signal out now, given that the institutional and budgetary challenges of the enlargement underway have not yet been resolved.

(Agence Europe, 2005)

There was a virtual agreement between the interviewees from the Commission, the Council of the EU, the EP, national officials from the member states and the candidate countries that the Dutch and French no-votes had significant implications for EU enlargement policy. Some of them even commented that Bulgaria and Romania were very fortunate to have signed the Accession Treaty with the EU in April 2005, just weeks before the grim and gloomy mood settled in Europe (Interview 6, 2009; Interview 21, 2009).

However, 2005 was not the only time when the Union was facing major challenges. The Commissioner for Enlargement accounted for the changing political environment at the presentation of the EU enlargement package in November 2008 by noting that:

[w]hat is interesting is the *new context* for our policy today. I present this package against the backdrop of the Russia-Georgia crisis and a renewed awareness of the strategic importance that countries like Turkey has for the EU – for our stability, security, energy supplies and contacts in the region. This underlines the value of maintaining our 'soft power', and a well managed enlargement policy. We also discuss enlargement against the backdrop of a global financial crisis, which again underlines the importance of keeping a steady course and this way help stabilise our partners in SEE.

(Rehn, 2008c)

The strong impact of external factors and crises on the development of the enlargement process was highlighted again in 2009. Rehn acknowledged the detrimental effect of the financial crisis by stating that '[t]oday, we are pursuing our enlargement policy in a context where the global economic crisis has shaken deeply our economies and taken centre-stage in both domestic and international politics' (Rehn, 2009a). Against this background, when many questioned the rational of the EU enlargement and advocated the slowing down or even the halting of the accession process, the Commissioner defended the enlargement project by remarking that 'I cannot imagine enlargement could be blamed for the economic crisis. Let's not blame Croatian workers for failures of financial capitalism which originated in Wall Street' (*Agence Europe*, 2009a). Furthermore, he insisted that:

> [w]hile combating the economic crisis, we cannot take a sabbatical from our work for stabilisation of Southeast Europe. It is much better to export stability to the Balkans than import instability from there... In the coming period; we must make the most of our size and strength as a Union. We need the political will of all Member States and a joint vision of how to promote stability and prosperity in our Southern and Eastern Neighbourhood.
>
> (Rehn, 2009b)

The Czech Foreign Minister Karel Schwarzenberg reflected on the difficult discussions in the Council regarding the enlargement policy of the Union by confirming that '[w]e managed to agree that despite the economic and financial crisis, we will not slow down the integration of the western Balkans' (*Agence Europe*, 2009a).

The discussion of the implications of the Balkan conflicts, the 'European paralysis' and the current financial crisis for the development of EU enlargement policy highlights the significant variation in the impact of external factors on the internal dynamic of the Union. Although all of the events shared the negative connotations associated with a crisis (humanitarian, institutional or economic), not all of them had negative consequences for the enlargement process. The EU's determination to overcome the legacies of the Balkans' troubled past has not only inspired a new comprehensive policy approach, but also led to the establishment of the membership perspective of the region. However, the European crisis following the failure of the ratification of the Constitutional treaty and the financial crisis have put significant strain on the efforts of the Commission and the Council to keep the enlargement policy on track.

Conclusions

The chapter confirms that the evolution of the EU enlargement conditionality towards Turkey and the Western Balkans is characterised by three distinct trends. Firstly, the scope and range of EU conditions illustrate the growing application of detailed, differentiated and targeted conditionality. Secondly, the eroded credibility of the accession process (particularly in the case of FYROM and Turkey) combined with the introduction of a range of *preventive and remedial sanctions* weakened the positivity of the pre-negotiation and negotiation incentive structure. The findings also underline the increasing relevance and multi-functionality of the monitoring reports.

In order to explain these developments, the multi-level analysis dissects the influence of a mix of institutional and external factors. The investigation confirms the essential relevance of EU institutions for the development of the scope and range of EU requirements. Furthermore, it illustrates the impressive entrepreneurship of the Commission for the introduction of individual country-specific conditions which in turn led to the increasing application of detailed, targeted conditionality. The study also reveals that the profile of the candidate countries influences the scope of EU requirements. Although neither the additional *conditions for opening accession negotiations* nor the sets of requirements included in the negotiation frameworks were actively engineered by the enlargement countries, these novelties reflect the Union's acknowledgement of the specific challenges which the applicants need to address and point to the relevance of group dynamics.

The evaluation of the factors affecting the developments of the incentive structure reveals a very complex picture. Similarly to the discussion of the evolution of EU conditions, the analysis confirms the crucial role of the institutional factors – EU member states and inter-institutional dynamics. The findings highlight the detrimental impact of open bilateral issues between candidate countries and member states on the advancement of the accession process. Furthermore, the analysis shows that the extensive application of benchmarks not only allows the member states to modify the scope and the range of EU conditions but also multiplies their veto power. However, the study also points to the growing influence of the Commission over shaping the development of the accession process. In addition to steering the accession negotiations into a more technical direction, the Commission has pursued a very active role in counteracting the damaging effects of bilateral disputes between candidate countries and member states.

The book confirms that the one of the EU's most successful policies is exposed to the pressures caused by external crises and shocks. Although it is difficult to precisely measure the intensity of their impact, the empirical evidence identified in this study shows that security crises such as the Kosovo crisis had a catalysing effect on the development of EU enlargement conditionality towards the Western Balkans and Turkey. However, external pressures cannot on their own account for the developments of the incentive structure. The same observation applies to the impact of candidate countries. The analysis shows that the lack of strong group dynamics among the candidate and potential countries can have a damaging impact on the advancement of the accession process. Nevertheless, the slow pace of the enlargement with the countries of South-Eastern Europe cannot be solely attributed to the lack of a large group of candidates at the same stage of the process. The chapter highlights the increasing significance of public opinion for the enlargement policy of the Union. Although the declining support for enlargement has not had a direct negative effect on the EU's incentive structure such as blocking the granting of *accession advancement rewards*, it could have and has the potential to do so. Furthermore, the examination confirms that the evolution of the monitoring instruments was exclusively modified by the Commission. The study stresses the growing relevance of the Progress Reports for the advancement of the accession process.

Despite the similarities in the EU's approach to Croatia, Turkey, FYROM, Montenegro, Serbia, Albania, Bosnia and Herzegovina and Kosovo and the ten CEECs, the Union introduced significant changes to the range and the scope of the conditions with which the candidate countries from South-Eastern Europe had to comply and further intensified the monitoring process. The developments provide more evidence for the evolutionary nature of EU enlargement policy. The comprehensive investigation on the basis of *stage-structured conditionality model* illustrates the increasing application of differentiated, targeted and detailed conditionality, which confirms the linear trajectory of development of EU requirements. Similarly, the intensification and specification of detail in the reports shows that evolution of monitoring represents a natural progression, whereas the evolution of the second element of EU enlargement conditionality is characterised by the weakening of the incentive structure.

The analysis confirms the leading role of the Commission and the Council for the development of the policy, but also points to the relevance of external factors. The research findings show that the impact of candidate countries is not a direct result of their bargaining power and that they can shape both the scope of EU conditions and the incentive structure. Furthermore, the chapter illustrates the catalysing effects of the external pressures caused by security crises on the advancement of the accession process. The study confirms that a single factor cannot account for the evolution of EU enlargement conditionality and highlights the advantages of the comprehensive approach, which allows us to examine the impact of a dense constellation of factors.

5
The Evolution of EU Enlargement Conditionality: Overview and Key Findings

The chapter draws together the key findings of the project, relates them to the two research themes of book and answers the main research questions:

- How has EU enlargement conditionality changed across different stages of the accession process and between different groups of enlargement applicants?
- Why has EU enlargement conditionality changed over time?

The analysis, which emphasises the strong comparative dimension of the study, unfolds in three steps. Firstly, on a basis of the *stage-structured conditionality model*, it discusses the evolution of EU enlargement conditionality across the stages of the accession process between the three groups of enlargement applicants. The first group includes the countries with which the EU completed the first phase of the fifth enlargement in 2004 – the Czech Republic, Estonia, Hungary, Poland, Latvia, Lithuania, Slovenia, Slovakia, Cyprus and Malta. The second group consists of Bulgaria and Romania, whose accession to the Union in 2007 led to the completion of the fifth enlargement round. The third group focuses on Croatia's accession and the ongoing enlargement process with Turkey, Montenegro, Serbia and FYROM, Albania, Bosnia and Herzegovina and Kosovo.

Secondly, the study investigates continuity and change in EU enlargement policy by analysing the developments of EU enlargement conditionality with reference to the following factors: (1) *EU member states*, (2) *EU inter-institutional dynamics*, (3) *public opinion in the EU*, (4) *enlargement countries* and (5) *external pressures caused by economic or security shocks and crises*. Finally, the study draws conclusions on the evolutionary nature of EU enlargement conditionality and the varying mechanisms for shaping the Union's most successful policy; and reflects on their wider implications for the ongoing enlargement process and the advancement of the research agenda on EU enlargement.

Analysing the evolution of EU enlargement conditionality

Pre-negotiation stage

The investigation of the evolution of EU conditionality during the pre-accession stage, which starts with the formal agreement of the European Council on the membership perspective of the potential candidate country and ends with the launch of the accession negotiations, focuses on the developments of the *conditions for applying for membership* and the *conditions for opening accession negotiations*; the changes in the *reward–threat balance* of the incentive structure and the transformation of the range and functions of the monitoring instruments.

The comparative analysis illustrates the remarkable transformation of the scope and the range of both sets of conditions with which applicant states need to comply. In order to apply for membership the CEECs had to meet the single condition of being a European country, however the changes introduced by the Amsterdam Treaty expanded the *conditions for applying for membership* by specifying that any European state 'which respects the principles set out in Article 6(1) may apply' (*Official Journal*, 1997b). The Lisbon Treaty amended them further by confirming that any European state 'which respects the values referred to in Article 1a **and is committed to promoting them may apply**' [emphasis added], the treaty also expanded the range of prerequisites (previously referred to in Article 6(1) by including human dignity and equality and specifically emphasising the significance of the rights of persons belonging to minorities[1] (*Official Journal*, 2007). Nevertheless, the EU has stringently avoided defining one of most essential, but also controversial requirements – the 'Europeanness' of the applicants, whilst Commissioner Rehn dismissed the debate on the geographical borders of the EU by insisting that: 'Geography sets the frame, but fundamentally it is values that make the borders of Europe' (Rehn, 2005). However, in the case of Western Balkan countries, the Union significantly expanded on the scope of the *conditions for applying for membership* by linking the evaluation of the membership applications to the progress in the SAP.

The *conditions for opening accession negotiations*, which underwent a series of dramatic transformations, confirm the gradual specification of EU conditions but also highlight another pronounced trend –

the growing application of differentiated and targeted conditionality. In 1997, the Union insisted that the recommendations for the start of the membership talks were to be based on the applicants' sufficient progress in satisfying all of the Copenhagen criteria in the medium term (European Commission, 1997: 38). Two years later, the Helsinki European Council took a remarkable U-turn by confirming that compliance with the Copenhagen political criteria was a prerequisite for opening accession negotiations. However, as discussed in Chapter 3, the EU differentiated the candidate countries by introducing additional country-specific conditions for Bulgaria and Romania. Although, at the time the move was seen as the solution, which allowed the Union to keep Sofia and Bucharest firmly on track towards accession, the ongoing enlargement with the Western Balkans and Turkey and confirms that the practice of setting out country-specific conditions (in addition to the political criteria) has become the norm rather than the exception. Furthermore, the EU's strategy towards Iceland,[2] a candidate country very distant from the other applicants, provides more evidence for the institutionalisation of this approach to establishing *the conditions for opening accession negotiations*.

The comparative analysis on the basis of the *stage-structured conditionality model* confirms that the second element of EU conditionality – the incentive structure – has also undergone several modifications. While, the Union maintained a strong commitment to encouraging and facilitating reforms by providing the applicant states with *financial rewards*, it introduced two important changes to the range of the *accession advancement rewards*, which reflect the progress of the applicant state in the enlargement process.

After the completion of the fifth enlargement, the EU extended the European journey of the new applicants from the Western Balkans by introducing an addition step – the category of potential candidate country – on the ladder of contractual relationships, leading to accession. As one senior official noted, 'There was no much distinction between a candidate country and a potential candidate country. You were either a candidate country or a candidate country negotiating with the EU' (Interview 23, 2014). The comparative analysis of the credibility of the membership perspective, which is examined with reference to a commitment to a target date/timetables for the advancement of the accession process, confirmed that member states were always wary of granting such a powerful, but also potentially self-fulfilling *accession advancement reward*. However, the start of the accession negotiations with Croatia and Turkey marked a significant departure, as the European

Council officially acknowledged that it would refrain from setting target dates for the current enlargement (Council of the European Union, 2004b). The new approach of the Union is in stark contrast with the EU's commitments to the timetables and target dates for the accession of the CEECs; and by taking away one of the most desirable *accession advancement rewards*, it undoubtedly reduces the positivity of the pre-negotiation incentive structure. However, much more concerning has been the EU's inability to deliver on its promise to reward candidates for their progress, particularly in the case of FYROM. Furthermore, the statement of Jean-Claude Juncker (2014) that the accession negotiations would continue, but 'no further enlargement will take place over the next five years' has made him the first President of the Commission to set a timetable for no further expansion of the Union. Although Juncker's position on the timing of the future expansion of the Union corresponds with the technical realities of the complex negotiation process, some including the outgoing Enlargement Commissioner raised concerns that the call for a pause on enlargement sent the wrong message to the Western Balkans and Turkey (*The Economist*, 2014). Juncker did not drop the enlargement portfolio, but made the priorities of new Commission clear, by appointing Johannes Hahn as a Commissioner for European Neighbourhood Policy and Enlargement Negotiations.

In addition to transforming the range of the rewards, granted during the initial stage of the accession process, the EU has changed the parameters of the incentive structure by extending the spectrum of threats. During the fifth enlargement round, the Union relied only on *financial sanctions* and *implicit threats*, which sanction non-compliance by delaying the receiving of the *accession advancement rewards*. However, as evident from the ongoing enlargement process, the EU introduced a range of *preventive and remedial sanctions*, which establish specific penalising measures such as the suspension of the application of the AAs. Furthermore, the conclusions of the Luxembourg European Council, which established two groups of candidate countries, namely 'ins' and 'pre-ins', but also the Union's decision to suspend the SAA negotiations with Serbia and to postpone the start of membership talks with Croatia show the EU's determination not only to establish but also to apply threats as a means of sanctioning insufficient compliance.

The comparative assessment of the third element of EU enlargement conditionality – monitoring – shows that the Commission gradually elaborated on the scope and functions of the Progress and Regular Reports. The Luxembourg European Council acknowledged the high relevance attached to the process of evaluating compliance with its conditions, particularly in the framework of the Copenhagen criteria and established regular monitoring as an integral part of its enlargement strategy. The analysis confirms that the early developments of the monitoring instruments followed a consistent pattern which provided firm foundations for tracking yearly progress. Furthermore, the Opinions and the reports of the Commission were based on a homogenous framework, which allowed the EU to comparatively evaluate progress across the candidate countries.

The comparative examination of the pre-negotiation conditionality, on the basis of the *stage-structured conditionality model* (see Table 5.1), highlights important evolutionary developments in the application of EU enlargement conditionality. The Union has clearly prioritised the relevance of the political requirements by incorporating the values of the EU in the *conditions for applying for membership* and institutionalising the Copenhagen political criteria as an essential part of the *conditions for opening accession negotiations*. Nevertheless, the analysis confirms that the Union has favoured and gradually developed a differentiated approach by introducing additional country-specific conditions for the start of the membership talks. Furthermore, the latter trend has been taking place in parallel with the increasing use of targeted conditionality.

The second element of EU enlargement conditionality has also undergone a series of transformations. Despite the fact that the pre-negotiation incentive structures provided by the Union for all of the case studies were dominated by *financial rewards* and *accession advancement rewards*; the EU shifted the *reward–threat balance* from strong positive to weak positive by taking away one of the most attractive *accession advancement rewards* – the credibility of the membership perspective – and introducing *preventive and remedial sanctions*. These changes mark the shift away from strong positive pre-negotiation, which the Union applied towards the Luxembourg six. The EU did not introduce any dramatic changes to its monitoring practices. However, as the Commission expanded the breadth of the monitoring reports and institutionalised their frequency, they became more than just instruments for assessment and provided the Union with an additional channel for applying political pressure.

The analysis of the evolution of the EU enlargement conditionality confirms that the pre-negotiation stage, which stresses the crucial importance of the Copenhagen political criteria, is characterised by the growing application of differentiated and targeted conditionality. Furthermore, the Union established firm links between compliance and

Table 5.1 Evolution of pre-negotiation conditionality

Elements of EU enlargement conditionality	Fifth enlargement: first phase (2004)	Fifth enlargement: second phase (2007)	Sixth enlargement: HR (2013)	Ongoing enlargement with TU, FY, ME, RS, AL
I. Conditions				
– Conditions for applying for membership	✓	✓	✓	✓
– Conditions for opening accession negotiations	✓	✓	✓	✓
– Additional country-specific conditions	–	✓	✓	✓
II. Incentive structure				
1. Rewards				
1.1. Accession advancement rewards				
– Providing membership perspective	✓	✓	✓	✓
– Granting potential candidate status	NA	NA	✓	✓
– Signing AA or SAA	✓	✓	✓	✓
– Implementing AA or SAA	✓	✓	✓	✓
– Granting candidate country status	✓	✓	✓	✓
– Credible membership perspective	✓	✓	–	–
– Opening accession negotiations	✓	✓	✓	✓
1.2. Financial rewards	✓	✓	✓	✓
2. Threats				
2.1. Explicit threats				
– Financial sanctions	✓	✓	✓	✓
– Preventive and remedial sanctions	–	–	✓	✓
2.2. Implicit threats	✓	✓	✓	✓
III. Monitoring				
– Progress/regular reports	✓	✓	✓	✓

advancement in the accession process. However, whilst expanding the scope of the conditions, the EU has also reduced the positivity of the incentive structure thus making the initial stage of the process much more demanding than it used to be.

Negotiation stage

This section discusses the evolution of EU enlargement conditionality during the negotiation stage, which begins with the launch of the accession negotiations and ends with their completion, and focuses on the development of opening benchmarks; the increasing number of negotiation chapters; the changes in the *reward–threat balance* of the incentive structure and the transformation of the range and functions of the monitoring instruments.

The comparative analysis underlines two important developments in the scope of the conditions with which the candidate countries need to comply during the negotiation stage: the increase in the number of negotiations chapters from 31 to 35 and the introduction of opening and interim benchmarks. The change in the negotiation chapters should not be treated as a pure organisational matter or a mere reflection of the expansion of the EU legislation. The establishment of a new chapter on Judiciary and Fundamental Rights, allowed the Union to incorporate the political membership criteria into the negotiations, which in turn influenced significantly the advancement of the enlargement process with Croatia. The urgency of addressing the issues related to the areas of Judiciary and Fundamental rights (Chapter 23) and Justice and Home Affairs (Chapter 24) is reflected by the New Approach to the accession negotiations, which revolutionised the conduct of the membership talks by making the advancement of process conditional on progress under Chapters 23 and 24 (European Commission, 2012a).

The introduction of opening and interim benchmarks further highlights the evolutionary nature of EU enlargement conditionality. These changes have also influenced significantly the dynamics of the accession negotiations by establishing a three-step negotiations process (for some of the chapters), which requires the unanimous decision from the member states on (1) the conditions for opening a chapter and (2) interim conditions (3) the conditions for the provisional closure of a chapter. Furthermore, the ongoing accession process with Turkey and the Western Balkan countries rekindled the debate on the relevance and the definition of the EU absorption capacity. Although, the Commission renamed it to 'integration capacity' and specified (for the first time) that 'it is first and foremost a functional concept', it followed a differentiating approach by noting that it would be 'a condition to be observed' in the case of Turkey, but not Croatia (Rehn, 2006d; European Commission, 2006g).

The comparative analysis confirms that the evolution of the negotiation incentive structure is characterised by the same three trends, observed during the pre-negotiation stage: continuous commitment to granting *financial rewards*; diminishment in the range of the *accession advancement rewards*; introduction of *preventive and remedial sanctions*. Following the completion of the fifth enlargement, the EU enhanced the coherence of the financial assistance by merging the existing pre-accession programmes under a single framework – Instrument for Pre-Accession Assistance (IPA). IPA II set a new framework for financial assistance for the period 2014–2020.

The Union provided the three groups of candidate countries with a range of *accession advancement rewards* such as opening and closing chapters. However, the EU's approach to one of the most attractive rewards – the credibility of the membership perspective – has changed significantly. In 2005 the Union defined the accession negotiations with Ankara and Zagreb as 'an open-ended process, the outcome of which cannot be guaranteed' which was a dramatic change from the previous definitions which highlighted 'the continuous, inclusive and irreversible nature of the enlargement process' (Council of the European Union, 2002, 2004b). Furthermore, the European Council in December 2006, which put a seal of approval on the renewed consensus on enlargement, added another layer of uncertainty by confirming that the Union would 'refrain from setting any target dates for accession until the negotiations are close to completion' (Council of the European Union, 2006a). The new approach towards Turkey and the Western Balkans marked a radical departure from the EU strategy towards CEECs, which were focused on timetables and target dates and contributed to the success of the fifth enlargement.

In addition to removing the credibility of the membership perspective from the available *accession advancement rewards*, the EU further altered the incentive structure by introducing new threats. Whereas, during the fifth enlargement, the Union relied only on *financial sanctions* and *implicit threats* in order to sanction non-compliance with its conditions; the negotiating framework for Turkey and Croatia provided for the suspension of the membership talks, thus introducing for the first time during the negotiation stage *preventive and remedial sanctions*. Furthermore, the partial suspension of negotiations with Turkey, illustrates the EU's determination not only to expand the scope of *explicit threats* but also apply them to sanction non-compliance. The EU has further transformed the nature of the accession process with the introduction of the disequilibrium clauses in the case of Montenegro and Serbia.

The comparative examination of the monitoring during the negotiation stages reveals that the key developments – expansion of the scope and level of detail, provided by the Progress Reports – are identical to the developments during the pre-negotiation stage. Furthermore, the analysis shows the Commission has been even more rigorous in its approach towards the Turkey and the Western Balkan countries. The publication of a separate interim report on Croatia's progress towards addressing the benchmarks of one of the most challenging chapters – Justice and Fundamental Rights highlights the growing intensification and high political relevance of the monitoring process. As the modification of monitoring is characterised by the further development of the trends observed in earlier stages, we can conclude that the evolution of monitoring instruments is a natural progression.

The comparative assessment of the third element of EU enlargement conditionality – monitoring – highlights the continuity in the Commission's approach to evaluating the candidate countries' compliance with EU conditions. The Commission gradually expanded the scope and the functions of the monitoring reports which reflected the Union's ambition to facilitate and improve the quality of the accession negotiations. The annual publication of the Regular Reports swiftly became a very important date in the political calendars of politicians in the candidate countries and the Commission was quick to transform the reports from technocratic assessment tools into an instrument for applying political pressure.

The comparative study of the negotiation conditionality, on the basis of the *stage-structured conditionality model* (see Table 5.2), highlights evolutionary developments, which are similar to the changes observed during the pre-negotiation stage. We can outline the growing list of EU demands, however, it should be noted that the expansion of the *acquis* is not the sole reason for the increase in the number of negotiation chapters. The Union further emphasised the significance of the Copenhagen political criteria by devising a new chapter aimed at enhancing the compliance of the candidate countries with the Copenhagen political criteria. In addition to expanding and elaborating on scope of the conditions, the EU followed a highly differentiated approach by introducing lists of country-specific conditions for the advancement of the membership talks with Croatia, Turkey, Montenegro and Serbia.

Table 5.2 Evolution of negotiation conditionality

Elements of EU enlargement conditionality	Fifth enlargement: first phase (2004)	Fifth enlargement: second phase (2007)	Sixth enlargement: HR (2013)	Ongoing enlargement with TU,FY,ME,RS,AL
I. Conditions				
– Copenhagen criteria	✓	✓	✓	✓
– Opening benchmarks	–	–	✓	✓
– Interim benchmarks	–	–	–	✓
– Closing benchmarks	✓	✓	✓	✓
II. Incentive structure				
1. Rewards				
1.1. Accession advancement rewards				
– Opening chapters	✓	✓	✓	✓
– Closing chapters	✓	✓	✓	✓
– Credible membership perspective	✓	✓	–	–
– Completing accession negotiations	✓	✓	✓	✓
– Signing Accession Treaty				
1.2. Financial rewards	✓	✓	✓	✓
2. Threats				
2.1. Explicit threats				
– Financial sanctions	✓	✓	✓	✓
– Preventive and remedial sanctions	–	–	✓	✓
2.2. Implicit threats	✓	✓	✓	✓
III. Monitoring				
– Progress/regular reports	✓	✓	✓	✓
– Interim report	–	–	✓	NA

The transformation of the incentive structure mimicked developments from the pre-negotiation stage. The alteration in the *reward–threat balance*, which respectively led to a shift away from strong positive was a product of two simultaneous trends: taking away one of the most attractive *accession advancement rewards* – the credibility of the membership perspective – and introducing *preventive and remedial sanctions*. The EU introduced only a tiny cosmetic change to the structure of the Regular Reports by publishing the conclusions in a separate document. Furthermore, the Union intensified the monitoring by publishing an additional interim report, which provided a detailed examination of Croatia's compliance with Chapter 23, and provided the basis for the completion of the accession negotiations and additional report for FYROM.

The comparative study of the developments during the negotiation stage confirms that EU enlargement conditionality is characterised by the increasing application of differentiated and targeted conditionality. Furthermore, the Union expanded the scope of the conditions by introducing new chapters and put a very strong emphasis on the track-record of implementation. However, whilst, extending the range of demanding requirements, the EU weakened the incentive structure thus making the successful completion of the negotiation stage a much more challenging endeavour for the ongoing enlargement with the Western Balkans and Turkey than it used to be for the CEECs and the two Mediterranean islands.

Accession stage

The section investigates the evolution of EU enlargement conditionality during the accession stage which refers to the period after the completion of the membership talks and before the formal accession of a country to the Union. As Turkey, Montenegro and Serbia have not completed the accession stage, the analysis is limited to first and the second wave of the fifth enlargement and the sixth enlargement with Croatia and focuses on the significance of individual country-specific benchmarks; the introduction of unprecedented 'super-safeguard' clauses and their implications for the *reward–threat balance*; and the intensification of the monitoring process.

Following the completion of the membership talks, the would-be member states are expected to finalise their preparations and meet all the Copenhagen criteria. However, it was during the accession stage that the EU moved away from its uniform approach to setting out conditions and provided the 'Laeken Ten' with a list of individual country-specific benchmarks. Although this remained the only time that the EU applied differentiated and targeted conditionality towards the countries from the first phase of the Eastern enlargement, the new approach became very pronounced in the Union's strategy towards Bulgaria and Romania. In the span of 12 months (September 2005–September 2006), the Commission prepared three sets of individual benchmarks, which Sofia and Bucharest were urged to address immediately, thus making differentiation a prominent feature of EU conditionality during the accession stage. It should be noted that the requirements for Croatia were characterised by a much higher level of detail and were aimed at three particularly challenging areas: the judiciary and fundamental rights; freedom, security and justice, and competition policy.

The findings reveal the remarkable transformation of the accession incentive structure, which have significant consequences for both dimensions of the evolution of EU enlargement conditionality: across the stages of the process and between different groups of candidate countries. The completion of the membership talks is a crucial turning point, which marks the beginning of the end of the European journeys of the applicant states. However, as the advancement of the accession process is inherently bound to 'strip' the Union of its *accession advancement rewards*, the finalisation of the negotiations limits significantly the range of the available rewards. Furthermore, the EU extended the application of *explicit threats* by introducing *preventive and remedial sanctions* in the form of safeguard measures. The combined effect of both trends (less *accession advancement rewards* compensated by more *explicit threats*) significantly altered the *reward–threat balance* during the accession stage and produced a negative incentive structure.

The Union sent shockwaves through the governments in Sofia and Bucharest by establishing the 'super' safeguard clause, which allowed for the postponement of the accession of either country by one year. However, in another unprecedented move, the Union tightened even further the screws on Romania by introducing the possibility of invoking the clause by a qualified majority vote in the Council in the case of serious shortcomings in the fulfilment of additional 11 requirements, specified in the Accession Treaty. Thus, the EU not only extended the scope of the *explicit threats* but also applied for the first time a highly differentiated approach to setting up the incentive structure by introducing stricter additional *preventive or remedial sanctions* for Bucharest. However, the Union did not follow the same approach in the case of

Croatia. Although the Accession Treaty provided for the application of corrective measures, it did not include a postponement clause. These developments suggest that the super safeguard clause was an ad hoc solution.

The study confirms that the third element of EU enlargement conditionality – monitoring – also underwent important changes. After the completion of the accession negotiations, the Union not only expanded but also intensified the monitoring instrument by preparing very detailed comprehensive monitoring reports which reflected on the progress of the candidates towards meeting all the criteria and included separate sections on the progress towards meeting the commitments agreed in the negotiation chapters. In addition to providing a basis for the Commission's recommendations regarding the advancement of the accession process, the reports introduced new conditions and threats. This trend became very noticeable in the case of Bulgaria and Romania, as well as Croatia.

As illustrated by Table 5.3, EU accession conditionality underwent a series of important evolutionary developments. Whereas, the application of differentiated conditionality was a novel development in the case of the CEECs, Cyprus and Malta, its transformation, particularly along the lines of more clarification and greater details in the case of Bulgaria, Romania, firmly established those elements as essential characteristics of EU enlargement conditionality. The Union followed a much more targeted and detailed approach in the case of Croatia.

Although it is difficult to pinpoint the single most significant change during the accession stage, the evolution of the incentive structure is probably the most striking one. Whereas, the alternation in the *reward–threat balance* which signified a marked shift from the positive incentive structures of the pre-negotiation and negotiation stage is most of all dictated by the intrinsic logic of the enlargement process. Furthermore, the high level of differentiation between Bulgaria and Romania is also an indication of the fluid and constantly changing nature of EU enlargement conditionality. The study also underlines the hike in the relevance of the monitoring for the successful completion of the accession process, which is reflected by the important developments in the range, scope, frequency and functionality of the monitoring reports. The evolution of the reports from assessment tools into instruments for continuous political pressure provides

Table 5.3 Evolution of accession conditionality

Elements of EU enlargement conditionality	Fifth enlargement: first phase (2004)	Fifth enlargement: second phase (2007)	Sixth enlargement: HR (2013)
I. Conditions			
– Copenhagen criteria	✓	✓	✓
– Areas of serious concern	✓	✓	✓
II. Incentive structure			
1. Rewards			
1.1. Accession advancement rewards			
– Treaty ratification	✓	✓	✓
– Accession	✓	✓	✓
1.2. Financial rewards	✓	✓	✓
2. Threats			
2.1. Explicit threats:			
– Financial sanctions	✓	✓	✓
– Preventive and remedial sanctions:			
• Internal market safeguard clause	✓	✓	✓
• JHA safeguard clause	✓	✓	✓
• Super safeguard clause	–	✓	–
2.2. Implicit threats			
III. Monitoring			
– Progress/regular reports	✓	✓	✓

more evidence for the growing application of targeted and differentiated conditionality.

Post-accession stage

The section discusses the evolution of EU enlargement conditionality during the post-accession stage. As specified by the *stage-structured conditionality model*, it starts with the accession of a state to the Union and ends with the suspension of any post-accession mechanism or, in the absence of any post-accession monitoring mechanism, with the expiry of the application of the safeguard measures included in the Accession Treaty. As the changes during the first stage of the fifth enlargement and the sixth enlargement with Croatia affected only the incentive structure, the analysis focuses predominantly on developments of the EU's approach towards Bulgaria and Romania, characterised by the growing significance of benchmarking; the alternations in the *reward–threat balance*; and the multi-purpose instrumentalisation of the monitoring.

The introduction of the CVM, providing for individual country-specific benchmarks which Bulgaria and Romania had to address after their accession to the Union, set a remarkable precedent in the history of the EU. Although the approach towards establishing the requirements followed the trajectories which previously emerged in the earlier stages: towards more differentiated, targeted and detailed conditionality, it was the period of application of the new instrument which made it uniquely distinct. The mechanism effectively singled out the two Balkan members of the Union by subjecting them to exclusive scrupulous monitoring of the progress in the particularly demanding areas of judicial reform and the fight against corruption and organised crime. Furthermore, the EU has continuously redefined and elaborated on the scope of the benchmarks by breaking them down into lists of tasks (see European Commission, 2009f, 2009g, 2010h, 2010i, 2011d, 2011e, 2014c, 2014d). Thus the developments during the post-accession stage highlight not only the growing interrelation between differentiation and targeting but also the very high level of specification of EU conditions.

The comparative analysis also illuminates the exceptional transformation of the incentive structure between the first and the second phase of the Eastern expansion. As the accession of the new member state to the Union marks the official completion of the enlargement process, the EU is not only 'stripped' of its of its strongest 'tool' for inducing compliance – the membership perspective – but also of all of the *accession advancement rewards*. Therefore, the first significant change in the

reward–threat balance (in comparison to the earlier stages of the accession process) is that the rewards provided by the Union for compliance
with its conditions are limited to *financial rewards*. These changes also
affect the second element of the incentive structure – as the *implicit
threats*, which are also no longer available; the EU relies exclusively
on *explicit threats* to induce compliance with its conditions. Although
both Accession Treaties (in 2003 and 2005) set the parameters of the
post-accession *preventive and remedial sanctions*, which the Union can
apply in order to punish the new member states, by introducing three
safeguard clauses,[3] the establishment of the CVM for an unspecified
period of time significantly expanded the scope of the *explicit threats*.
Furthermore, the implication of the unorthodox monitoring mechanism extended beyond the areas it was designed for. Despite the lack
of formal links between the requirements of CVM and the Schengen criteria, the Netherlands and Finland blocked the accession of Bulgaria and
Romania to the border-free area on the grounds of insufficient progress
in the fight against corruption and organised crime.

The book also highlights the far-reaching transformation of the monitoring instruments. As previously mentioned the EU's decision to monitor both Balkan states after their accession to the Union set an important
precedent. However, the unusual but also controversial time frame of
the application of the CVM was not the only striking development.
It should be noted that, in contrast to the early stages of the enlargement
process during which the Commission prepares reports on an annual
basis, the post-accession period is characterised by the remarkable intensification of the monitoring, which is reflected by the number of reports
as well as the level of detail. The Commission is expected to assess the
progress of Sofia and Bucharest 'at least every six months'; and has so far
prepared 14 sets of reports (European Commission, 2006b, 2006c). Furthermore, it has developed an array of additional instruments such as
technical updates, thus dramatically enhancing the level of detail of its
assessments. Most of all, the post-accession progress reports best capture
the unique evolution of monitoring because in addition to illustrating
the increasing frequency and breadth of the assessments, they exem-
plify the growing multi-functionality of the monitoring instruments.
Whereas in the early stages of the process the sole purpose of monitoring
was to evaluate progress, the CVM shows that reports can also establish
conditions and threats but more importantly have become a significant
factor in EU enlargement policy, which in turn has transformed them
from an assessment tool into an instrument for continuous political
pressure.

Table 5.4 Evolution of post-accession conditionality

Elements of EU enlargement conditionality	Fifth enlargement: first phase (2004)	Fifth enlargement: second phase (2007)	Sixth enlargement: HR (2013)
I. Conditions			
– Individual country-specific benchmarks	–	✓	–
II. Incentive structure			
1. Rewards			
1.1. Accession advancement rewards	–	–	–
1.2. Financial rewards	✓	✓	✓
2. Threats			
2.1. Explicit threats			
– Financial sanctions	✓	✓	✓
– Preventive and remedial sanctions	✓	✓	✓
• Economic safeguard clause	✓	✓	✓
• Internal market safeguard clause	✓	✓	✓
• JHA safeguard clause	✓	✓	–
2.2. Implicit threats			
III. Monitoring			
– Progress reports	–	✓	–
– Interim reports	–	✓	–
– Technical updates	–	✓	–
– Fund management reports	–	✓	–

The comparative examination of the post-accession conditionality (see Table 5.4) outlines a number of unique developments and provides further evidence for its evolutionary nature. The EU not only extended the application of differentiated and targeted conditionality after accession but also elaborated on the scope of the requirements by introducing three lists of individual country-specific tasks. The analysis of the incentive structure confirms the trend, noted during the accession stage, that the *reward–threat balance* is dominated by *explicit threats* and therefore the EU relies on negative conditionality to induce compliance with its conditions. However, the introduction of the scrupulous monitoring mechanism has had much more tangible implications for Bulgaria and Romania than the three safeguard clauses had for the ten countries which joined in 2004. The publication of the CVM reports has not only significantly damaged the reputation of the two Balkan countries, which as pointed out by most of the interviewees would take a long time to be restored, it has also compromised their accession to the Schengen area. However, the developments during the post-accession stage have much more widespread effects on EU enlargement conditionality. The Commission confirmed that the early focus on sensitive issues such as judicial reform, the fight against crime and corruption and the rigorous monitoring of the candidate and potential candidate countries, were based on its previous experiences from the fifth enlargement.

Conclusions

The comparative study of the evolution of EU enlargement conditionality across the stages of the accession process between three groups of case studies illustartes the key developments which have become firmly integrated into EU enlargement policy. It also allows us to reflect on distinctly pronounced trends such as the increasing application of differentiated, targeted and detailed conditionality.

The research shows that the EU gradually expanded and elaborated on the scope of the conditions. Furthermore, the early stages of the accession process are characterised by a high degree of uniformity. The EU confirmed that Europeanness and respect for the values on which the Union is based, constitute the core of the *conditions for applying for membership*. In a similar manner, the EU made the Copenhagen criteria, initially designed for the CEECs, universally applicable to any potential or candidate country. The EU took another step to uniformity by firmly cementing the priority of the Copenhagen political criteria by confirming its status as a *condition for opening accession negotiations*.

However, the comparative investigation demonstartes that with the advancement of the accession process, the scope of the conditions with which the candidate country needs to comply became increasing heterogeneous. Although initially viewed as an exception (particularly in the case of Bulgaria and Romania), this approach has become fully integrated into the enlargement strategy of the Union; and has been particularly pronounced during the ongoing enlargement round. In addition to extending the scopes of the individual country-specific conditions, the EU gradually shifted the focus towards establishing particular targets rather than codifying broad lists of requirements. Bulgaria's and Romania's post-accession experience exemplifies the high degree of interconnection between differentiated and targeted conditionality. These developments are also complemented by the increasing level of detail and specification of EU conditions as evidenced by Croatia's accession and the ongoing enlargement with Turkey and the Western Balkans. Although these trends originated at different stages of the process for the three groups of enlargement applicants, their consistent application (towards all groups of candidate and potential candidate countries) makes them essential characteristics of EU enlargement conditionality. Another development which the Union has now fully integrated into its enlargement strategy is the gradual expansion of the list of requirements which the candidate and potential candidate need to satisfy during the early stages of the process thus making the pre-negotiation and negotiation stage much more challenging for Montenegro, Serbia, FYROM, Bosnia and Herzegovina, Albania, Kosovo and Turkey than they used to be for the countries of the fifth enlargement round. Furthermore, the findings demonstrate an important progression in the EU demands: from the adoption of the *acquis* and the alignment with the Union's policies to ensuring the sustainability of the reforms through credible track records of implementation.

The study confirms the emergence of consistent patterns in the development of the incentive structure. Although the research findings unequivocally support the relevance of the stages of the accession process for the transformations of each of the key elements of EU enlargement conditionality, they seem to be highly significant for the evolution of the incentive structure. This trend is largely a product of the inherent logic of EU enlargement. The advancement of the accession process limits significantly the range of the *accession advancement rewards* which the Union can use in order to induce compliance with its conditions. The completion of the accession negotiations 'strips' the Union of almost all of its *accession advancement rewards* and negates the *reward–threat balance*, which marks the shift from positive to negative incentive structure.

In addition to outlining the broad categories of conditionality, the *stage-structured conditionality model* allows for a more nuanced analysis. The recent developments towards Turkey and the Western Balkans are characterised by two trends: less *accession advancement rewards* and more *explicit threats*. Although the incentive structure during the early stages is still dominated by a range of accession advancement rewards, the EU has decisively removed one of its most powerful and desired rewards – the credibility of the membership perspective by refusing to make any commitments to timetables or target dates. The Union has also introduced and applied a number of *explicit threats* (which in the case of the fifth enlargement were only applicable to the accession and pre-accession stage). The combined effect of these new trends has reduced the positivity of the incentive structure.

The comparative examination of third element of EU conditionality – monitoring – also highlights the emergence of interrelated trends. Since the publication of the Commission's opinions on membership applications of the CEECs in 1997, the EU has dramatically intensified the monitoring process. Simultaneously, the Commission has gradually expanded the scope of the monitoring reports but more importantly it skilfully elaborated on their functions, thus transforming them from assessment tools into instruments for applying political pressure.

Explaining the evolution of EU enlargement conditionality

With a view to analysing the evolution of EU enlargement conditionality, the book specifies that *EU enlargement policy is a function of differentiated influences from multiple actors and external pressures*. The definition highlights the complex constellations of actors involved in the accession process and emphasises their relevance by focusing on the influence which they can exert rather than their competences. Although the book stresses the leading role of the main EU institutions, it delves deeper into policy dynamics by analysing key policy developments with reference to the following factors: (1) *EU member states*, (2) *EU inter-institutional dynamic*, (3) *public opinion in the EU*, (4) *enlargement countries* and (5) *external pressures caused by economic or security shocks and crises*.

EU member states

This section discusses the impact of the Council of the EU on the development of EU enlargement conditionality by looking into the influence of individual member states. Although it acknowledges the scope of the competences of the Council, the research is concerned with examining more subtle channels for applying political pressure and focuses on two key aspects:

- the impact of member states' preferences for the advancement of the accession process; and
- the implications of bilateral issues between member states and candidate countries.

The high relevance of member states for the accession process is based on the fact that enlargement policy requires unanimity, which gives each member state the veto powers to block any step on the long road to accession. Consequently, member states influence the incentive structure through their exclusive control over the granting of the *accession advancement rewards*. However, as the Union has fostered a culture of decision-making, based on compromise, the failure to reach a consensus usually leads to the postponement of the decision, whereas the use of veto power is applied as a last resort. In contrast to reflecting on vetoed decisions on EU enlargement, analysing the channels though which a member state can improve the incentive structure and accelerate the advancement of the accession process is more demanding (not least due to the fact that the Union has not established any such formal procedures). In order to examine the intensity and the direction of the influence applied by the member states on EU enlargement conditionality, the analysis drew heavily on the information gathered from extensive interviews with high-ranking EU and national officials and news articles.

The comparative analysis across the three groups of case studies confirms that member states can successfully channel political attitudes into political influence. There is a virtual agreement among the interviewees that relationship between member states and candidate countries matter for the development of EU enlargement policy. EU and national official acknowledged the importance of good and particularly strong relationships for the advancement of the accession process and highlighted the high relevance of patronage by reflecting on: Germany's strong and continuous support for Poland; Greece's sponsorship for the accession of Cyprus; the strong push from the Scandinavian countries for the Baltic States. Although their efforts were directed at improving the incentive structure by securing the granting of the *accession advancement rewards*, member states used a variety of strategies to channel political pressure: from lobbying for the start the start of accession negotiations with a candidate country (Finland, Sweden, Denmark) to advocating inclusive screening process (Denmark, Sweden) and threatening to block the fifth enlargement round (Greece).

The ongoing enlargement round confirms that member states' opposition to the accession of a candidate country is undoubtedly worse than the absence of proactive supporters. Although such developments are rare, the emergence of strong anti-Turkey sentiments in some member states shows that they can have tangible implications for the accession process. Austria's opposition to opening accession negotiations with Ankara led to a compromise which transformed the membership talks into 'an open-ended process, the outcome of which cannot be guaranteed in advance' thus inevitably eroding the credibility and irreversibility of the process (Council of the European Union, 2004b). However, other member states also voiced their reservations: France and Germany called for offering Ankara privileged membership. EU and national officials acknowledged the negative impact of the proposal, even Commissioner Rehn addressed the issue and warned that that 'those who talked continuously about privileged partnership are creating a vicious circle of reversed commitment, weakened conditionality and stalled reforms' (Rehn, 2006b). Nevertheless, France did not hesitate to translate rhetoric into action, in an unprecedented move, Paris blocked the opening of the five negotiation chapters with Ankara on the grounds that negotiations on Chapters: 11, 17, 22, 33 and 34 assume the accession of the country.

Turkey's European journey shows that negative attitudes can have serious implications for the advancement of the accession process. However, it should be noted that that even the most outspoken opponents refrained from using their veto power to break off the accession negotiations with Ankara and used different strategies to channel political pressure: from weakening the credibility of the membership perspective to blocking the opening of negotiation chapters.

In addition to analysing the implications of the member states' preferences, the comparative study allows us to look into to the effects of another essential feature of the relations between member states and candidate countries – bilateral issues. The fifth enlargement of the Union was not free from bilateral problems, but they did not derail the accession process. Nevertheless, some of the interviewees noted that two issues – the disputes over the Beneš decrees between the Czech Republic and Germany, Austria and Hungary; and the Czech-Austrian row over Temelín nuclear power plant – put a severe strain on the accession negotiations. Despite tensions running high on both sides (particularly Prague and Vienna), the problems were resolved without any tangible implications for the completion of the enlargement round.

In stark contrast, the damaging consequences of the unresolved disputes on the European journeys of Ankara, Zagreb and Skopje confirm that bilateral issues can compromise significantly the advancement of the accession process. There is a virtual agreement among the interviewees that the complications caused by bilateral problems in the current enlargement round with Turkey and the Western Balkans are of an unprecedented scale.

The analysis confirms that blocking the granting of the *accession advancement rewards* is a common strategy for applying political pressure. Greece blocked the implementation of the second phase of the SAA agreement with FYORM and put the decision for the start of the accession negotiations on hold. Cyprus hindered the opening of several negotiation chapters with Turkey. Slovenia blocked the accession negotiations with Croatia for almost 12 months. However, the impact of member states is not confined to altering the balance of the incentive structure, as most of the member states trapped in bilateral disputes tried to advance their position through engineering the scope of EU conditions. Austria was keen to make the conclusions following the argument over Temelín nuclear plant an essential part of the conditions for the conclusion of the accession negotiations on the energy chapter but also insisted on their incorporation in the Accession Treaty. Similarly, both Greece and Slovenia tried to favour their positions, respectively prior to the start of the accession negotiations with Turkey and during the escalation of the border dispute with Croatia. Although the EU did not include the resolution of the name issues between FYROM and Greece as a formal condition for the advancement of the accession process with Skopje, it confirmed that it was 'essential' (Council of the European Union, 2014).

The EU's response to the unresolved disputes between candidate countries and member states provides even more evidence for their increasingly damaging impact on the accession process. The Commission not only did acknowledge that 'Bilateral questions, including border issues, are increasingly affecting the enlargement process' but also became actively involved in the border issue between Croatia and Slovenia through providing its facilitation services (European Commission, 2009d). The latest EU enlargement strategy further highlights the relevance of bilateral issues and urges that they 'should be tackled as early as possible and not hold up the accession process'; as 'blockages linked to bilateral issues can compromise the transformative power of the enlargement process' (European Commission, 2011b).

The discussion of the responsibilities of the Council confirms that decisions regarding the granting of the *accession advancement rewards* lie with the member states. However, the study reveals that the influence of the member states on the accession process is not confined to their veto powers during the accession process. The analysis shows that member states' preferences are highly relevant for EU enlargement conditionality as strong support improves the incentive structure by securing the granting of the *accession advancement rewards*, whereas strong opposition to a candidate country negates the incentive structure. The research also highlights the growing relevance of outstanding bilateral issues between member states and candidate countries for EU enlargement. The recent developments during the ongoing enlargement round illustrate their full potential to severely disrupt the dynamics of the accession process by blocking partially or completely its advancement. Furthermore, the strong comparative dimension of the book shows that most of the member states have proactively shaped the development of the enlargement policy and that the policy it is not under the control of a few.

Inter-institutional dynamics

This section reviews the impact of institutional factors on the evolution of EU enlargement conditionality. It complements the analysis of the influence on member states by discussing the complexity of the inter-institutional dynamics of the Union. Although the Council of the EU is ultimately responsible for the advancement of the accession process, it is not the only EU institution which can influence the enlargement process, as the Commission, the EP and the Presidency of the EU can also engineer policy changes. The analysis acknowledges the leading role of the Council in decision-making but focuses predominantly on the development brought about by the Commission and the Parliament.

The review of the competences of the Council, on the basis of the *stage-structured conditionality model*, shows variations in the relevance of its influence on the different elements of EU enlargement conditionality. As all decisions – from confirming the membership perspective of the applicant state to signing the Accession Treaty – require a unanimous decision, we can conclude that the role of the Council is essential for the second element of EU enlargement conditionality – the incentive structure. Similarly, the model confirms the pertinence of the Council for another element – EU conditions – as it decides on, but also elaborates and amends their scope. Although some of the member states might rely on their own sources to monitor candidate countries' compliance, the Council does not prepare any monitoring reports, therefore, it cannot directly influence the third element – monitoring.

The analysis of the Presidency of the Council of the EU also referred to as the Presidency of the EU complements the examination of the role of the Council and gives more insight into the complex inter-institutional dynamics of the Union. Although the presidency is considered to be on the margins of policy-making, as its main responsibilities include agenda-setting and policy co-ordination, its position is crucial for mediating inter-institutional bargaining and brokering compromise between member states. There was a virtual agreement among the members of the working group on enlargement that the presidencies' monopoly over the agenda has significant implications for the advancement of the accession process. The vast majority of the interviewees noted the amazing job done by the Swedish presidency in 2001 for boosting the accession negotiations with the 12 candidate countries, which is also reflected by the number of the chapters opened and provisionally closed. However, most national officials also acknowledged that the influence of the Presidency is constrained by the member states' preferences and pointed out that despite its strong support and ambitious agenda for the development of the enlargement process, the Czech presidency managed to achieve only very moderate success.

Despite the fact that power is primarily concentrated in the Council, the Commission has firmly cemented its role as a driving force for the development of EU enlargement policy through its active leadership in policy initiation, formulation and coordination. In order to highlight the increasing relevance and growing influence of the Commission, the study analyses its impact on four landmark developments: the Luxembourg European Council conclusions which launched the historical enlargement process with the CEECs; the Helsinki European

Council U-turn; the establishment of the CVM – the unprecedented post-accession monitoring mechanism for Bulgaria and Romania; the introduction of the renewed consensus on enlargement and the New approach to the accession negotiations.

The decision of the Luxembourg European Council to launch accession negotiations with the Czech Republic, Estonia, Hungary, Poland, Slovenia and Cyprus, signified a highly significant step not only for the development of Union but also for the role of the Commission in the accession process. The Commission's recommendations for the start of the membership talks with only six of the applicant states provoked very strong reactions among the member states and the CEECs. Despite the heated debates and strong pressure from most of the member states, the Council unanimously agreed to follow the Commission's proposal.

Two years later, the Commission played a crucial role in another landmark decision of the Union – the opening of the accession negotiations with all candidate countries fulfilling the Copenhagen political criteria. Although this development confirmed by the Helsinki European Council cannot be attributed to a single factor, the analysis confirms the leading position of the new Commission, which for the first time had a Commissioner for enlargement and respectively a separate DG for managing and engineering the key modalities of the enlargement process.

The completion of the 2004 enlargement did not lead to a decrease in the Commission's activism; on the contrary, it continued to actively engineer new policy developments, as evidenced by the introduction of the unprecedented special post-accession monitoring mechanism for Sofia and Bucharest. The unique nature of the CVM highlights the leading role of the Commission not only in finding workable solutions, but also in shaping the enlargement policy of the Union even after the accession of the EU hopefuls.

The renewed consensus on enlargement and the New Approach to the accession negotiations provide more evidence for the strong influence of the Commission and confirms the evolutionary nature of EU enlargement conditionality. Although some EU officials noted that the new approach was more technocratic than the previous strategies, others commented that its rigidity was aimed at boosting the position of the Commission vis-à-vis an increasing enlargement-lukewarm Council.

The analysis illustrates that the Commission has skilfully navigated the course of the development of the enlargement process and policy through influencing the decisions of the Council but also through active policy initiation and formulation. The Commission has also played a key role in monitoring the compliance with EU conditions and transformed the reports from assessment tools into instruments for political pressure. Furthermore, it has managed to successfully balance demanding responsibilities; earned the trust of both – member states and applicants – and firmly established its position as the dominant policy driver.

The findings show that the EP can also exert strong influence on the advancement of the accession process despite its limited competences in the area of enlargement policy. Its main official role is to give assent to the Accession Treaty before it can be signed and ratified, but the Parliament is also involved in the process through its powers over the EU budgetary process and its monitoring responsibilities. The analysis outlines two instances of strong Parliamentary activism which revealed its potential to shape the development of the enlargement policy. The EP played a crucial role in the establishment of the target date for the first phase of the Eastern expansion, as it continuously urged the EU institutions, member states and candidate countries to 'do everything in their power' to ensure that the accession would allow the new member states to participate in the European Parliament elections in 2004 (European Parliament, 2000).

In addition to altering the incentive structure by galvanising support for setting timetables and target dates, the EP showed that it could increase its influence over the advancement of accession through its monitoring responsibilities. Although the Regular and Progress Reports published by the Commission provide the basis for the decisions of the Council, the 2004 Monitoring report prepared by the EP rapporteur on Romania – Baroness Emma Nicholson – revealed that the Parliament could disrupt the accession process. Baroness Nicholson heavily criticised Bucharest and asked for the suspension of the accession negotiations. Although the Union did not freeze the membership talks, the report had a tangible effect on the relationship between the Balkan state and the Union. Furthermore, it emphasised the importance of the judiciary reform and showcased the growing potential of the EP to shape the Union's most successful foreign policy.

The comparative study of the inter-institutional dynamics of the EU and its implications for the development of EU enlargement policy shows that the influence of the main EU institutions – the Council of the EU, the Commission and the EP – is not a direct function of their competences and responsibilities. The examination acknowledges the leading role of the Council in decision-making. However, it also illustrates the increasing relevance and growing influence of the Commission, which has established itself as the dominant driving force behind the evolution of the policy. Furthermore, the research confirms that the Parliament, which is the least powerful of the three main institutions with regard to enlargement, can nonetheless successfully channel political pressure and shape significantly the advancement of the accession process. The book shows that both the Commission and the EP have expanded their influence over the development of enlargement policy, but this has not diminished the position of the Council in the inter-institutional dynamics. In addition to highlighting the unquestioned relevance of the Presidents of the Commission, the Commissioners for enlargement, EP rapporteurs for the development of EU enlargement policy, the analysis also acknowledges the influence of the individual EU and national officials.

Public opinion

The comparative investigation of public opinion across the three groups of case studies draws heavily on the Standard Eurobarometer surveys, which were published in the period between 1990 and 2014. The impressive scope of the data from the 24-year period allows us to conclusively identify three key trends and reflect on their relevance and implication for the development of EU enlargement policy:

- Public support for enlargement depended on which country the respondents come from;
- Public attitudes towards enlargement depended on the candidate country in question; and
- Average levels of support for EU enlargement used to be relatively consistent, but since 2011 support for further enlargement has decreased.

The comparative examination of public opinion confirms that the support for enlargement varied and varied greatly depending on which country the respondents come from. In some of the member states, particularly in Sweden, Denmark and Greece (before 2005); and Poland, Latvia and Romania (after 2005), attitudes towards enlargement were quite favourable and support was generally above the EU average. In other countries like France and Austria, anti-enlargement sentiments have been very strong and the levels of support – consistently below the EU average. Although the support for EU enlargement varied over time, it is evident that the public opinion in the countries which joined the Union in 2004, 2007 and 2013 was more enthusiastic about further enlargement.

Secondly, attitudes towards enlargement varied also depending on the candidate country in question. In the run up to the completion of the fifth enlargement, support was consistently highest for Malta, Hungary and Poland, whereas Slovenia and Romania were the least supported candidates in the group of 12. However, other candidate countries – such as Slovakia, Estonia, Latvia, Bulgaria and Lithuania – also did not manage to secure the approval of the EU public all the time (see Appendix IV). Although attitudes towards the 12 candidates changed over time, most of the variations were within ±5%. The preferences of the EU citizens were much more varied with reference to Turkey and the Western Balkans. Although public opinion in the EU was initially opposed to the accession of all three countries, there was a significant shift in the attitudes towards Croatia and since 2005 the trend has been reversed, whereas the opposition to Turkey's membership has increased. The EU citizens in favour of the accession of Serbia, Montenegro, Bosnia and Herzegovina, Albania, Kosovo and Turkey were always outnumbered by those against their membership.

The comparative study of the public opinion also confirms that the average support for EU enlargement has never been particularly high. As illustrated by Appendix III it has remained relatively steady around 40%. It peaked twice above 50% in period between the autumn 2001 and autumn 2002 and in the autumn of 2004. However, since 2011 support for further expansions has plummeted, whereas anti-enlargement sentiments have become very prominent not only in EU15.

The analysis of the developments of EU conditionality confirms that public opinion did not have any substantial positive or negative effect on the fifth enlargement. The levels of support did not reflect the conclusions of the Luxembourg European Council, which established two groups of candidate countries ('ins' and 'pre-ins'). Furthermore, neither declining support, nor growing opposition to some of the candidate countries seemed to have affected the advancement of the accession process; and in particular the EU's decisions with which countries and when to close the accession negotiations and sign an Accession Treaty. Similarly, the low levels of EU public support for Turkey and the countries from the Western Balkans did not compromise the establishment of the membership perspective of the region.

The renewed consensus on enlargement, which provided the basis for the new enlargement strategy of the Commission, insisted that 'It is essential to ensure public support for enlargement' (European Commission, 2006g). However, the more stringent and demanding approach towards Turkey and the Western Balkans cannot be attributed to public attitudes, as the averaged support for enlargement increased and even in the case of the old member states it did not plummet but remained at level similarly to those in the late 1990s.

The vast majority of the interviewees commented on the significance of the 'No' votes on the constitution in France and the Netherlands and identified it as a turning point, which marked the increasing relevance of public opinion for EU policy-making. In addition to the Commission's repeated demands to get the public on board, some of the member states took concrete steps to taking account of public attitudes by empowering their citizens. France amended its constitution to impose an automatic referendum on any accession after Croatia, Austria also promised to hold a referendum on Turkey's accession. While there were speculations that those changes and promises reflect the strong anti-Turkey sentiment in both countries and should not be viewed as a threat to the enlargement process as a whole, the Slovenian referendum on the border arbitration deal with Croatia showed that public opinion has the potential to be a crucial factor in EU enlargement policy. Although a slim majority of 51.5% was in favour, a No vote could have had detrimental impact on Zagreb's membership talks (*Financial Times*, 2010). Some high-ranking Commission officials also speculated in the summer of 2009, prior to the settlement of the border issue, how devastating the consequences of a negative Slovenian referendum on Croatia's accession might be. The evidence points to the growing relevance of support for individual candidate countries, however general support for EU enlargement policy has not affected the advancement of the ongoing enlargement despite the growing opposition to the policy.

The assessment of the impact of public opinion on the development of EU enlargement policy confirms that it was not a decisive factor in the case of the fifth enlargement, as it did not influence any of the decisions of the Union regarding the advancement of the process. However, the recent developments introduced by constitutional amendments (or firm promises for amendments), have not only increased the relevance of public opinion but also empowered the public in some of the member states to determine the outcome of the accession process by approving or rejecting the accession of a country to the Union. Although the findings highlight a significant shift in the pertinence of public opinion for the completion of the process, public attitudes have not had immediate effects on the development of the policy. It is evident that the analysis of this factor alone cannot account for the evolution of EU conditionality.

Enlargement countries

Despite the growing body of literature on the impact on EU enlargement conditionality on candidate and potential candidate countries, the relationship between the profile of the applicant states and the nature of EU conditionality has not been investigated. Although enlargement takes place in an environment of power asymmetry and applicant states have very limited bargaining power in the accession process, they can condition the development of EU enlargement policy. In order to analyse the relationship between the profile of the candidate countries and EU enlargement conditionality, the book focuses on the two aspects:

- the impact of the problematic issues and reform challenges (the applicants need to address) on the scope and range of the EU conditions; and
- the implications of the existence or lack of group dynamics (which is examined with reference to the number of applicant states at the same stage of the accession process) for the development of the incentive structure, particularly with reference to the *accession advancement rewards*.

The comparative study of three groups of candidates over a period of almost 20 years reveals that candidates have significantly influenced the scope of the membership conditions. It is important to acknowledge that there are competing but not mutually excluding explanations for the development of the EU conditions, particularly for the establishment of the Copenhagen criteria. Although some have argued that the conditions were set out in order to protect the achievements of the Union (Smith, 2003), we can also advance the argument that the membership conditions reflect the key challenges which the former communist countries were facing in early 1990s, as all of the CEECs were to deal with major political and economic reforms. The distinct approach of the Commission towards the CEECs and Cyprus, Malta and Turkey, manifested in the preparation of separate enlargement strategies provides further evidence for the relevance of the individual problematic issues and challenging reforms. The 2007 enlargement offers more insights into the relationship between the profile of the candidate countries and the scope and range of the EU conditions.

The introduction of additional country-specific conditions with which Bulgaria and Romania had to comply was not limited to the early stages of the process. By establishing sets of individual benchmarks for Sofia and Bucharest, the CVM highlights not only the evolutionary nature but also the increasing application of differentiated and targeted conditionality. Furthermore, the incorporation of the SAP conditionality in the accession process with the Western Balkan countries and the establishment of additional individual conditions for the opening of the accession negotiations with Turkey, Croatia and FYROM provide more evidence for the EU's increasing differentiating approach. It is evident that the profile of the candidate countries (and more precisely the range of the problematic issues they need to deal with) has a substantial impact on the scope of the EU conditions and it has led to the growing use of differentiated and targeted conditionality.

In order to investigate another channel for influencing the development of EU enlargement, the book looks into the relationship between the existence of lack of group dynamics among the candidate countries and the development of the incentive structure, particularly with reference to the *accession advancement rewards*. The definition of group dynamics is not limited to the number of countries, it is also conditioned by their advancement in the accession process.

The comparative analysis of the fifth enlargement identifies various configurations of groups. Initially, it was the Visegrád three, then they were joined by Bulgaria and Romania in a group of five associate countries; after the Luxembourg European Council, there were – the 'ins' and 'pre-ins'. The Helsinki summit altered the dynamics by establishing one group of 12 negotiating countries, but soon Bulgaria and Romania were separated from the 'Laeken Ten'. The detailed discussions in Chapter 2 and Chapter 3 confirm that the decisions regarding the granting of key *accession advancement rewards* – such as the opening and closing of the accession negotiations were also affected by the existence of group dynamics. Furthermore, EU officials reflected on the relevance of the group dynamics for another accession advancement reward – commitment to a credible membership perspective – and confirmed that although candidate countries continuously asked for target dates, it was their unprecedentedly high number which facilitated the establishment of timetables and target dates. The interviewees also confirmed the link between the decision of the Council to establish 2007 as the target date for the accession of Bulgaria and Romania and the group dynamics established by the 12 negotiating countries. The examination of the ongoing enlargement, which includes small states at different stages of the process, provides more evidence for the relevance of the number of candidate and potential candidate countries and level of advancement of their relations with the Union. In contrast with the fifth enlargement round, the Union acknowledged that there would be 'no enlargement with a large number of countries in the future' and confirmed that it would refrain from setting any target dates (Council of the European Union, 2006a). Commissioner Hahn described the 'the current trend of two-tier enlargement with frontrunners and laggards moving in opposite directions' as a major challenge (European Parliament, 2014b). Nevertheless, there is a virtual agreement among EU and national officials that Turkey is in a group of its own.

The book confirms that although applicant states have a narrow scope for manoeuvring in the accession process, they do indirectly shape the development of EU enlargement policy. The strong comparative dimension of the study reveals that the impact of the profile of the candidate countries (particularly the problematic issues or the deficiencies that they need to address or improve) on the range and scope of EU conditions was not limited to a single enlargement wave. As evidenced by a number of novel developments such as the additional conditions for Bulgaria and Romania, SAP conditionality, the introduction of the CVM, candidate countries have substantially shifted the scope and the range of EU conditions. Furthermore, the study confirms that the existence or the lack of group dynamics influences the incentive structures. Whereas strong group dynamics can accelerate the advancement of the accession process, lack of group dynamics can jeopardise the credibility of the membership perspective with reference to the EU's commitments to target dates. The findings confirm that despite their limited bargaining power in the accession negotiations, candidate countries can exert strong influence on the development of EU enlargement policy which is reflected by the increasing application of differentiated and targeted conditionality.

External pressures

This section contributes the analysis of the external factors shaping the development of EU enlargement conditionality by reflecting on the influence of external pressures caused by economic and security shocks or crises. The examination follows a selective approach and focuses on pivotal events, whose significance for the transformation of Europe is undeniable: the end of the Cold War, the Yugoslav wars, and the Eurozone crisis. Thus, the selection allows us to concentrate and draw conclusions on the relevance and the implications of two broad themes: security and economic threats to the stability and integrity of the Union.

Although the EU has developed a unique and complex system of its own which provides multiple arenas for interaction between different constellations of actors, it also operates within the boundaries of bigger international systems, therefore, it is not surprising that the Union is not immune to external shocks. The findings highlight a significant variation in their impact on the internal dynamic of the EU. In addition to the variation in the intensity of the impact, the comparative analysis illustrates a variation in the direction of the impact and reveals two consistent patterns:

- security shocks and crises have a catalysing effect on the development of EU enlargement conditionality
- economic shocks and crises have a decelerating effect on the development of EU enlargement conditionality

Despite the negative connotations attributed to political developments which pose security threats, the study confirms that their impact on EU enlargement was positive. They were highly relevant for the development of the policy. More importantly, they acted as catalysts for the initiation and the advancement of the Union's enlargement policy.

The consequences of the end of the Cold War, which prompted the emergence of new political landscape, were neither limited to the European continent nor to one single policy dimension. However, as the end of the bipolar rivalry inevitably raised serious security concerns we can include it under the security shocks/crises category. The study confirms that the end of the Cold War was one of the key factors which contributed immensely to the EU's crucial decision to establish accession of the former communist states as a shared objective, which marked the beginning of a new approach to the EU's enlargement policy. Similarly, the Yugoslav conflicts had a significant impact on the development of the policy and lent momentum to the advancement of the accession process.

The Commission underlined 'the dramatic changes in the European political landscape, mainly as a consequence of the crises in the Balkan region' as its principal motivation for redefining the scope of the *conditions for opening accession negotiations* and recommending the start of the membership talks with all of the candidate countries which met the Copenhagen political criteria (European Commission, 1999). Although the Kosovo crisis had wider implications for Bulgaria and Romania (as immediate neighbours), the vast majority of the interviewees agreed that it influenced the EU decision to launch membership talks with Sofia and Bucharest but noted that the conflict was not the sole or the most important factors which affected the Union's approach. By contrast, there was a virtual agreement that the EU's engagement with the Western Balkans, initially in the framework of the Regional approach and subsequently the introduction of SAP was a direct response to the devastating Yugoslav conflicts. Furthermore, they highlighted the strong link between the EU's determination to overcome the legacies of the Balkans' troubled past and the establishment of the membership perspective of the region.

The Russia–Georgia crisis in August 2008 provides more evidence for the catalysing effect of security shocks. Although the conflict had much more tangible implications for the developments of the EU neighbourhood policy and led to the introduction of a new instrument – the Eastern Partnership. The conflict also highlighted the strategic importance of Ankara and the need to draw Turkey closer to the European family. Furthermore, some of the interviewees also reflected on the mobilising impact of a potential security threat by speculating that another crisis in the Western Balkans was highly likely to dramatically intensify the EU's engagement with the region.

The discussion of the economic crises is limited to the examination of the Eurozone crisis which emerged in 2009. However, its persistence and damaging effect on the EU economy made it a dominant factor, shaping national and international politics. The impact of the crisis has not been constrained to the stability of the euro zone, and it emerged as a crucial point of reference for the development of the wide spectrum of EU policies. The increasingly hostile environment to the advancement of the accession process was noted by Commissioners for enlargement, who vehemently disagreed with those advocating the slowing down or halting the process. Rehn and Füle defended the enlargement project and worked tirelessly towards keeping it firmly on track. The Commission also highlighted the negative implications of the crisis and insisted that enlargement would contribute to the recovery of the economy rather than exacerbate the situation by noting that: 'It is essential to explain to the public how pursuing the enlargement agenda can help the EU attain its objectives linked to the economic crisis, jobs, the environment and climate change, safety, and migration' (European Commission, 2011b).

The Eurozone crisis did not formally freeze the advancement of the ongoing accession process, but it contributed to the emergence of very hostile political climate towards its further advancement. The crisis also forced the Union to revise its key priority areas. Although the ongoing accession process with Turkey and the Western Balkans remained on the EU agenda, enlargement is not one of the top priorities of the Union, which was previously the case with the fifth enlargement.

The comparative analysis across the three groups of applicant confirms that external pressures affect the political environment and actors included in the enlargement process, therefore, we can conclude that external shocks and crises are important factors shaping the development of EU enlargement. Furthermore, the research findings reveal a significant degree of variation in both the intensity and the direction of the impact. The examination of the end of the Cold War, the Yugoslav wars and the Russia–Georgia conflict illustrate that political developments which introduce security threats to the Union have a catalysing effect on the development of EU enlargement policy, whereas the Eurozone crisis shows that economic shocks dilute the relevance of the enlargement project and significantly weaken the consensus for its advancement. As evidenced by the consequences of the Kosovo crisis, the impact of external pressures on EU enlargement is also relative, as it can have wider implications for one country than for the others. Although the influence of economic and security shocks and crises gives important insights into the implications of the external context on EU internal dynamics and political climate, the examination of external pressures does not provide a complete picture of the development of EU enlargement policy and should be analysed in conjuncture with other factors.

Conclusions

The comparative investigation on the basis of the *stage-structured conditionality model* allows us to analyse thoroughly and systematically the transformations of the key elements of EU enlargement conditionality across the stages of the accession process and between three groups of enlargement applicants. The two-step approach of the book generates comprehensive findings which allow us to identify and account for the emergence of stable patterns of development and draw conclusions on the evolutionary nature of EU enlargement conditionality and the varying mechanisms for shaping the Union's most successful foreign policy.

The comparative study of the scope and range of EU conditions reveals three complimentary trajectories of developments, which mark the gradual shift from uniform, broad and vague conditionality to more differentiated, targeted and specific conditionality. Initially, the inter-related trends illustrated the transformation of the conditions across the stages the accession process. However, the analysis of the 2007 and 2013 enlargements and the ongoing enlargement with Turkey and the Western Balkans confirms that the Union has fully integrated these developments into its strategy, thus making them essential features of the evolution of EU conditionality. The investigation also shows that the Union has redistributed the workload across the stages of the process and made the pre-negotiation and negotiation stage more demanding by expanding the scope of *conditions for applying for membership, conditions for opening accession negotiations* and extending the range of negotiation chapters.

The evaluation of the incentive structure provided by the Union to induce compliance with its conditions confirms the emergence of more consistent patterns of development. The first trend – the transformation of the incentive structure from positive to negative – is mainly a product of the advancement of the accession process which 'strips' the Union of its *accession advancement rewards*. The alternation of the *reward-threat balance* is illustrated by the shift from positive conditionality, applied during the early stages of the process (pre-negotiation and negotiation) to negative conditionality during the accession and post-accession stage. Furthermore, the ongoing accession process which is characterised by less *accession advancement rewards* and more *explicit threats* points to the emergence of another trend – the weakening of the incentive structure.

The comparative assessment of third element of EU conditionality – monitoring – also highlights the emergence of interrelated trends. Since the publication of the Commission's opinions on membership applications of the CEECs in 1997, the EU has dramatically intensified the monitoring process. Simultaneously, the Commission has gradually expanded the scope of the monitoring reports but more importantly it skilfully elaborated on their functions, thus transforming them from assessment tools into instruments for applying political pressure. The intensification and specification of detail in the reports shows that evolution of monitoring represents a natural progression

We can conclude that as a result of the new developments of EU enlargement conditionality the EU has become more demanding by expanding and elaborating on the scope of the conditions with which the applications stages need to comply, thus making the accession process much more challenging. However, these developments have not been matched by the strengthening of the incentive structure. On the contrary, the Union weakened the *reward–threat balance* by taking away one of the most desired *accession advancement rewards* – the credibility of the membership perspective – and introducing more *explicit threats.* Furthermore, the growing multi-functionality of the monitoring instruments provided the EU with an additional channel for applying political pressure through rigorous scrutiny. In order to account for the emergence of these trajectories of development, the study specifies that *EU enlargement policy is a function of differentiated influences from multiple actors and external pressures.*

The book confirms the leading role of institutional factors for establishing the scope and range of EU requirements. Furthermore, it illustrates the impressive entrepreneurship of the Commission which has not only led to the growing application of detailed, targeted conditionality but also firmly cemented the links between the conditions which need to be met and the *accession advancement rewards* available. The analysis also points to the intensified attempts of the member states to shape the scope of EU conditions. The trend is very pronounced among the EU states involved in bilateral disputes with candidate countries. Croatia's experience and the ongoing accession process with Turkey and FYROM shows that some of the member states are determined to favour their stance and willing to integrate their demands in EU conditions. However, the research findings reveal that the development of EU requirements is not fully monopolised by institutional factors, as enlargement countries influence the scope of the requirements. Although the increasing application of differentiated conditionality is not actively engineered by the EU hopefuls, but constitutes the Union's acknowledgement of the specific challenges which the applicants need to address, it points to the growing relevance of external factors. Furthermore, it proves that despite their limited bargaining power in the accession process candidate countries are a decisive factor, shaping the evolution of EU enlargement conditionality.

The examination of the factors affecting the developments of the incentive structure reveals a highly complex picture. Similarly to the discussion of the evolution of EU conditions, the study confirms the crucial role of the institutional factors – member states' preferences and inter-institutional dynamics. The research findings highlight the decreasing enthusiasm and support for the enlargement project among member states as one of the key reasons for the gradual weakening of the incentive structure. One of the most notable changes with reference to the *accession advancement rewards* was the EU's refusal to set timetables and target dates. As this shift in the EU's approach is classified as one of the lessons learnt from the previous enlargement, we cannot attribute it to a single actor or institution. However, the findings reveal that the transformation of the accession negotiations into an open-ended process is a direct result of member states' preferences. The study also points to the growing influence of the Commission over shaping the development of the accession process. It has firmly cemented its position as a policy driver, which is reflected not only by its responsibilities for the preparation of the Union's enlargement strategies but also by its impact on the Council. Since the establishment of the membership perspective of the CEECs in 1993, the Council has followed all the Commission's recommendations with the exception of one – the proposal to open accession negotiations with FYROM – due to objections from Greece related to the unresolved name dispute. The fact that the Union has put the decision on hold for more than six years fully illustrates the destructive potential of bilateral issues between member states and candidate countries.

In addition to reflecting on the institutional dimension, the book highlights the relevance of external factors. The research findings confirm that EU enlargement policy is exposed to the pressures caused by external crises and shocks. Although it is difficult to precisely measure the intensity of their impact, the empirical evidence identifies two consistent patterns, based on the type of threats that they generate. While security shocks and crises have a catalysing effect on the development of EU enlargement conditionality, economic shocks and crises have a decelerating effect on the development of EU enlargement conditionality. However, as previously acknowledged external pressures cannot on their own account for the developments of the incentive structure. The same observation applies to the impact of candidate countries. The analysis confirms the relevance of group dynamics for the incentive structure. As evidenced by the first phase of the fifth enlargement strong group dynamics can accelerate the advancement process; whereas lack of group dynamics can compromise the credibility of the membership perspective. Furthermore, the research confirms the emergence of another external factor which has the potential to play for crucial role for the outcome of the accession process. Although public opinion in the EU has always been carefully surveyed, it was not consulted directly, as member states relied on the their national parliaments to ratify the Accession Treaties, the amendments of the French constitution and the firm promised of other member states to hold referendums on future enlargement put significant power in the hands of the general public. These new developments have significantly increased the number of actors which can influence the incentive structure, provided by the EU to applicant states in order to induced compliance with its conditions. The high concentration of relevant interrelated actors is the key to understanding the nonlinear trajectory of the development of the second element of EU enlargement conditionality.

The Commission has almost exclusively modified the EU monitoring instruments. However, it is important to also acknowledge the role of the critical voices in the Council, which are aware of the strong impact of monitoring reports not only on the enlargement process but also on national politics in both applicant and member states. It should also be noted that the groups dynamics generated by the candidate countries and more precisely their number has also had implications for the transformations of the monitoring tools into instrument for political pressure.

The book links two important dimensions of research on EU enlargement by contextualising the study of EU conditionality with reference to EU policy-making. Furthermore, the study makes an original contribution to the literature on EU on European integration by designing a rigorous conceptual framework for comparative analysis of EU enlargement conditionality which allows us to examine its evolving nature at two levels – between different groups of enlargement applicants and across different stages of the accession process. On the basis of the *stage-structured conditionality model*, the study provides the first comprehensive comparative analysis of the development of EU enlargement conditionality across four different enlargement waves – the first (2004) and the second (2007) phase of the Eastern enlargement, the EU enlargement to Croatia (2013) and the ongoing enlargement round with the Western Balkans and Turkey.

The detailed examination of the EU enlargement conditionality highlights its complex and evolutionary nature. The systematic and thorough analysis shows that the transformation of EU conditions and monitoring has followed linear and logical trajectories of development and as a result, the ongoing enlargement round with Turkey and the Western Balkans is characterised by the use of detailed, targeted and differentiated conditionality and intensified rigorous monitoring process. Whereas the developments of the incentive structure show that Union has become much more cautious and reluctant to make any firm commitments not only to target dates but even to the outcome of the process. These empirical findings are consistent with those reported in earlier studies on change and continuity in EU enlargement policy (see Pridham, 2007; İçener, Phinnemore and Papadimitriou, 2010).

Conceptually, the *stage-structured conditionality model* presents a strong case for establishing monitoring as a key element of EU enlargement conditionality and linking the study of EU enlargement conditionality to the stages of the accession process. The relevance of the model is not limited to the macro level of EU enlargement policy, as it establishes a highly comprehensive framework which allows us also to trace the evolution of the EU's enlargement strategy in specific policy areas (such as environment, energy and justice and home affairs). Furthermore, the applicability of the model extends to another research area – the effectiveness of the EU conditionality. Most academic studies specify that the clarity of the EU conditions, the credibility of the membership perspective and the size of the rewards determine the impact of EU enlargement policy on domestic politics (Schimmelfennig and Sedelmeier, 2004; Grabbe, 2006; Sedelmeier, 2011). As the *stage-structured conditionality model* introduces a systematic approach to analysing the scope and range of EU conditions and the transformation of the incentive structure, it provides a suitable basis for tracing the development of key dependent variable explaining the variations in the EU's influence.

The book traces EU enlargement policy evolution beyond the scope of key historical milestones (such as the Union's decision to enlarge eastwards) and develops a comprehensive approach to policy dynamics. The study confirms the leading role of the member states and the Commission for the development of EU enlargement policy. The findings correspond with the observations of detailed studies of the Eastern enlargement (see Sedelmeier, 2005; O'Brennan, 2006). The strong relevance of the EP and the Presidency of the European Council for the advancement of the accession process confirms that the analysis of EU institutions should focus on the influence which they can exert rather than on their competences. In addition to investigating EU inter-institutional dynamics, the study also highlights the relevance of external factors. The rich empirical evidence builds a strong case for establishing the profile of the candidate countries as a relevant variable influencing the evolution of EU enlargement conditionality. The book illustrates the volatile nature of the EU citizens' preferences and stresses the growing relevance of public support for the ongoing accession process with Turkey and the Western Balkans. Furthermore, analysis of the public attitudes towards the accession of Croatia shows that negative trends can be reversed and presents a very interesting empirical case for further investigation. The study also demonstrates that the security shocks and crises have acted as windows of opportunity for policy development in the EU. Furthermore, the book confirms that a single factor cannot account for the evolution of EU enlargement conditionality and highlights the advantages of the comprehensive approach, which allows us to examine the impact of a dense constellation of factors.

The findings of the book show that EU enlargement policy has evolved dramatically since 1993 when the Union embarked on one of its most adventurous endeavours – to reunite the continent. Although the underlying principles of the policy remain the same, the New Approach to the accession negotiations which firmly cemented the fundamental significance of the rule of law and the need for solid track records has changed the nature of the enlargement process. These developments demonstrate a very important progression in the EU's requirements for accession: from demanding the adoption of the *acquis* and alignment with the Union's policies to insisting on the development of solid track records and irreversible reforms. As the candidate and potential candidate countries have a long way to go before they join the Union, it is clear that EU enlargement conditionality will continue to evolve. It will be interesting to follow the work of the new DG Neighbourhood Policy and Enlargement Negotiations (DG NEAR) particularly in the context of growing anti-EU sentiments across Europe. The development and the effectiveness of the New Approach, the normalisation process between Serbia and Kosovo and the new approach to Bosnia and Herzegovina provide exciting avenues to examine the EU's approach towards highly sensitive and problematic issues such as fight against organised crime and corruption, judiciary reform and bilateral disputes. These dimensions are of particular significance because they allow us not only to analyse the growing entrepreneurship of the Commission, but also provide an intriguing testing ground for studying the effectiveness of EU conditionality. Furthermore, the launch of EU Justice Scoreboard and EU Anti-Corruption Report, modelled on instruments developed in the framework of EU enlargement conditionality outlines another important area for future research – the impact of EU enlargement policy for policy-making in the Union.

Appendix I: List of Negotiating Chapters

1. Free movement of goods
2. Free movement for workers
3. Right of establishment and freedom to provide services
4. Free movement of capital
5. Public procurement
6. Company law
7. Intellectual property law
8. Competition policy
9. Financial services
10. Information society and media
11. Agriculture and rural development
12. Food safety, veterinary and phytosanitary policy
13. Fisheries
14. Transport policy
15. Energy
16. Taxation
17. Economic and monetary policy
18. Statistics
19. Social policy and employment
20. Enterprise and industrial policy
21. Trans-European networks
22. Regional policy and coordination of structural instruments
23. Judiciary and fundamental rights
24. Justice, freedom and security
25. Science and research
26. Education and culture
27. Environment
28. Consumer and health protection

29. Customs union
30. External relations
31. Foreign, security and defence policy
32. Financial control
33. Financial and budgetary provisions
34. Institutions
35. Other issues

Appendix II: Commissioners Responsible for Enlargement

Time in Office	Directorate-General	Commissioner
1970–1973	Co-ordination of Enlargement Negotiations and Development Aid	Jean-François Deniau
1977–1981	Enlargement, Protection of the Environment, Nuclear Safety, Contacts with Member Governments and Public Opinion on Preparation for Direct Elections to the European Parliament (until 1979)	Lorenzo Natali (Vice-President)
1981–1985	Mediterranean policy, Enlargement and Information	Lorenzo Natali (Vice-President)
1989–1993	External Relations and Trade Policy, Cooperation with other European Countries	Frans Andriessen (Vice-President)
1993–1994	External Political Relations, Common Foreign and Security Policy and Enlargement Negotiations	Hans van den Broek
1995–1999	External Relations	Hans van den Broek
1999–2004	Enlargement	Günter Verheugen
2004–2009	Enlargement	Olli Rehn
2009–2014	Enlargement and Neighbourhood Policy	Štefan Füle
2014–2019	European Neighbourhood Policy and Enlargement Negotiations (DG NEAR)	Johannes Hahn

Appendix III: Public Supports for Enlargement in EU Member States: 1996–2006

Member states	Spring 1996	Spring 1998	Autumn 1998	Spring 1999	Autumn 1999	Spring 2000	Autumn 2000	Spring 2001	Autumn 2001	Spring 2002	Autumn 2002	Spring 2003	Autumn 2003	Spring 2004	Autumn 2004	Spring 2005	Autumn 2005	Spring 2006	Autumn 2006
SE	53	**63**	**63**	56	**62**	**61**	**59**	50	69	**60**	**65**	56	54	54	44	51	48	49	53
DK	41	61	61	**62**	60	58	55	50	69	57	60	63	63	59	43	48	46	51	48
EL	52	56	61	58	57	55	57	**70**	**74**	59	58	**71**	**65**	**66**	62	60	**74**	56	**71**
NL	**57**	57	51	55	55	49	46	42	58	42	47	48	50	44	50	45	48	43	45
FI	50	56	52	51	49	48	45	45	54	52	54	50	53	48	45	45	45	35	43
ES	51	54	51	51	48	49	46	55	61	50	51	60	54	59	67	56	55	55	51
IT	50	47	48	45	49	43	49	51	61	46	50	59	61	55	61	59	53	48	47
IE	37	44	41	45	47	41	41	59	60	43	55	60	59	60	54	52	54	45	48
PT	34	46	42	38	40	41	41	52	57	40	45	60	52	52	51	76	55	47	54
UK	40	43	44	40	41	35	34	35	41	32	38	36	38	31	50	48	43	44	36
LU	**29**	38	36	45	41	34	38	43	53	44	50	53	45	37	38	33	31	**27**	32
DE	35	36	34	38	38	34	35	35	47	36	37	42	38	**28**	36	33	36	28	**30**
FR	**29**	35	35	33	**34**	30	**28**	33	**39**	**25**	**29**	**31**	**34**	37	39	**31**	**29**	31	34
AU	**29**	33	30	**29**	35	**26**	**28**	**33**	46	36	41	43	41	34	**28**	**31**	**29**	**27**	**31**
BE	31	**32**	**28**	39	42	38	33	44	49	40	40	38	43	38	50	50	47	45	46
EU15	**41**	**44**	**42**	**42**	**43**	**38**	**39**	**43**	**51**	**39**	**42**	**46**	**47**	**42**	**49**	**45**	**44**	**41**	**41**

Note: Bold numbers indicate the highest, the average and the lowest level of support for enlargement.

(Continued)

Member states	Spring 1996	Spring 1998	Autumn 1998	Spring 1999	Autumn 1999	Spring 2000	Autumn 2000	Spring 2001	Autumn 2001	Spring 2002	Autumn 2002	Spring 2003	Autumn 2003	Spring 2004	Autumn 2004	Spring 2005	Autumn 2005	Spring 2006	Autumn 2006
EU25															53	50	49	45	46
NMS															68	68	65	60	67
PL															78	76	72	72	76
LT															76	69	69	60	68
SI															75	79	74	73	74
SK															69	73	67	58	69
CZ															66	66	67	58	65
LV															65	64	62	54	63
EE															63	56	51	50	59
HU															63	66	66	59	65
CY															61	70	67	59	66
MT															61	63	57	56	66

Note: Bold numbers indicate the highest, the average and the lowest level of support for enlargement.
Source: Eurobarometer (1996, 1998a, 1998b, 1999a, 1999b, 2000a, 2000b, 2001a, 2001b, 2002a, 2002b, 2003a, 2003b, 2004a, 2004b, 2005a, 2005b, 2006a, 2006b).

Appendix IV: EU Public Attitudes to the 13 Applicant Countries: 1996–2002

Applicant countries	Spring 1996		Autumn 1997		Spring 1998		Autumn 1998		Spring 1999		Autumn 1999		Spring 2000		Autumn 2000		Autumn 2001		Spring 2002	
	+	−	+	−	+	−	+	−	+	−	+	−	+	−	+	−	+	−	+	−
MT	50	29	−	−	52	25	52	25	50	26	49	27	50	26	48	30	51	28	47	30
HU	57	30	47	29	53	24	50	28	46	31	47	31	46	31	46	32	50	30	48	31
PL	49	33	43	34	49	29	47	32	43	35	44	34	44	34	44	36	47	34	44	35
CY	43	36	40	33	46	29	45	31	42	33	43	33	44	32	42	35	46	33	43	34
CZ	44	36	41	33	48	28	45	31	40	35	42	35	41	35	42	36	45	34	43	35
SK	38	41	36	37	43	32	40	36	35	39	37	38	37	38	38	39	40	38	38	38
EE	37	40	35	37	41	32	39	36	36	38	37	38	36	38	37	38	40	38	37	38
LV	38	39	35	37	41	32	39	36	35	38	37	38	36	38	37	38	39	38	37	38
BG	37	42	36	38	42	33	33	39	36	35	35	40	36	39	36	39	35	42	38	40
LT	37	40	35	37	41	33	38	36	35	39	36	39	35	38	37	39	39	38	36	38
RO	38	42	33	41	39	37	37	40	32	43	34	42	34	42	34	42	33	45	36	43
SI	34	43	33	40	39	35	36	38	32	42	34	41	34	40	35	41	37	40	35	40
TU	36	44	−	−	−	−	−	−	29	47	30	47	30	47	30	47	30	48	34	46

Note: Bold numbers indicate that the people opposed to the membership of the applicant country were more than those in favour of it.
Source: Eurobarometer (1996, 1997, 1998a, 1998b, 1999a, 1999b, 2000a, 2000b, 2001a, 2001b, 2002a, 2002b).

Appendix V: Public Support for Enlargement in EU Member States: 2007–2014

Member states	Spring 2007		Autumn 2007		Spring 2008		Autumn 2008		Spring 2009		Autumn 2009		Spring 2010		Autumn 2010		Spring 2011		Autumn 2011		Spring 2012		Autumn 2012		Spring 2013		Autumn 2013		Spring 2014		Autumn 2014	
±	+	–	+	–	+	–	+	–	+	–	+	–	+	–	+	–	+	–	+	–	+	–	+	–	+	–	+	–	+	–	+	–
BE	44	53	47	49	50	48	45	53	44	53	47	49	50	48	45	53	42	56	33	63	36	61	33	63	36	61	35	62	33	62	34	60
DK	51	43	49	44	54	41	49	50	51	43	49	44	54	41	49	50	43	52	42	52	44	50	40	50	43	53	45	51	40	52	38	53
DE	34	59	28	66	33	58	33	65	28	59	28	66	33	58	26	65	22	71	17	76	20	74	20	73	18	75	23	69	21	71	24	68
EL	56	43	53	46	62	38	49	50	56	43	53	46	62	38	50	50	45	48	44	47	44	48	51	51	42	53	44	51	44	50	43	52
ES	65	13	59	18	62	16	57	23	65	13	59	18	62	16	57	23	51	30	45	36	41	39	46	35	43	38	37	51	49	28	52	28
FR	32	60	32	59	31	60	31	62	32	60	32	59	31	60	31	62	32	61	23	71	25	70	26	68	22	71	23	70	23	69	26	65
IE	42	38	45	35	46	31	36	41	42	38	45	35	46	31	36	41	30	50	24	54	31	54	34	44	34	48	42	46	40	47	26	45
IT	48	34	43	43	41	37	39	42	48	34	43	43	41	37	39	42	42	55	37	45	31	52	34	50	34	52	29	59	33	44	30	52
LU	25	68	25	65	33	59	25	68	25	68	25	65	33	59	25	68	29	64	34	62	27	66	27	70	31	66	31	64	26	65	25	67
NL	50	44	48	40	50	46	48	47	50	44	48	40	50	46	48	47	35	59	31	64	34	62	36	60	28	68	33	64	32	62	35	59
AT	28	64	24	67	27	63	25	67	28	64	24	67	27	63	25	67	23	72	18	77	21	73	23	72	23	69	17	76	25	67	26	67
PT	51	30	48	27	51	31	43	31	51	30	48	27	51	31	43	31	46	36	37	44	44	41	40	46	33	50	38	49	42	44	44	44
FI	39	56	43	52	46	50	41	54	39	56	43	52	46	50	41	54	31	66	27	70	26	71	29	67	26	70	32	65	28	63	33	58
SE	52	38	54	35	55	36	56	37	52	38	54	35	55	36	56	37	59	38	47	49	51	45	48	48	47	50	56	40	48	42	55	36
UK	41	48	36	49	36	50	40	48	41	48	36	49	36	50	40	48	37	53	29	59	29	60	33	59	33	58	32	65	32	52	38	49

Note: Bold numbers indicate that the people opposed to further enlargement of the EU were more than those in favour of it.

(Continued)

Member states	Spring 2007		Autumn 2007		Spring 2008		Autumn 2008		Spring 2009		Autumn 2009		Spring 2010		Autumn 2010		Spring 2011		Autumn 2011		Spring 2012		Autumn 2012		Spring 2013		Autumn 2013		Spring 2014		Autumn 2014	
	+	−	+	−	+	−	+	−	+	−	+	−	+	−	+	−	+	−	+	−	+	−	+	−	+	−	+	−	+	−	+	−
EU27/28	43	45	46	40	47	39	44	43	43	45	46	40	47	39	44	43	42	**47**	36	**53**	36	**53**	38	**52**	37	**53**	37	**52**	37	**49**	39	**48**
CY	65	20	57	24	64	23	54	30	65	20	57	24	64	23	54	30	49	36	44	**45**	40	**48**	35	**53**	30	**56**	32	**56**	39	**47**	37	**51**
CZ	64	28	62	28	63	26	57	33	64	28	62	28	63	26	57	33	47	43	38	**54**	41	**51**	39	**53**	45	**50**	44	**50**	44	**46**	42	**49**
EE	55	32	55	34	63	25	60	26	55	32	55	34	65	25	60	26	44	45	46	45	47	44	47	42	53	38	51	40	48	37	48	32
HU	64	28	64	26	65	23	55	32	64	28	64	26	65	23	55	32	65	28	56	35	54	35	54	30	55	33	60	32	58	33	55	37
LV	56	33	52	31	57	26	54	33	56	33	52	31	57	26	54	33	53	37	45	45	48	41	49	36	51	36	48	38	49	35	51	36
LT	68	17	67	17	69	16	63	20	68	17	67	17	69	16	63	20	61	21	60	26	58	27	62	24	62	24	64	20	65	19	65	23
MT	62	22	61	17	65	15	57	20	62	22	61	17	65	15	57	20	54	19	50	26	48	32	50	30	51	30	60	25	61	24	63	23
PL	76	14	76	12	74	12	69	15	76	14	76	12	74	12	69	15	69	17	69	21	62	26	69	22	71	20	61	26	55	23	64	18
SK	59	30	59	27	63	28	63	24	59	30	59	27	63	28	63	24	60	33	48	44	52	42	46	46	52	40	51	42	49	41	50	40
SI	67	29	66	27	74	21	70	21	67	29	66	27	74	21	70	24	55	40	50	44	56	38	61	34	57	39	52	42	58	34	54	35
BG	58	15	55	11	67	8	57	11	58	15	55	11	67	8	57	11	58	20	54	21	56	22	58	24	54	25	55	29	53	21	51	25
RO	67	9	64	10	67	8	60	16	67	9	64	10	67	8	60	16	64	15	58	21	58	18	58	21	61	20	64	18	70	16	72	14
HR																											71	22	64	25	56	33

Note: Bold numbers indicate that the people opposed to further enlargement of the EU were more than those in favour of it.
Source: Eurobarometer (2007a; 2007b; 2008a; 2008b; 2009a; 2009b; 2010a; 2010b; 2011a; 2011b; 2012a; 2012b; 2013a; 2013b; 2014a; 2014b).

Notes

Introduction

1. This designation is without prejudice to positions on status and is in line with UNSCR 1244/99 and the ICJ Opinion on the Kosovo declaration of independence. Hereinafter referred to as Kosovo.

1 Conditionality and EU Enlargement: A Conceptual Overview

1. Croatia, FYROM, Albania, Bosnia and Herzegovina, Montenegro, Serbia and Kosovo (under the UNSCR 1244).
2. See Zagreb Declaration (2000).
3. The SAAs were signed with FYROM (April 2001), Croatia (October 2001), Albania (June 2006), Montenegro (October 2007), Serbia (April 2008) and Bosnia and Herzegovina (June 2008).
4. The EU confirmed the membership perspective of the applicant countries of CEE at the Copenhagen European Council in June 1993. For details on the dates of application, see Table 1.1.
5. Although opening and closing benchmarks are not publicly available, the Commission listed the benchmarks which Croatia had to meet for the provisional closure of negotiations on Chapter 23 (Judiciary and Fundamental Rights) in its Interim Report (see European Commission, 2011c).
6. Poland and Hungary: Assistance for Reconstructing their Economies (PHARE) was originally created in 1989 and expanded from Poland and Hungary to cover all CEECs. Special Accession Programme for Agriculture and Rural Development (SAPARD) and Instrument for Structural Policies for Pre-Accession (ISPA) were established in June 1999, with the aim of addressing specific priorities, identified in the Accession Partnerships between the EU and the CEECs. Since 2007, the EU introduced a single framework for financial assistance – Instrument for Pre-Accession Assistance (IPA).

2 EU Conditionality in the Context of the 2004 Enlargement

1. With the exception of the post-accession stage section which examines only the incentive structure as the other two elements of conditionality are not applicable to this stage.
2. TCAs were signed with Hungary (September 1988), Czechoslovakia (December 1988) Poland (September 1989), Bulgaria (May 1990), Romania (October 1990), Estonia (May 1992), Latvia (May 1992) and Lithuania (May 1992) and Slovenia (April 1993).

3. The summary lists the objectives which were included in the TCA with Poland, Hungary, Bulgaria Czechoslovakia, Romania, Estonia, Latvia and Lithuania, the TCA with Slovenia was signed on 15 April 1993 and did not follow the structure and the content of the TCAs signed with the other countries.

4. Some of the requirements specified in the White Paper included adjustment of the sequence and the pace of the legislative approximation, further progress with privatisation and consolidation of judicial reform.

5. Presented on 16 July 1997.

6. Since the entry into force of the Treaty of Amsterdam in May 1999, these requirements have been enshrined as constitutional principles in the Treaty on European Union, and have been emphasised in the Charter of Fundamental Rights of the European Union, that was proclaimed at the Nice European Council in December 2000.

7. Ibid.

8. Bulgaria, the Czech Republic, Cyprus, Estonia, Hungary, Latvia, Lithuania, Poland, Slovakia, Slovenia and Romania.

9. This clause is included in all the Accession Partnership between the EU and the 12 applicant countries of the fifth enlargement.

10. Ibid.

11. Statistics, telecommunications, industrial policy, consumer protection, research, small and medium-sized enterprises, and education and training.

12. Singed in 1999.

13. Article 36 (see *Official Journal*, 2003a).

14. Cyprus, the Czech Republic, Estonia, Hungary, Latvia, Lithuania, Malta, Poland, Slovakia, and Slovenia may also apply for the authorisation to take protective measures with regard to other member states.

15. For details, see the section 'Accession Stage' of the chapter.

16. Respondents were shown a map of Europe containing 43 countries and asked – if given the choice – which of them they think should be part of the EC by the year 2000.

17. Absolute majorities of Danes and Dutch would like to see all three Baltic states be members by the year 2000.

3 EU Conditionality in the Context of the 2007 Enlargement

1. Hungary, Czechoslovakia and Poland singed TCAs in the late 1980s. The agreements with Sofia and Bucharest were signed in 1990.

2. Published in 1998 and 1999.

3. Annex IX of the Accession Treaty identified the following areas: (1) the implementation of the Schengen Action Plan; (2) control and surveillance at the future external borders of the Union; (3) the implementation of the Action Plan and Strategy for the Reform of the Judiciary; (4) the enforcement of anti-corruption legislation and the effective independence of the National Anti-Corruption Prosecutors' Office; (5) the full implementation of the National Anti-Corruption Strategy; (6) improvements in the operations of the gendarmerie and the police; and (7) the implementation

of the strategy to protect victims of trafficking (see *Official Journal*, 2005b).

4. Annex IX of the Accession Treaty indentified the following areas: (1) further investigations into accusations of state aid to the energy sector; (2) the strengthening of the state aid enforcement record; (3) the submission of a revised steel restructuring plan; and (4) the strengthening of the financial means and human resources of the Competition Council (see *Official Journal*, 2005b).
5. Article 36 (see *Official Journal*, 2005a).
6. Bulgaria and Romania may also apply for the authorisation to take protective measures with regard to other member states.
7. Fight against corruption was an area established only established for Bulgaria.
8. One general and two specific safeguard clauses.
9. In January 2013, the Commission presented only one report to follow up on the ten specific recommendations aimed at resolving the controversies on the rule of law and judicial independence in Romania.
10. Respondents were shown a map of Europe containing 43 countries and asked – if given the choice – which of them they think should be part of the EC by 2000.
11. With the exception of Estonia and Malta.

4 EU Conditionality in the Context of the South-Eastern Enlargements

1. Since the entry into force of the Treaty of Amsterdam in May 1999, these requirements have been enshrined as constitutional principles in the Treaty on European Union, and these have been emphasised in the Charter of Fundamental Rights of the European Union that was proclaimed at the Nice European Council in December 2000.
2. Six pieces of legislation included Laws on Association, Penal Code, Law on Intermediate Courts of Appeal, Code of Criminal Procedures and Law on Execution of Punishments.
3. As specified by the European Council at Helsinki in December 1999.
4. OSCE – Organisation for Security and Co-operation in Europe.
5. The OSCE-Office for Democratic Institutions and Human Rights (ODIHR) provides support, assistance and expertise to participating States and civil society to promote democracy, rule of law, human rights and tolerance and non-discrimination.
6. Regarding ethnic discrimination for representation in the institutions of the country for persons not belonging to one of the three constituent peoples (Bosniak, Serb and Croat).
7. Trans-European Networks and Energy; Agriculture and Rural Development; and Food Safety, Veterinary and Phytosanitary Policy.
8. Presented together with the Progress Reports.
9. Judiciary and public administration; fight against corruption and organised crime; and minority rights, including the refugee return, war crime trials (see European Commission, 2006d, 2007a, 2008a, 2009a, 2010a).

10. Freedom of expression, rights of non-Muslim religious communities, women's rights, trade union rights, civilian oversight of the security forces and implementation of the Additional Protocol to the Association Agreement (see European Commission, 2006e, 2007b, 2008b, 2009b, 2010b).
11. Article 36 (see *Official Journal*, 2005a).
12. Bulgaria and Romania may also apply for the authorisation to take protective measures with regard to other member states.

5 The Evolution of EU Enlargement Conditionality: Overview and Key Findings

1. Furthermore, Article 1a specified that the societies of EU member states are characterised by 'pluralism, non-discrimination, tolerance, justice, solidarity and equality between women and men' (*Official Journal*, 2007).
2. See European Commission (2009c).
3. A general economic safeguard clause, a specific internal market safeguard clause and a specific justice and home affairs safeguard clause. See *Official Journal* (2003a, 2005a).

Bibliography

Agence Europe (1997a) EU/Enlargement. Applicant Countries that Have Made Further Progress Do Not Have to Wait for Others, Say Mr Kinkel and Mr Schussels, 23 July.

Agence Europe (1997b) EU/Enlargement – Italy Wants Negotiations to Open at the Same Time with All Applicant Countries, 23 July.

Agence Europe (1997c) EU/Enlargement/Baltic States. Baltic States Have to Negotiate Together Mrs. Hjelm-Wallen Tells Mr Van den Broek – Mr Vagnorius Raises Problem of Russia's Attitude Before EPP (Which in Favour of Rapid Accession for Baltic States), 11 September.

Agence Europe (1997d) EU/Enlargement – Majority of Council Supports Commission Evaluation of Applicant Countries, 7 October.

Agence Europe (1997e) EU/Enlargement – Fourteen in Line, 25 November.

Agence Europe (1997f) EU/Enlargement, 26 November.

Agence Europe (1997g) EU/Enlargement – Joint Proposal by Denmark and Sweden on the Start-up of Negotiations, 2 December.

Agence Europe (1998a) EU/Enlargement, 10 November.

Agence Europe (1998b) EU/Enlargement – Differences in Council over Signal to Be Sent Out to 'Second Group' Applicants, 8 December.

Agence Europe (2004) EU/Enlargement: Bulgaria Finalises Membership Talks after Having Had to Accept Strengthened Safeguard Clause Allowing EU to Delay Accession until 2008 if Serious Problems Arise – Romania May Complete Negotiations by End of Year, 16 June.

Agence Europe (2005) EU/Enlargement /Balkans: Differences of Opinion on Candidate Country Status for FYROM – Jack Straw Refutes Link 'Established by Certain Countries' with Financial Perspectives – France Wants Wider Debate on Enlargement, 13 December.

Agence Europe (2008) EU/Enlargement: Referendum Remains Compulsory in France for All New EU Accessions, after that of Croatia, 5 July.

Agence Europe (2009a) EU/Enlargement: Process of Enlargement Should Not Slow down but There Should Be Conditions, Say EU27, 31 March.

Agence Europe (2009b) EU/Enlargement: Accession of Balkan Countries and Turkey Will Not Necessarily Prevent Deepening of EU, States Rehn, 30 April.

Albi, A. (2005) *EU Enlargement and the Constitutions of Central and Eastern Europe*, Cambridge: Cambridge University Press.

Anadolu Agency (2014) EU Slows Turkey's Accession: Bozkir, 11 November, http://www.aa.com.tr/en/turkey/418865–certain-eu-states-blocking-turkeys-accession-turkeys-eu-head-says, date accessed 1 December 2014.

Anastasakis, O. (2008) 'The EU's Political Conditionality in the Western Balkans: Towards a More Pragmatic Approach', *Southeast European and Black Sea Studies*, 8 (4): 366–377.

Andonova, L. (2003) *Transnational Politics of the Environment: The European Union and Environmental Policy in Central and Eastern Europe*, Cambridge, MA: MIT Press.

Avery, G. (2009) 'Uses of Time in the EU's Enlargement Process', *Journal of European Public Policy*, 16 (2): 256–269.

Bache, I. (2010) 'Europeanization and Multi-Level Governance: EU Cohesion Policy and Pre-Accession Aid in Southeast Europe', *Southeast European and Black Sea Studies*, 10 (1): 1–12.

Baldwin, R. (1995) 'The Eastern Enlargement of the European Union', *European Economic Review*, 39 (3–4): 474–481.

Baldwin, R., Francois, J. and Portes, R. (1997) 'The Costs and Benefits of Eastern Enlargement: The Impact on the EU and Central Europe', *Economic Policy*, 12 (24): 125–176.

Barroso (2012) *Statement by President Barroso following the adoption of the Cooperation and Verification Mechanism Reports for Romania and Bulgaria*, Speech 12/565, Brussels, 18 July.

Baun, M. (2002) 'EU Regional Policy and the Candidate States: Poland and the Czech Republic', *Journal of European Integration*, 24 (3): 261–280.

Bellier, I. (2004) 'The European Commission between the Acquis Communautaire and Enlargement', in D. Dimitrakopoulos (ed.) *The Changing European Commission*, Manchester: Manchester University Press, pp. 138–152.

Bieber, F. (eds.) (2012) *EU Conditionality in the Western Balkans*, Abingdon: Routledge.

Blair, T. (1999) *Speech to the Romanian Parliament*, Bucharest, 4 May, http://webarchive.nationalarchives.gov.uk/20090101050155/number10.gov.uk/page1312, date accessed 1 May 2012.

Börzel, T. A. (2010) 'Why You Don't Always Get What You Want: EU Enlargement and Civil Society in Central and Eastern Europe', *Acta Politica*, 45 (1–2): 1–10.

Börzel, T. A. and Risse, T. (2009) Diffusing (Inter-) Regionalism: The EU as a Model of Regional Integration, KFG Working Paper Series, No. 7, September 2009, Kolleg-Forschergruppe (KFG), The Transformative Power of Europe, Free University Berlin, http://userpage.fu-berlin.de/kfgeu/workingpapers/WorkingPaperKFG_7.pdf, date accessed 1 May 2012.

Börzel, T. A. and Risse, T. (2012a) 'From Europeanisation to Diffusion: Introduction', *West European Politics*, 35 (1): 1–19.

Börzel, T. A. and Risse, T. (2012b) 'When Europeansation Meets Diffusion: Exploring New Territory' *West European Politics*, 35 (1): 192–207.

Bruszt, L. (2008) 'Multi-Level Governance – The Eastern Versions: Emerging Patterns of Regional Development Governance in the New Member States', *Regional and Federal Studies*, 18 (5): 607–627.

Bulletin of the European Economic Community (1961) *The United Kingdom's Application for Membership to the EEC, September-October 1961*, Luxembourg.

Bulletin of the European Community (1982) *Supplement 8/82*, Luxembourg.

Buzan, B. and Diez, T. (1999) 'The European Union and Turkey', *Survival*, 41 (1): 41–57.

Carmin, J. and VanDeveer, S. (eds.) (2004) *EU Enlargement and the Environment: Institutional Change and Environmental Policy in Central and Eastern Europe, vol. 13 of Environmental Politics* (Special Issue), Portland, OR: Frank Cass.

Casier, T. (2010) 'The European Neighbourhood Policy: Assessing the EU's Policy towards the Region', in F. Bindi (ed.) *The Foreign Policy of the European Union. Assessing Europe's Role in the World*, Washington: Brookings Press, pp. 99–115.

Casier, T. (2011) 'To Adopt or Not to Adopt. Explaining Selective Rule Transfer under the European Neighbourhood Policy', *Journal of European Integration*, 33 (1): 37–53.

Chiva, C. (2007) 'The Institutionalisation of Post-Communist Parliaments: Hungary and Romania in Comparative Perspective', *Parliamentary Affairs*, 60 (2): 187–211.

Christophersen, H. (1994) *Europe's Future Role in International Relations*, Speech 94/40, 26 April, Washington.

Churchill, W. (1946) *Speech Delivered at the University of Zurich*, 19 September.

Commission of the European Communities (1976) *Opinion on Greek Application for Membership*, COM (76)30 final, Brussels: Commission of the European Communities.

Commission of the European Communities (1989) *Commission Opinion on Turkey's Request for Accession to the Community*, SEC (89) 2290 final/2, Brussels: Commission of the European Communities.

Council of the European Communities (1976) *Press Release on Greece's Application for Accession to the European Communities*, 9 February 1976, Brussels: Council of the European Communities.

Council of the European Communities (1978) *Conclusions – The European Council [Copenhagen Summit 1978]: 7–8 April*, Brussels: Council of the European Communities.

Council of the European Communities (1990) *Conclusions of the Presidency – The European Council [Rome Summit 1990]: 14–15 December*, Brussels: Council of the European Communities.

Council of the European Communities (1992) *Conclusions of the Presidency – The European Council [Lisbon Summit 1992]: 26 – 27 June*, Brussels: Council of the European Communities.

Council of the European Union (1993) *Presidency Conclusions – Copenhagen European Council: 21 – 22 June*, Brussels: Council of the European Union.

Council of the European Union (1994a) *Presidency Conclusions – Corfu European Council: 24 – 25 June*, Brussels: Council of the European Union.

Council of the European Union (1994b) *Presidency Conclusions – Essen European Council: 9 – 10 December*, Brussels: Council of the European Union.

Council of the European Union (1995a) *Presidency Conclusions – Cannes European Council: 26 – 27 June*, Brussels: Council of the European Union.

Council of the European Union (1995b) *Presidency Conclusions – Madrid European Council: 15 – 16 December*, Brussels: Council of the European Union.

Council of the European Union (1996) *Presidency Conclusions – Dublin European Council: 13 – 14 December*, Brussels: Council of the European Union.

Council of the European Union (1997a) *Presidency Conclusions – Luxembourg European Council: 12 – 13 December*, Brussels: Council of the European Union.

Council of the European Union (1997b) *2003rd Council Meeting General Affairs*, C97/129, 29–30 April, Luxembourg.

Council of the European Union (1998) *2148th Council Meeting General Affairs*, C98/431, 6–7 December, Brussels.

Council of the European Union (1999a) *Presidency Conclusions – Cologne European Council: 3 – 4 June*, Brussels: Council of the European Union.

Council of the European Union (1999b) *Presidency Conclusions – Helsinki European Council: 10 – 11 December*, Brussels: Council of the European Union.

Council of the European Union (1999c) *2192nd Council Meeting General Affairs*, C 99/198, 21–22 June, Luxembourg.

Council of the European Union (2000a) *Presidency Conclusions – Santa Maria da Feira European Council: 19 – 20 June*, Brussels: Council of the European Union.

Council of the European Union (2000b) *Presidency Conclusions – Nice European Council: 7 – 10 December*, Brussels: Council of the European Union.

Council of the European Union (2001a) *Presidency Conclusions – Göteborg European Council: 15 – 16 June*, Brussels: Council of the European Union.

Council of the European Union (2001b) *Presidency Conclusions – Laeken European Council: 14 – 15 December*, Brussels: Council of the European Union.

Council of the European Union (2002) *Presidency Conclusions – Copenhagen European Council: 12 – 13 December*, Brussels: Council of the European Union.

Council of the European Union (2003a) *Presidency Conclusions – Thessaloniki European Council: 19 – 20 June*, Brussels: Council of the European Union.

Council of the European Union (2003b) *Presidency Conclusions – Brussels European Council: 12 – 13 December*, Brussels: Council of the European Union.

Council of the European Union (2003c) *2518th Council Meeting, General Affairs and External Relations, External Relations*, C/03/166, 16 June, Brussels.

Council of the European Union (2004a) *Presidency Conclusions – Brussels European Council: 16 – 17 June*, Brussels: Council of the European Union.

Council of the European Union (2004b) *Presidency Conclusions – Brussels European Council: 16 – 17 December*, Brussels: Council of the European Union.

Council of the European Union (2005a) *Presidency Conclusions – Brussels European Council: 16 – 17 June*, Brussels: Council of the European Union.

Council of the European Union (2005b) *Presidency Conclusions – Brussels European Council: 15 – 16 December*, Brussels: Council of the European Union.

Council of the European Union (2005c) *2649th Council Meeting, General Affairs and External Relations, General Affairs*, C/05/44, 16 March, Brussels.

Council of the European Union (2005d) *2678th Council Meeting, General Affairs and External Relations, General Affairs*, C/05/241, 3 October, Luxembourg.

Council of the European Union (2006a) *Presidency Conclusions – Brussels European Council: 14 – 15 December*, Brussels: Council of the European Union.

Council of the European Union (2006b) *2770th Council Meeting, General Affairs and External Relations, General Affairs*, C/06/352, 11 December, Brussels.

Council of the European Union (2008) *Presidency Conclusions – Brussels European Council: 19 – 20 June*, Brussels: Council of the European Union.

Council of the European Union (2009) *The Third Enlargement: Spain's and Portugal's Accession to the ECC. Report on the Council of Ministers Archival Material*, Brussels.

Council of the European Union (2010) *Introduction to the Fonds of the Central Archives relating to the First Enlargement of the European Economic Community, 1960–1973*, SN 4143/10, Brussels, http://www.consilium.europa.eu/uedocs/cmsUpload/archives-Report_Enlargement.pdf, date accessed 1 May 2012.

Council of the European Union (2011a) *Council Conclusions on Enlargement and Stabilisation and Association Process, 3132 General Affairs Council Meeting, Brussels, 5 December 2011*, Brussels: Council of the European Union.

Council of the European Union (2011b) *Presidency Conclusions – European Council: 8 – 9 December*, Brussels: Council of the European Union.

Council of the European Union (2011c) *Third Meeting of the Accession Conference with Iceland at Ministerial Level, Brussels, 12 December 2011*, Brussels: Council of the European Union.

Council of the European Union (2012) *Presidency Conclusions – European Council: 1 – 2 March*, Brussels: Council of the European Union.

Council of the European Union (2013) *Council Conclusions on Enlargement and Stabilisation and Association Process, 3287 General Affairs Council Meeting, Brussels, 17 December 2014*, Brussels: Council of the European Union.

Council of the European Union (2014) *Council Conclusions on Enlargement and Stabilisation and Association Process, 3362 General Affairs Council Meeting, Brussels, 16 December 2014*, Brussels: Council of the European Union.

Cremona, M. (2003) *The Enlargement of the European Union*, Oxford: Oxford University Press.

Crisis Group (2009) *Macedonia's Name: Breaking the Deadlock*, Crisis Group Europe Briefing No 52, 12 January, http://www.crisisgroup.org/~/media/Files/europe/b52_macedonias_name__breaking_the_deadlock.pdf, date accessed 1 May 2012.

Dalhman, C. (2004) 'Turkey's Accession to the European Union: The Geopolitics of Enlargement', *Eurasian Geography and Economics*, 45 (8): 553–574.

De Vreese, C. H. and Boomgardeen, H. G. (2006) 'Media Effects on Public Opinion about the Enlargement of the European Union', *Journal of Common Market Studies*, 44 (2): 419–436.

Dimier, V. (2006), 'Constructing Conditionality: The Bureaucratization of EC Development Aid', *European Foreign Affairs Review*, 11 (2): 263–280.

Dimitrova, A. (2002) 'Enlargement, Institution-Building and the EU's Administrative Capacity Requirement', *West European Politics*, 25 (4): 171–190.

Dimitrova, A. and Pridham, G. (2004) 'International Actors and Democracy Promotion in Central and Eastern Europe: The Integration Model and Its Limits', *Democratization*, 11 (5): 91–112.

Dimitrova, A. and Toshkov, D. (2009) 'Post-Accession Compliance between Administrative Co-Ordination and Political Bargaining', *European Integration Online Papers*, 13 (2), 19, http://eiop.or.at/eiop/texte/2009-019a.htm, date accessed 1 May 2012.

Droutsas, D. (2010) *Foreign Minister Droutsas's Press Conference at the General Affairs and Foreign Affairs Councils*, Brussels, 14 December 2010, http://www2.mfa.gr/www.mfa.gr/GoToPrintable.aspx?UICulture=en-US&GUID={A5B5D35D-35C7-41AD-BF4E-EC35F2BA2CE2}, date accessed 1 May 2012.

Dyson, K. (ed.) (2006) *Enlarging the Euro Area: External Empowerment and Domestic Transformation in East Central Europe*, Oxford: Oxford University Press.

Dyson, K. (2007) 'Euro Area Entry in East-Central Europe: Paradoxical Europeanisation and Clustered Convergence', *West European Politics*, 30 (3): 417–442.

The Economist (2014) In the Queue, 27 September, http://www.economist.com/news/europe/21620264-door-membership-remains-open-region-must-do-more-get-it-queue, date accessed 1 December 2014.

Eichenberg, R. and Dalton, R. (1993) 'Europeans and European Community: The Dynamics of Public Support for European Integration', *International Organization*, 47 (4): 507–534.

Elbasani, A. (2013) *European Integration and Transformation in the Western Balkans: Europeanization or Business as Usual?* Abingdon: Routledge.

Epstein, R. and Johnson, J. (2010) 'Uneven Integration: Economic and Monetary Union in Central and Eastern Europe', *Journal of Common Market Studies*, 48 (5): 1237–1260.

EUObserver (2009) Slovenia Wants Changes to Croatia Border Resolution Plan, 19 May, http://euobserver.com/15/28153, date accessed 1 May 2012.

EUObserver (2010) Turkey Allies Speak out after EU Accession Talks Stall, 15 December, http://euobserver.com/15/31507, date accessed 1 May 2012.

EUObserver (2011a) Corruption in Bulgaria and Romania Still Unpunished, EU Says, 20 June, http://euobserver.com/9/32643, date accessed 1 May 2012.

EUObserver (2011b) EU May Impose Monitoring System on Candidate Croatia, https://euobserver.com/enlargement/32381, date accessed 1 May 2012.

EUObserver (2012) Bosnia-Herzegovina Appoints New PM, 13 January, http://euobserver.com/1016/114875, date accessed 1 May 2012.

EurActiv (2004) Commission Wants More Reform in Romania, 3 December, http://www.euractiv.com/enlargement/commission-wants-reform-romania/article-133046, date accessed 1 May 2012.

EurActiv (2009a) Slovenia Waves Referendum Card at Croatia, 8 January, http://www.euractiv.com/enlargement/slovenia-waves-referendum-card-croatia/article-178349, date accessed 1 May 2012.

EurActiv (2009b) Bulgaria, Romania Remain under Commission Scrutiny, 23 July, http://www.euractiv.com/enlargement/bulgaria-romania-remain-commission-scrutiny/article-184311, date accessed 1 May 2012.

EurActiv (2010a) EU Negotiator: 'Main Difficulty of German Reunification Was Its Speed', 4 October, http://www.euractiv.com/future-eu/insider-main-difficulty-german-reunification-was-its-speed-interview-498395, date accessed 1 May 2012.

EurActiv (2010b) Slovenian Vote Clears Main Obstacle to EU Accession, 7 June, http://www.euractiv.com/enlargement/slovenian-vote-clears-croatia-s-main-obstacle-eu-accession-news-494916, date accessed 1 May 2012.

EurActiv (2011a) Austria Mulls Turkey Referendum, Ankara Unimpressed, 6 May, http://www.euractiv.com/enlargement/austria-mulls-turkey-referendum-ankara-unimpressed-news-504579, date accessed 1 May 2012.

EurActiv (2011b) EU Bets on Montenegro Keep Enlargement Alive, 12 October, http://www.euractiv.com/enlargement/eu-bets-montenegro-keep-enlargement-alive-news-508306, date accessed 1 May 2012.

EurActiv (2011c) As EU Presidency Nears End, Poland Vents Frustrations, 16 December, http://www.euractiv.com/future-eu/eu-presidency-nears-poland-vents-frustrations-news-509788, date accessed 1 May 2012.

EurActiv (2012) Bosnia and Herzegovina Readies EU Membership Bid, 22 February, http://www.euractiv.com/enlargement/bosnia-herzegovina-readies-eu-membership-bid-news-511026, date accessed 1 May 2012.

EurActiv (2013a) Iceland Walks Out on EU Membership Talks, 23 August, http://www.euractiv.com/enlargement/iceland-quits-eu-talks-news-529923, date accessed 1 May 2014.

EurActiv (2013b) The Netherlands Vetoes Albania's EU Candidate Status, 13 December, http://www.euractiv.com/enlargement/netherlands-vetoes-albania-eu-ca-news-532360, date accessed 1 December 2014.

EurActiv (2014) EU-Serbia Relations, http://www.euractiv.com/enlargement/eu-serbia-relations, date accessed 1 December 2014.

EURATOM Treaty (1957) *Treaty Establishing the European Atomic Energy Community (EURATOM)*, 25 March, http://www.proyectos.cchs.csic.es/euroconstitution/library/historic%20documents/Rome/TRAITES_1957_EURATOM.pdf, date accessed 1 May 2012.

Eurobarometer (1990) *Eurobarometer No 33*, Brussels: Commission of the European Communities.

Eurobarometer (1991a) *Eurobarometer No 35*, Brussels: Commission of the European Communities.

Eurobarometer (1991b) *Eurobarometer No 36*, Brussels: Commission of the European Communities.

Eurobarometer (1992) *Eurobarometer No 38*, Brussels: Commission of the European Communities.

Eurobarometer (1994) *The First Year of the New Union, Report on Standard Eurobarometer 42*, Brussels: European Commission.

Eurobarometer (1996) *Report Number 45*, Brussels: European Commission.

Eurobarometer (1997) *Eurobarometer – Public Opinion in the European Union, Report Number 48*, Brussels: European Commission.

Eurobarometer (1998a) *Eurobarometer – Public Opinion in the European Union, Report Number 49*, Brussels: European Commission.

Eurobarometer (1998b) *Eurobarometer – Public Opinion in the European Union, Report Number 50*, Brussels: European Commission.

Eurobarometer (1999a) *Eurobarometer – Public Opinion in the European Union, Report Number 51*, Brussels: European Commission.

Eurobarometer (1999b) *Eurobarometer – Public Opinion in the European Union, Report Number 52*, Brussels: European Commission.

Eurobarometer (2000a) *Eurobarometer – Public Opinion in the European Union, Report Number 53*, Brussels: European Commission.

Eurobarometer (2000b) *Eurobarometer – Public Opinion in the European Union, Report Number 54*, Brussels: European Commission.

Eurobarometer (2001a) *Eurobarometer – Public Opinion in the European Union, Report Number 55*, Brussels: European Commission.

Eurobarometer (2001b) *Eurobarometer – Public Opinion in the European Union, Report Number 56*, Brussels: European Commission.

Eurobarometer (2002a) *Eurobarometer – Public Opinion in the European Union, Eurobarometer 57, Spring 2002*, EU 15 Report, Brussels: European Commission.

Eurobarometer (2002b) *Eurobarometer – Public Opinion in the European Union, Report Number 58*, Brussels: European Commission.

Eurobarometer (2003a) *Eurobarometer 59 – Public Opinion in the European Union, Spring 2003*, Brussels: European Commission.

Eurobarometer (2003b) *Eurobarometer 60 – Public Opinion in the European Union, Autumn 2003*, Brussels: European Commission.

Eurobarometer (2004a) *Eurobarometer Spring 2004 – Public Opinion in the European Union*, Brussels: European Commission.

Eurobarometer (2004b) *Eurobarometer 62 – Public Opinion in the European Union,* Brussels: European Commission.

Eurobarometer (2005a) *Eurobarometer 63 – Public Opinion in the European Union,* Brussels: European Commission.

Eurobarometer (2005b) *Eurobarometer 64 – Public Opinion in the European Union,* Brussels: European Commission.

Eurobarometer (2006a) *Eurobarometer 65 – Public Opinion in the European Union,* Brussels: European Commission.

Eurobarometer (2006b) *Eurobarometer 66 – Public Opinion in the European Union,* Brussels: European Commission.

Eurobarometer (2007a) *Eurobarometer 67 – Public Opinion in the European Union,* Brussels: European Commission.

Eurobarometer (2007b) *Eurobarometer 68 – Public Opinion in the European Union,* Brussels: European Commission.

Eurobarometer (2008a) *Eurobarometer 69 – Public Opinion in the European Union,* Brussels: European Commission.

Eurobarometer (2008b) *Eurobarometer 70 – Public Opinion in the European Union,* Brussels: European Commission.

Eurobarometer (2009a) *Eurobarometer 71 – Public Opinion in the European Union,* Brussels: European Commission.

Eurobarometer (2009b) *Eurobarometer 72 – Public Opinion in the European Union, Report,* Brussels: European Commission.

Eurobarometer (2010a) *Eurobarometer 73 – Public Opinion in the European Union, Report, Volume 1,* Brussels: European Commission.

Eurobarometer (2010b) Eurobarometer 74, Autumn 2010 – Public Opinion in the European Union, Report, Brussels: European Commission.

Eurobarometer (2011a) *Eurobarometer 75, Spring 2011 – Public Opinion in the European Union, Report,* Brussels: European Commission.

Eurobarometer (2011b) *Eurobarometer 76, Autumn 2011 – Public Opinion in the European Union, Report,* Brussels: European Commission.

Eurobarometer (2012a) *Eurobarometer 77, Spring 2012 – Public Opinion in the European Union, Report,* Brussels: European Commission.

Eurobarometer (2012b) *Eurobarometer 78, Autumn 2012 – Public Opinion in the European Union, Report,* Brussels: European Commission.

Eurobarometer (2013a) *Eurobarometer 79, Spring 2013 – Public Opinion in the European Union, Report,* Brussels: European Commission.

Eurobarometer (2013b) *Eurobarometer 80, Autumn 2013 – Public Opinion in the European Union, Report,* Brussels: European Commission.

Eurobarometer (2014a) *Eurobarometer 81, Spring 2014 – Public Opinion in the European Union, Report,* Brussels: European Commission.

Eurobarometer (2014b) *Eurobarometer 82, Autumn 2014 – Public Opinion in the European Union, Report,* Brussels: European Commission.

Europa Press Releases (1996) *Relations EU/Croatia,* MEMO 96/57, Brussels.

Europa Press Releases (2007) *Translation: Where Do We Stand Two Years after the Fifth Enlargement?* MEMO 07/76, Brussels.

Europa Press Releases (2014) *EU Candidate Status for Albania,* MEMO 14–439, Brussels.

European Commission (1993a) *Commission Opinion on Malta's Application for Membership,* COM (93) 312 final, Brussels: European Commission.

European Commission (1993b) *Commission Opinion on the Application by the Republic of Cyprus for Membership*, COM (93) 313 final, Brussels: European Commission.

European Commission (1994) *Commission Opinion on the Applications for Accession to the European Union by the Republic of Austria, the Kingdom of Sweden, the Republic of Finland and the Kingdom of Norway*, COM (94) 148 final, Brussels: European Commission.

European Commission (1995) *White Paper – Preparation of the Associated Countries of Central and Eastern Europe for Integration into the Internal Market of the Union*, COM (95) 163 final, Brussels: European Commission.

European Commission (1997) *Agenda 2000: Vol. I: For a Stronger and Wider Union, Vol. II: the Challenge of Enlargement*, COM (97) 2000 final, Brussels: European Commission.

European Commission (1998a) *Commission Staff Working Document – Regional Approach to the Countries of South-Eastern Europe: Compliance with the Conditions in the Council Conclusions of 29 April 1997, Bosnia and Herzegovina Croatia, Federal Republic of Yugoslavia, Former Yugoslav Republic of Macedonia and Albania*, SEC(98) 1727, Brussels: European Commission.

European Commission (1998b) *Composite Paper, Reports on Progress towards Accession by Each of the Candidate Countries*, COM (98) 700–712 final, Brussels: European Commission.

European Commission (1999) *Composite Paper, Reports on Progress towards Accession by Each of the Candidate Countries*, COM (99) 500 final, Brussels: European Commission.

European Commission (2000a) *Enlargement Strategy Paper, Reports on Progress towards Accession by Each of the Candidate Countries*, COM (2000) 700 final, Brussels: European Commission.

European Commission (2000b) *2000 Regular Report from the Commission on Turkey's Progress towards Accession*, Brussels: European Commission.

European Commission (2001) *Making a Success of Enlargement - Strategy Paper and Report of the European Commission on the Progress towards Accession by Each of the Candidate Countries*, COM (2002) 700 final, Brussels: European Commission.

European Commission (2002a) *Towards the Enlarged Union - Strategy Paper and Report of the European Commission on the Progress towards Accession by Each of the Candidate Countries*, COM (2002) 700 final, Brussels: European Commission.

European Commission (2002b) *2002 Regular Report on Bulgaria's Progress towards Accession*, COM (2002) 700 final, Brussels: European Commission.

European Commission (2002c) *2002 Regular Report on Romania's Progress towards Accession*, SEC (2002) 700 final, Brussels: European Commission.

European Commission (2002d) *2002 Regular Report on Turkey's Progress towards Accession*, COM (2002) 700 final, Brussels: European Commission.

European Commission (2003) *Comprehensive Monitoring Report of the European Commission on the State of Preparedness for EU Membership of the Czech Republic, Estonia, Cyprus, Latvia, Lithuania, Hungary, Malta, Poland, Slovenia and Slovakia*, COM (2003) 675 final, Brussels: European Commission.

European Commission (2004a) *Communication from the Commission – Opinion on Croatia's Application for Membership of the European Union*, COM (2004) 257 final, Brussels: European Commission.

European Commission (2004b) *Communication from the Commission to the Council and the European Parliament – Strategy Paper of the European Commission on Progress in the Enlargement Process*, COM (2004) 657 final, Brussels: European Commission.

European Commission (2004c) *Enlargement of the European Union – Guide to the Negotiations – Chapter by Chapter*, Brussels: European Commission.

European Commission (2004d) *Report from the Commission - The Stabilisation and Association Process for South East Europe - Third Annual Report*, COM (2004) 202 final, Brussels: European Commission.

European Commission (2004e) *2004 Regular Report on Bulgaria's Progress towards Accession*, COM (2004) 657 final, Brussels: European Commission.

European Commission (2004f) *2004 Regular Report on Romania's Progress towards Accession*, COM (2004) 657 final, Brussels: European Commission.

European Commission (2004g) *2002 Regular Report on Turkey's Progress towards Accession*, COM (2002) 700 final, Brussels: European Commission.

European Commission (2005a) *Bulgaria - 2005 Comprehensive Monitoring Report*, COM (2005) 534 final, Brussels: European Commission.

European Commission (2005b) *Communication from the Commission – Opinion on the Application from the Former Yugoslav Republic of Macedonia for Membership of the European Union*, COM (2005) 257 final, Brussels: European Commission.

European Commission (2005c) *Communication from the Commission – 2005 Enlargement Strategy Paper*, COM (2005) 561 final, Brussels: European Commission.

European Commission (2005d) *Negotiating Framework for Croatia*, Brussels: European Commission.

European Commission (2005e) *Negotiating Framework for Turkey*, Brussels: European Commission.

European Commission (2005f) *D Romania - 2005 Comprehensive Monitoring Report*, COM (2005) 534 final, Brussels: European Commission.

European Commission (2006a) *Bulgaria – May 2006 Monitoring Report*, COM (2006) 214 final, Brussels: European Commission.

European Commission (2006b) *Commission Decision of 13 December 2006 Establishing a Mechanism for Cooperation and Verification of Progress in Bulgaria to Address Specific Benchmarks in the Areas of Judicial Reform and the Fight against Corruption and Organised Crime*, C(2006) 6570, Brussels: European Commission.

European Commission (2006c) *Commission Decision of 13 December 2006 Establishing a Mechanism for Cooperation and Verification of Progress in Romania to Address Specific Benchmarks in the Areas of Judicial Reform and the Fight against Corruption and Organised Crime*, C(2006) 6569, Brussels: European Commission.

European Commission (2006d) *Commission Staff Working Document – Croatia 2006 Progress Report*, SEC (2006) 1385, Brussels: European Commission.

European Commission (2006e) *Commission Staff Working Document – Turkey 2006 Progress Report*, SEC (2006) 1390, Brussels: European Commission.

European Commission (2006f) *Communication from the Commission - Monitoring Report on the State of Preparedness for EU Membership of Bulgaria and Romania*, COM (2006) 214 final, Brussels: European Commission.

European Commission (2006g) *Communication from the Commission to the European Parliament and the Council – Enlargement Strategy and Main Challenges*

2006–2007, Including Annexed Special Reports on EU's Capacity to Integrate New Members, COM (2006) 649 final, Brussels: European Commission.

European Commission (2006h) *C: Monitoring Report on the State of Preparedness for EU Membership of Bulgaria and Romania*, COM (2006) 549 final, Brussels: European Commission.

European Commission (2006i) *Romania – May 2006 Monitoring Report*, COM (2006) 214 final, Brussels: European Commission.

European Commission (2007a) *Commission Staff Working Document – Croatia 2007 Progress Report Accompanying the Communication from the Commission to the European Parliament and the Council: Enlargement Strategy and Main Challenges 2007–2008*, SEC (2007) 1431, Brussels: European Commission.

European Commission (2007b) *Commission Staff Working Document – Turkey 2007 Progress Report Accompanying the Communication from the Commission to the European Parliament and the Council: Enlargement Strategy and Main Challenges 2007–2008*, SEC (2007) 1436, Brussels: European Commission.

European Commission (2007c) *Understanding Enlargement: The European Union's Enlargement Policy*, Brussels: European Commission.

European Commission (2008a) *Commission Staff Working Document – Croatia 2008 Progress Report accompanying the Communication from the Commission to the European Parliament and the Council: Enlargement Strategy and Main Challenges 2008–2009*, SEC (2008) 2694, Brussels: European Commission.

European Commission (2008b) *Commission Staff Working Document – Turkey 2008 Progress Report accompanying the Communication from the Commission to the European Parliament and the Council: Enlargement Strategy and Main Challenges 2008–2009*, SEC (2008) 2699, Brussels: European Commission.

European Commission (2008c) *Communication from the Commission to the Council and to the European Parliament – Enlargement Strategy and Main Challenges 2008–2009*, COM (2008) 674 final, Brussels: European Commission.

European Commission (2008d) *Communication from the Commission to the Council and to the European Parliament – Western Balkans: Enhancing the European Perspective*, COM (2008) 127 final, Brussels: European Commission.

European Commission (2009a) *Commission Staff Working Document – Croatia 2009 Progress Report Accompanying the Communication from the Commission to the European Parliament and the Council: Enlargement Strategy and Main Challenges 2009–2010*, SEC (2009) 1333, Brussels: European Commission.

European Commission (2009b) *Commission Staff Working Document – Turkey 2009 Progress Report Accompanying the Communication from the Commission to the European Parliament and the Council: Enlargement Strategy and Main Challenges 2009–2010*, SEC (2009) 1334, Brussels: European Commission.

European Commission (2009c) *Commission Staff Working Document – The Former Yugoslav Republic of Macedonia 2009 Progress Report*, SEC (2009) 1335 final, Brussels: European Commission.

European Commission (2009d) *Communication from the Commission to the European Parliament and the Council – Enlargement Strategy and Main Challenges 2009–2010*, COM (2009) 533 final, Brussels: European Commission.

European Commission (2009e) *Enlargement Newsletter*, 13 January 2009, http://ec.europa.eu/enlargement/press_corner/newsletter/130109_en.htm, date accessed 1 May 2012.

European Commission (2009f) *Report from the Commission to the European Parliament and the Council on Progress in Bulgaria under the Co-operation and Verification Mechanism*, COM (2009) 402 final, Brussels: European Commission.

European Commission (2009g) *Report from the Commission to the European Parliament and the Council on Progress in Romania under the Co-operation and Verification Mechanism*, COM (2009) 401 final, Brussels: European Commission.

European Commission (2010a) *Commission Staff Working Document – Croatia 2010 Progress Report Accompanying the Communication from the Commission to the European Parliament and the Council: Enlargement Strategy and Main Challenges 2010–2011*, SEC (2010) 1326, Brussels: European Commission.

European Commission (2010b) *Commission Staff Working Document – Turkey 2010 Progress Report Accompanying the Communication from the Commission to the European Parliament and the Council: Enlargement Strategy and Main Challenges 2010–2011*, SEC (2010) 1327, Brussels: European Commission.

European Commission (2010c) *Communication from the Commission to the European Parliament and the Council – Commission Opinion on Albania's Application for Membership of the European Union*, COM (2010) 680 final, Brussels: European Commission.

European Commission (2010d) *Communication from the Commission to the European Parliament and the Council – Commission Opinion on Iceland's Application for Membership of the European Union*, COM (2010) 62 final, Brussels: European Commission.

European Commission (2010e) *Communication from the Commission to the European Parliament and the Council – Commission Opinion on Montenegro's Application for Membership of the European Union*, COM (2010) 670 final, Brussels: European Commission.

European Commission (2010f) *Communication from the Commission to the European Parliament and the Council – Enlargement Strategy and Main Challenges 2010–2011*, COM (2010) 660 final, Brussels: European Commission.

European Commission (2010g) *Negotiating Framework for Iceland*, Brussels: European Commission.

European Commission (2010h) *Report from the Commission to the European Parliament and the Council on Progress in Bulgaria under the Co-operation and Verification Mechanism*, COM (2010) 400 final, Brussels: European Commission.

European Commission (2010i) *Report from the Commission to the European Parliament and the Council on Progress in Romania under the Co-operation and Verification Mechanism*, COM (2010) 401 final, Brussels: European Commission.

European Commission (2011a) *Communication from the Commission to the European Parliament and the Council – Commission Opinion on Serbia's Application for Membership of the European Union*, COM (2011) 668 final, Brussels: European Commission.

European Commission (2011b) *Communication from the Commission to the European Parliament and the Council – Enlargement Strategy and Main Challenges 2011–2012*, COM (2011) 666 final, Brussels: European Commission.

European Commission (2011c) *Interim Report from the Commission to the European Parliament and the Council: On the Reforms in Croatia in the Field of Judiciary and Fundamental Rights (Negotiation Chapter 23)*, COM (2011) 110, Brussels: European Commission.

European Commission (2011d) *Report from the Commission to the European Parliament and the Council on Progress in Bulgaria under the Co-operation and Verification Mechanism*, COM (2011) 459 final, Brussels: European Commission.

European Commission (2011e) *Report from the Commission to the European Parliament and the Council on Progress in Romania under the Co-operation and Verification Mechanism*, COM (2011) 460 final, Brussels: European Commission.

European Commission (2012a) *Communication from the Commission to the European Parliament and the Council – Enlargement Strategy and Main Challenges 2012–2013*, COM (2012) 600 final, Brussels: European Commission.

European Commission (2012b) *Communication from the Commission to the European Parliament and the Council – On the Main Findings of the Comprehensive Monitoring Report on Croatia's State of Preparedness for EU Membership*, COM (2012) 601 final, Brussels: European Commission.

European Commission (2012c) *Negotiating Framework for Montenegro*, Brussels: European Commission.

European Commission (2012d) *Pre-Accession Relations: EU-Bulgaria, EU-Bulgaria Negotiations*, http://ec.europa.eu/bulgaria/abc/pre_accession/negotiations/index_en.htm, date accessed 1 May 2012.

European Commission (2014a) *Communication from the Commission to the European Parliament, the Council, the European Economic and Social Committee and the Committee of the Regions – Enlargement Strategy and Main Challenges 2014–2015*, COM (2014) 700 final, Brussels: European Commission.

European Commission (2014b) *Negotiating Framework for Serbia*, Brussels: European Commission.

European Commission (2014c) *Report from the Commission to the European Parliament and the Council on Progress in Bulgaria under the Co-operation and Verification Mechanism*, COM (2014) 36 final, Brussels: European Commission.

European Commission (2014d) *Report from the Commission to the European Parliament and the Council on Progress in Romania under the Co-operation and Verification Mechanism*, COM (2014) 37 final, Brussels: European Commission.

European Parliament (2000) *Resolution on the Enlargement of the European Union*, A5–0250, 4 October, Strasbourg.

European Parliament (2005) *European Parliament on Opening Accession Negotiations with Turkey*, P6 TA (2005) 0350, 28 September, Strasbourg.

European Parliament (2014a) *Hearing of European Commissioners-designate: Frans Timmermans First Vice-President –Better Regulation, Inter-Institutional Relations, the Rule of Law and Charter of Fundamental Rights*, Brussels, October 2014.

European Parliament (2014b) *Hearings of European Commissioners-Designate: Johannes Hahn European Neighbourhood Policy and Enlargement Negotiations*, Brussels, September 2014.

Europa Press Releases (2012) *Positive EU-Turkey Agenda Launched in Turkey*, Brussels: Europa Press.

European Voice (2009) *Slovenia Ready to Lift Veto on Croatia's EU Bid*, 11 September.

European Voice (2011) *Croatia Completes EU Talks*, 30 June.

European Voice (2012a) *Serbia and Kosovo Strike a Name Deal*, 24 February.

European Voice (2012b) *EU Grants Candidate Status to Serbia*, 28 February.

European Voice (2012c) *What Is in a Name?* 1 March.

Fagan, A. (2005) 'Taking Stock of Civil-Society Development in Post-Communist Europe: Evidence from the Czech Republic', *Democratization*, 12 (4): 528–547.

Field, H. (2000) 'Awkward States: EU Enlargement and Slovakia, Croatia and Serbia', *Perspectives on European Politics and Society*, 1 (1): 123–146.

Fierke, K. and Wiener, A. (1999) Constructing Institutional Interests: EU and NATO Enlargement, *Journal of European Public Policy*, 6 (3): 727–742.

Financial Times (2004a) Defiant EU Commission Says Romania Not Ready, 2 December, http://www.ft.com/cms/s/0/9b06 4874- 4491- 11d9- 9f6a- 00000e 2511c8.html#axzz1uqdJV5ia, date accessed 1 May 2012.

Financial Times (2004b) EU Envoy Agree Entry Terms with Romania, 9 December, http://www.ft.com/cms/s/0/2a9bcaee-4a1a-11d9-b065-00000e2511c8. html#axzz1uqdJV5ia, date accessed 1 May 2012.

Financial Times (2010) Slovenians Approve Border Deal with Croatia, 6 June, http://www.ft.com/cms/s/0/18cf2722-7163-11df-8eec-00144feabdc0. html#axzz1uqdJV5ia, date accessed 1 May 2012.

Freyburg, T. and Richter, S. (2010) National Identity Matters: The Limited Impact of EU Political Conditionality in the Western Balkans, *Journal of European Public Policy*, 17 (2): 262–280.

Füle, Š. (2012) *Policy Address at the Plenary Debate on the Former Yugoslav Republic of Macedonia*, Speech 12/186 European Parliament, 14 March, Strasbourg.

Goetz, K. (2005) 'The New Member States and the EU: Responding to Europe', in S. Bulmer and C. Lequesne (eds.) *The Member States of the European Union*, Oxford: Oxford University Press, pp. 254–284.

Government of Croatia (2011) *Progress at EU-Croatia Negotiations at a Glance*, http://www.eu- pregovori.hr/DOWNLOAD/2011/09/14/Progress_in_ EU- Croatia_accession_negotiations- 2011- 06- 16- M.pdf, date accessed 1 May 2012.

Government of the Republic of Serbia (2015) *Candidacy for Membership and European Commission Questionnaire*, available at http://www.seio.gov.rs/info-service/questions-and-answers.258.html

Government of Turkey (2011) *Turkey-EU Relations*, http://www.mfa.gov.tr/relations-between-turkey-and-the-european-union.en.mfa, date accessed 1 May 2012.

Grabbe, H. (2001) 'How Does Europeanisation Affect CEEC Governance? Conditionality, Diffusion and Diversity', *Journal of European Public Policy*, 8 (6): 1013–1031.

Grabbe, H. (2002) 'European Union Conditionality and the Acquis Communautaire', *International Political Science Review*, 23 (3): 249–268.

Grabbe, H. (2006) *The EU's Transformative Power. Europeanization through Conditionality in Central and Eastern Europe*, Basingstoke: Palgrave Macmillan.

Granell, F. (1995) 'The European Union Accession Negotiations with Austria, Finland, Norway and Sweden', *Journal of Common Market Studies*, 33 (1): 117–141.

Henderson, K. (ed.) (1999) *Back to Europe: Central and Eastern Europe and the European Union*, London: UCL Press.

Hille, P. and Knill, C. (2006) ' "It's the Bureaucracy, Stupid": The Implementation of the Acquis Communautaire in EU Candidate Countries, 1999–2003', *European Union Politics*, 7 (4): 531–552.

Hughes, J. and Sasse, G. (2003) 'Monitoring the Monitors: EU Enlargement Conditionality and Minority Protection in the CEECs', *Journal on Ethnopolitics and Minority Issues in Europe*, (1): 1–37.

Hughes, J., Sasse, G. and Gordon, C. (2004) 'Conditionality and Compliance in the EU's Eastward Enlargement: Regional Policy and the Reform of Sub-National Government', *Journal of Common Market Studies*, 42 (3): 523–551.

Hyde-Price, A. (2000) *Germany and European Order: Enlarging NATO and the EU*, Manchester: Manchester University Press.

İçener, E. (2009) 'Understanding Romania and Turkey's Integration with the European Union: Conditionality, Security Considerations and Identity', *Perspectives on European Politics and Society*, 10 (2): 225–239.

İçener, E., Phinnemore, D. and Papadimitriou, D. (2010) Continuity and Change in the European Union's Approach to Enlargement: Turkey and Central and Eastern Europe Compared, *Southeast European and Black Sea Studies*, 10 (2): 207–223.

Inotai, A. (1997) What is Novel about the Eastern Enlargement of the Union? The Costs and Benefits of the Eastern Enlargement of the Union, Working Paper No 87, *Institute for World Economics*, Budapest: Hungarian Academy of Sciences.

Interview 1 (2009) Official, Mission of Croatia, Brussels, August 2009.

Interview 2 (2009) Official, Mission of Turkey, Brussels, July 2009.

Interview 3 (2009) Official, European Commission, DG III, Brussels, July 2009.

Interview 4 (2009) Official, European Commission, DG II, Brussels, June 2009.

Interview 5 (2009) Official, European Commission, DG I, Brussels, June 2009.

Interview 6 (2009) Official, European Commission, DG II, Brussels, May 2009.

Interview 7 (2009) Official, European Commission, DG II, Brussels, July 2009.

Interview 8 (2009) Official, European Commission, DG II, Brussels, July 2009.

Interview 9 (2009) Official, European Commission, DG II, Brussels, May 2009.

Interview 10 (2009) Official, European Commission, DG II, Brussels, June 2009.

Interview 11 (2009) Official, General Secretariat of the Council of the European Union, Brussels, June 2009.

Interview 12 (2009) Official, European Commission, DG II, Brussels, June 2009.

Interview 13 (2009) Official, Permanent Representation (New Member State), Brussels, June 2009.

Interview 14 (2009) Official, European Commission, DG II, Brussels, May 2009.

Interview 15 (2009) Official, European Commission, DG II, Brussels, June 2009.

Interview 16 (2009) MEP, Brussels, July 2009.

Interview 17 (2009) Official, Permanent Representation (Old Member State), Brussels, June 2009.

Interview 18 (2009) Official, European Commission, DG I, Brussels, July 2009.

Interview 19 (2009) Official, General Secretariat of the Council of the European Union, Brussels, July 2009.

Interview 20 (2009) Official, European Commission, DG I, Brussels, July 2009.

Interview 21 (2009) Official, European Commission, DG IV, Brussels, July 2009.

Interview 22 (2013) Official, General Secretariat of the Council of the European Union, Brussels, November 2013.

Interview 23 (2014) Official, European Commission, DG II, Brussels, November 2014.

Interview 24 (2014) Official, European Commission, DG II, Brussels, November 2014.

Interview 25 (2014) Official, Permanent Representation (New Member State), Brussels, November 2014.

Johnson, J. (2008) 'The Remains of Conditionality: The Faltering Enlargement of the Euro Zone', *Journal of European Public Policy*, 15 (6): 826–841.

Juncker, J-C. (2014) *New Start for Europe: My Agenda for Jobs, Growth, Fairness and Democratic Change*, Strasbourg.

Kubicek, P. (ed.) (2003) *The European Union and Democratization*, London: Routledge.

Kujundžić, M. (2011) *Relations with the EU: Experience of a Candidate Country*, CDL-UDT (2011) 018, http://www.venice.coe.int/docs/2011/CDL-UDT%282011%29018-e.pdf, date accessed 1 May 2012.

Lass-Lennecke, K. and Werner, A. (2009) 'Policies, Institutions and Time: How the European Commission Managed the Temporal Challenge of Eastern Enlargement', *Journal of European Public Policy*, 16 (2): 270–285.

Lavenex, S. (2008) 'A Governance Perspective on the European Neighbourhood Policy: Integration Beyond Conditionality?', *Journal of European Public Policy*, 15 (6): 938–955.

Lewis, P. (2008) 'Changes in the Party Politics of the New EU Member States in Central Europe: Patterns of Europeanization and Democratization', *Journal of Southern Europe and the Balkans*, 10 (2): 151–165.

Lewis, P. and Mansfeldová, Z. (eds.) (2006) *The European Union and Party Politics in Central and Eastern Europe*, Basingstoke: Palgrave Macmillan.

Lippert, B., Umbach, G. and Wessels, W. (2001) 'Europeanization of CEE Executives: EU Membership Negotiations as a Shaping Power', *Journal of European Public Policy*, 8 (6): 980–1012.

Macmillan, H. (1961) On UK's application for Membership, http://www.cvce.eu/en/education/unit-content/-/unit/02bb76df-d066-4c08-a58a-d4686a3e68ff/a125033c-90ee-4355-a320-b38e7aaf4cca/Resources#a5c95873-aca0-4e9f-be93-53a36918041d_en&overlay, date accessed 1 December 2014.

Maier, J. and Rittberger, B. (2008) 'Shifting Europe's Boundaries: Mass Media, Public Opinion and the Enlargement of the EU', *European Union Politics*, 9 (2): 243–267.

Mattli, W. and Plumper, T. (2002) 'The Demand-Side Politics of EU Enlargement: Democracy and the Application for EU Membership', *Journal of European Public Policy*, 9 (4): 550–574.

Müftüler-Baç, M. (2000) 'The Impact of the European Union on Turkish Politics', *East European Quarterly*, 34 (2): 159–179.

Müftüler-Baç, M. (2009) 'The European Union's Accession negotiations with Turkey from a Foreign Policy Perspective', in E. Jones and S. van Genugten (eds.) *The Future of European Integration*, London: Routledge, pp.60–75.

Noutcheva, G. (2009) 'Fake, Partial and Imposed Compliance: The Limits of the EU's Normative Power in the Western Balkans', *Journal of European Public Policy*, 16 (7): 1065–1084.

Noutcheva, G. and Bechev, D. (2008) 'The Successful Laggards: Bulgaria and Romania's Accession to the EU', *East European Politics and Societies*, 22 (1): 114–144.

Nugent, N. (eds.) (2004) *European Union Enlargement*, Basingstoke: Palgrave Macmillan.

O'Brennan, J. (2006) *The Eastern Enlargement of the European Union*, Abingdon: Routeledge.

Official Journal (1961) *Agreement establishing an Association between the European Economic Community and Greece*, 294/83, 18 February.

Official Journal (1964) *Agreement establishing an Association between the European Economic Community and Turkey*, L 217, 29 December.

Official Journal (1992) *Treaty on European Union*, C 191, 29 July.

Official Journal (1993a) *Europe Agreement Establishing an Association between the European Communities and Their Member States, of the One Part, and the Republic of Hungary, of Other Part*, L 347, 31 December.

Official Journal (1993b) *Europe Agreement Establishing an Association between the European Communities and Their Member States, of the One Part, and the Republic of Poland, of Other Part*, L 348, 31 December.

Official Journal (1994a) *Agreement on Free Trade and Trade-Related Matters between the European Community, the European Atomic Energy Community and the European Coal and Steel Community, of the One Part, and the Republic of Estonia, of the Other Part*, L 373, 31 December.

Official Journal (1994b) *Agreement on Free Trade and Trade-Related Matters between the European Community, the European Atomic Energy Community and the European Coal and Steel Community, of the One Part, and the Republic of Latvia, of the Other Part*, L374, 31 December.

Official Journal (1994c) *Agreement on Free Trade and Trade-Related Matters between the European Community, the European Atomic Energy Community and the European Coal and Steel Community, of the One Part, and the Republic of Lithuania, of the Other Part*, L375, 31 December.

Official Journal (1994d) *Europe Agreement Establishing an Association between the European Communities and their Member States, of the One Part, and the Republic of Bulgaria, of Other Part*, L 358, 31 December.

Official Journal (1994e) *Europe Agreement Establishing an Association between the European Communities and their Member States, of the One Part, and Romania, of Other Part*, L 357, 31 December.

Official Journal (1997a) *Cooperation Agreement and Financial Protocol between the European Community and the Former Yugoslav Republic of Macedonia*, L 348, 18 December.

Official Journal (1997b) *Treaty of Amsterdam*, C 340, 10 November.

Official Journal (1998) *Council Regulation (EC) No 622/98 of 16 March 1998 on the Assistance to the Applicant States in the Framework of the Pre-Accession Strategy, and in Particular on the Establishment of Accession Partnerships*, L 85, 20 March.

Official Journal (1999) *Council Regulation (EC)No 1266/ 1999 of 21 June 1999 on Coordinating Aid in the Applicant Countries in the Framework of the Pre-Accession Strategy and Amending Regulation(ECC) No 3906/89*, L 161/68, 26 June.

Official Journal (2000) *Council Regulation (EC) No 2666/2000 of 5 December 2000 on Assistance for Albania, Bosnia and Herzegovina, Croatia, the Federal Republic of Yugoslavia and the Former Yugoslav Republic of Macedonia, Repealing Regulation (EC) No 1628/96 and Amending Regulations (EEC) No 3906/89 and (EEC) No 1360/90 and Decisions 97/256/EC and 1999/311/EC*, L 306, 7 December.

Official Journal (2001) *Council Decision (EC) No 2001/235 of 8 March 2001 on the Principles, Priorities, Intermediate Objectives and Conditions Contained in the Accession Partnership with the Republic of Turkey*, L 85, 24 March.

Official Journal (2003a) *Act Concerning the Conditions of Accession of the Czech Republic, the Republic of Estonia, the Republic of Cyprus, the Republic of Latvia, the Republic of Lithuania, the Republic of Hungary, the Republic of Malta, the Republic of Poland, the Republic of Slovenia and the Slovak Republic and the Adjustments to the Treaties on which the European Union is Founded,* L 236, 23 September.

Official Journal (2003b) *Treaty... Concerning the Accession of the Czech Republic, Estonia, Cyprus, Latvia, Lithuania, Hungary, Malta, Poland, Slovenia and Slovakia to the European Union,* L 236, 23 September.

Official Journal (2005a) *Act Concerning the Conditions of Accession of the Republic of Bulgaria and Romania and the Adjustments to the Treaties on Which the European Union is Founded,* L 157, 21 June.

Official Journal (2005b) *Treaty... Concerning the Accession of the Republic of Bulgaria and Romania to the European Union,* L 157, 21 June.

Official Journal (2007) *Treaty of Lisbon amending the Treaty on European Union and the Treaty establishing the European Community, signed at Lisbon, 13 December 2007,* C 306, 17 December.

Official Journal (2012) *Treaty... Concerning the Accession of the Republic of Croatia to the European Union,* L 112, 24 April.

Papadimitriou, D. (2002) *Negotiating the New Europe: The European Union and Eastern Europe,* Aldershot: Ashgate.

Papadimitriou, D. and Phinnemore, D. (2004) 'Europeanization, Conditionality and Domestic Change: The Twinning Exercise and Administrative Reform in Romania', *Journal of Common Market Studies,* 42 (3): 619–639.

Papadimitriou, D. and Phinnermore, D. (2009) *Romania and the European Union: From Marginalization to Membership,* London: Routledge.

Phinnemore, D. (2001) 'Romania and Euro-Atlantic Integration since 1989: A Decade of Frustration?' in D. Light and D. Phinnermore (eds.) *Post-Communist Romania: Coming to Terms with Transition,* Basingstoke: Palgrave Macmillan, pp. 245–269.

Phinnemore, D. (2010) 'And We'd Like to Thank...: Romania's Integration into the European Union, 1989–2007', *Journal of European Integration,* 32 (3): 291–308.

Piedrafita, S. (2007) 'Setting EU Eastern Enlargement Policy: Spain's Preferences for an Inclusive Process', *South European Society and Politics,* 12 (2): 203–220.

Pinheiro, J. (1993) *Speech by Commissioner Pinheiro at the Conference the European Community and the Balkans,* Speech 93/82, Corfu, 4 July.

Pippan, C. (2004) 'The Rocky Road to Europe: The EU Stabilisation and Association Process For the Western Balkans and the Principle of Conditionality', *European Foreign Affairs Review,* 9 (2): 219–245.

Pop-Eleches, G. (2007) 'Between Historical Legacies and the Promise of Western Integration: Democratic Conditionality after Communism', *East European Politics and Societies,* 21 (1): 142–161.

Pridham, G. (2001) 'Romania and European Union Accession: The Domestic Dimension', *Romanian Journal of Society and Politics,* 1 (2): 21–48.

Pridham, G. (2002) 'The European Union's Democratic Conditionality and Domestic Politics in Slovakia: The Mečiar and Dzurinda Governments Compared', *Europe-Asia Studies,* 54 (2): 203–227.

Pridham, G. (2005) *Designing Democracy: EU Enlargement and Regime Change in Post-Communist Europe,* Basingstoke: Palgrave Macmillan.

Pridham, G. (2007) 'Change and Continuity in the European Union's Political Conditionality: Aims, Approach, and Priorities', *Democratization*, 14 (3): 446–471.

Prodi, R. (1999) *On Enlargement*, Speech 99/130, European Parliament, 13 October.

Prodi, R. (2000) *Statement on Enlargement*, Speech 00/287, European Parliament, Strasbourg, 6 September.

Raik, K. (2006) 'The EU as a Regional Power: Extended Governance and Historical Responsibility', in H. Meyer and H. Vogt (eds.) *A Responsible Europe? Ethical Foundations of EU External Affairs*, Hampshire: Palgrave Macmillan, pp. 76–97.

Rechel, B. (2008) 'What Has Limited the EU's Impact on Minority Rights in Accession Countries?' *East European Politics and Societies*, 22 (1): 171–191.

Rehn, O. (2005) *Values Define Europe, Not Borders*, 4 January, http://www.ft.com/cms/s/0/26bde788-5df5-11d9-ac01-00000e2511c8.html#axzz1uwuEWpbb, date accessed 1 May 2012.

Rehn, O. (2006a) *Beyond Homogeneity*, Speech 06/561, Conference at the Central European University, Budapest, 9 February.

Rehn, O. (2006b) *Europe's Next Frontiers*, Speech 06/561, Lecture at Bilkent University, Ankara, 4 October.

Rehn, O. (2006c) *Europe's Next Frontiers*, Speech 06/654, Lecture at the Finnish Institute of International Affairs, Helsinki, 27 October.

Rehn, O. (2006d) *Enlargement Package*, Speech 06/727, European Parliament, Foreign Affairs Committee, Brussels, 21 November.

Rehn, O. (2006e) *Challenges and Opportunities on the Path to the European Union*, Speech 06/767, University of Osijek, Faculty of Economy, Osijek, 1 December.

Rehn, O. (2007) *A Strong Europe with its Gaze Fixed on the South-East: Our European Future*, Speech 07/594, Sciences Po, Paris, 4 October.

Rehn, O. (2008a) *Communication on the Western Balkans: Enhancing the European Perspective*, Speech 08/140, Western Balkans, Workshop, Brussels, 11 March.

Rehn, O. (2008b) *A Stronger Union through Deeping and Widening*, Speech 08/184, EPP Conference on Enlargement and Consolidation of the European Union, Brussels, 8 April.

Rehn, O. (2008c) *The Enlargement Package*, Speech 08/592, European Parliament, Foreign Affairs Committee, Brussels, 5 November.

Rehn, O. (2009a) *Future of EU Enlargement in South-East Europe*, Speech 09/87, EU Observer Conference Western Balkans, Brussels, 3 March.

Rehn, O. (2009b) *Enlargement and the EU's Role in World*, Speech 09/368, University of Copenhagen, Copenhagen, 8 September.

Richardson, J. (ed) (2012) Constructing a Policy-Making State? Policy Dynamics in the EU, Oxford University Press.

Ruiz-Jiménez, A. and Torreblanca, J. (2007) European Public Opinion and Turkey's Accession: Making Sense of Arguments For and Against, European Public Institutes Network (EPIN) Working Paper 16.

Sadurski, W. (2004) 'Accession's Democracy Dividend: The Impact of the EU Enlargement upon Democracy in the New Member States of Central and Eastern Europe', *European Law Journal*, 10 (4): 371–401.

Santer, J. (1997) *A Time for Vision – A Time for Partnership*, Speech 97/42, CSIS Conference Brussels, 21 February.

Sasse, G. (2005) 'EU Conditionality and Minority Rights: Translating the Copenhagen Criterion into Policy', *EUI Working Papers RSCAS*, (2005/16): 1–21.

Sasse, G. (2008) 'The Politics of EU Conditionality: The Norm of Minority Protection During and Beyond EU Accession', *Journal of European Public Policy*, 15 (6): 842–860.

Schimmelfennig, F. (1998) Liberal Norms and the Eastern Enlargement of the European Union: A Case for Sociological Institutionalism, *Österreichische Zeitschrift für Politikwissenschaft*, 27 (4): 459–472.

Schimmelfennig, F. (2001) 'The Community Trap: Liberal Norms, Rhetorical Action and the Eastern Enlargement of the European Union', *International Organization*, 55 (1): 47–80.

Schimmelfennig, F. and Scholtz, H. (2008) 'EU Democracy Promotion in the European Neighbourhood: Political Conditionality, Economic Development and Transnational Exchange', *European Union Politics*, 9 (2): 187–215.

Schimmelfennig, F. and Sedelmeier, U. (2002) 'Theorizing Enlargement: Research Focus, Hypotheses, and the State of Research', *Journal of European Public Policy*, 9 (6): 500–528.

Schimmelfennig, F. and Sedelmeier, U. (2004) 'Governance by Conditionality: EU Rule Transfer to the Candidate Countries of Central and Eastern Europe', *Journal of European Public Policy*, 11 (4): 661–679.

Schimmelfennig, F. and Sedelmeier, U. (eds.) (2005) *The Politics of European Union Enlargement: Theoretical Approaches*, Abingdon: Routledge.

Schimmelfennig, F. and Trauner, F. (eds.) (2009) 'Post-Accession Compliance in the EU's New Member States', *European Integration Online Papers (EIoP)*, Special Issue 2 (13).

Schimmelfennig, F., Engert, S. and Knobel, H. (2003) 'Cost, Commitment and Compliance: The Impact of EU Democratic Conditionality on Latvia, Slovakia and Turkey', *Journal of Common Market Studies*, 41 (3): 495–518.

Schoen, H. (2008) 'Turkey's Bid for EU Membership, Contrasting Views of Public Opinion, and Vote Choice: Evidence from the 2005 German Federal Elections', *Electoral Studies*, 27 (2): 344–355.

Schukkink, M. and Niemann, A. (2010) Portugal and the EU's Eastern Enlargement: A Logic of Identity Endorsement, European Foreign Policy Unit (EFPU), Working Paper 2010/1, http://www2.lse.ac.uk/internationalRelations/centresandunits/EFPU/EFPUpdfs/EFPUworkingpaper2010-1.pdf, date accessed 1 May 2012.

Schuman Declaration (1950) The Schuman Declaration – 9 May, http://europa.eu/about-eu/basic-information/symbols/europe-day/schuman-declaration/index_en.htm, date accessed 1 May 2012.

Scrivener, C. (1994) *USA and Europe: Why We Need Each Other*, Speech 94/44, Geneva, 29 April.

Sedelmeier, U. (2005) *Constructing the Path to Eastern Enlargement: The Uneven Policy Impact of EU Identity*, Manchester: Manchester University Press.

Sedelmeier, U. (2008) 'After Conditionality: Post-Accession Compliance with EU Law in East Central Europe', *Journal of European Public Policy*, 15 (6): 806–825.

Sedelmeier, U. (2011) 'Europeanisation in New Member and Candidate States', *Living Rev. Euro. Gov 6*, http://europeangovernance.livingreviews.org/Articles/lreg-2011-1/, date accessed 1 May 2012.

Sedelmeier, U. (2012) 'Is Europeanization through conditionality sustainable? Lock-in of Institutional Change after EU accession', *West European Politics*, 35 (1): 20–38.

Sjursen, H. (2002) 'Why Expand? The Question of Legitimacy and Justification in the EU's Enlargement Policy?' *Journal of Common Market Studies*, 40 (3): 491–513.

Sjursen, H. (ed.) (2006) *Questioning EU Enlargement: Europe in Search of Identity*, London: Routledge.

Skålnes, L. (2005) 'Geopolitics and the Eastern Enlargement of the European Union', in F. Schimmelfennig and U. Sedelmeier (eds.) *Theoretical Approaches to the Politics of EU Enlargement*, London: Routledge.

Smith, K. E. (1998) 'The Use of Political Conditionality in the EU's Relations with Third Countries: How Effective?' *European Foreign Affairs Review*, 3 (2): 253–274.

Smith, K. E. (2003) 'The Evolution and Application of EU Membership Conditionality', in M. Cremona (ed.) *The Enlargement of the European Union*, Oxford: Oxford University Press, pp. 105–140.

Smith, K. E. (2004) *The Making of EU Foreign Policy: The Case of Eastern Europe*, Basingstoke: Palgrave Macmillan.

Tewes, H. (1998) 'Between Deepening and Widening: Role Conflict in Germany's Enlargement Policy', *West European Politics*, 21 (2): 117–133.

Toshkov, D. (2007) 'In Search of the Worlds of Compliance: Culture and Transposition Performance in the European Union', *Journal of European Public Policy*, 14 (6): 933–959.

Toshkov, D. (2008) 'Embracing European Law: Compliance with EU Directives in Central and Eastern Europe', *European Union Politics*, 9 (3): 379–402.

Treaty of Paris (1951) *Treaty Establishing the Coal and Steel Community and Annexes I–III*, 18 April, http://www.proyectos.cchs.csic.es/euroconstitution/library/historic%20documents/Paris/TRAITES_1951_CECA.pdf, date accessed 1 May 2012.

Treaty of Rome (1957) *Treaty Establishing the European Economic Community*, 25 March, http://www.proyectos.cchs.csic.es/euroconstitution/library/historic%20documents/Rome/TRAITES_1957_CEE.pdf, date accessed 1 May 2012.

Vachudová, M. (2005) *Europe Undivided: Democracy, Leverage and Integration after Communism*, Oxford: Oxford University Press.

Van den Broek, H. (1993) *Europe Revisited: The New Europe and the Lessons of History*, Speech 93/68, Tilburg, 4 June.

Van den Broek, H. (1994) *The Challenge of a Wider Europe*, Speech 94/25, Brussels, 17 March 1994.

Van den Broek, H. (1997a) *The Challenge of a Wider Europe*, Speech 97/132, Win Conference, Montreux, 5 June.

Van den Broek, H. (1997b) *The Prospect for EU Enlargement*, Speech 97/264, Conference Organised by the International Press Institute 'The Future of Europe', Brussels, Centre Borschette, 27 November.

Van den Broek, H. (1998) *National Press Club Morning Newsmaker*, Speech 98/75, Washington, DC, 16 April.

Verheugen, G. (1999) *Enlargement: Speed and Quality*, Speech 99/151, Conference 'The Second Decade towards New and Integrated Europe', Den Haag, 4 November.

Verheugen, G. (2000) *Enlargement Is Irreversible*, Speech 00/351, Debate on Enlargement, European Parliament, Strasbourg, 3 October.

Verheugen, G. (2003) *EU Membership, a Driving Force in the Reform Process*, Speech 03/107, EU Enlargement Seminar with UK Parliamentarians, London, 4 March.

Vermeersch, P. (2002) 'Ethnic Mobilisation and the Political Conditionality of European Union Accession: The Case of the Roma in Slovakia', *Journal of Ethnic and Migration Studies*, 28 (1): 83–101.

Vermeersch, P. (2003) 'EU Enlargement and Minority Rights Policies in Central Europe: Explaining Shifts in the Czech Republic, Hungary and Poland', *Journal on Ethnopolitics and Minority Issues in Europe*, 1 (4): 1–32.

Verney, S. (2007) 'The Dynamics of EU Accession: Turkish Travails in Comparative Perspective', *Journal of Southern Europe and the Balkans Online*, 9 (3): 307–322.

Zagreb Declaration (2000) *The Declaration of the Zagreb Summit*, http://ec.europa.eu/enlargement/enlargement_process/accession_process/how_does_a_country_join_the_eu/sap/zagreb_summit_en.htm, date accessed 1 May 2012.

Index

Lightning Source UK Ltd.
Milton Keynes UK
UKOW06n0634061215

264110UK00003B/85/P